SPIRIT SPEECH

Martha,

May the spirit blow
on you os you
read.

Grace + Peace,

[signature]

"Luke Powery's excellent discussion of the Spirit will help preachers from all traditions in their sermons to reach to the depth of human suffering and soar to the heights of God's praise. His book is informative and inspiring, and gives practical guidance to manifestations of the Spirit—a must-read."
—**PAUL SCOTT WILSON**, Professor of Homiletics, Emmanuel College, University of Toronto

"Luke Powery has done us a great favor. In this book he demonstrates that it is possible to discern and describe the presence of the Holy Spirit in preaching. He is very convincing. He studs his argument with theological insight and practical observation. The book sizzles with examples of 'Spirit speech' drawn from the sermons of powerful contemporary preachers. Powery traces the Spirit's movement with a deft hand and in doing so starts an important new conversation for preachers and scholars."
—**JANA CHILDERS**, Professor of Homiletics and Speech-Communication, San Francisco Theological Seminary

"Professor Powery has provided us with the next overdue installment of reflection on preaching as distilled in the African American church tradition. But more, his contribution is a much needed discourse on the Holy Spirit, the true subject in any preaching that has power. His work is indispensable for all who would teach this fine art or learn to do it well. This book promises to be a treasure for those who love the word. Luke deserves our deepest gratitude."
—**W. C. TURNER**, Associate Professor of the Practice of Homiletics, Duke University Divinity School

SPIRIT SPEECH
LAMENT AND CELEBRATION IN PREACHING

Luke A. Powery

ABINGDON PRESS
NASHVILLE

SPIRIT SPEECH
LAMENT AND CELEBRATION IN PREACHING

Library of Congress Cataloging-in-Publication Data

Powery, Luke A., 1974-
  Spirit speech : lament and celebration in preaching / Luke A. Powery.
    p. cm.
  Includes bibliographical references (p.   ) and index.
  ISBN 978-0-687-65974-6 (binding: pbk., adhesive, perfect : alk. paper)
  1. Preaching. 2. African American preaching. 3. Joy—Religious aspects—Christianity. 4. Grief—Religious aspects—Christianity. 5. Holy Spirit. I. Title.
  BV4208.U6P69 2009
  251.0089'96073—dc22

                                                                      2009027999

09 10 11 12 13 14 15 16 17 18—10 9 8 7 6 5 4 3 2 1

MANUFACTURED IN THE UNITED STATES OF AMERICA

*For Christiana (1995–2005),
my niece, who lives in the Spirit*

CONTENTS

ACKNOWLEDGMENTS

I cannot help but think of these words as I acknowledge those who have influenced the shape of my life and this work: "Gratefulness is flowing from my heart." These words from "Grateful," a gospel song by Hezekiah Walker, are a lyrical and musical synopsis of what I am about to say. As I write each word, I imagine "Grateful" being repeated over and over again as the *cantus firmus* for this prose. The following words are like a linguistic descant over that one solid melodious message: gratefulness.

I am grateful for Emmanuel College of Victoria University in the University of Toronto. It was there where I providentially was mentored by Paul Scott Wilson, a tremendous homiletics scholar, pastor, and friend. Indeed, "God has smiled on me" through my relationship with Paul, whose unfailing support for my work and this project in particular was evident through its early and later stages. On the earlier version of this book as a dissertation, his homiletical wisdom was complemented by Carol B. Duncan, a gifted sociologist of black religion, who was a "God-send" as a wonderful cultural conversation partner throughout my doctoral program in Toronto. Arthur Van Seters, Dale P. Andrews, and Pamela Klassen also provided helpful feedback and critical insight on the earlier version of this work, which has hopefully strengthened the present manifestation of this project. Other homiletics colleagues in Toronto deserve honorable mention for their collegiality and stirring dialogue about preaching: David Schnasa Jacobsen, Stephen Johnson, Emily Rodgers, Robert Brewer, Alan Rudy-Froese, and Casey Barton. All of these individuals made my stay in Canadian "exile" feel like "home."

My work in Toronto would have been impossible without the financial support of the Fund for Theological Education (FTE) and Dr. Sharon Watson Fluker, Vice President of Doctoral Programs and Administration. Sharon's ongoing encouragement and advice was and is a bright light in the corridors of academe. I am grateful to her and the entire "FTE family" who ignite the flames of my intellectual curiosity and stoke the fires for cultural and spiritual vitality. If I had ten thousand tongues, I could not say enough about my FTE colleagues and friends, especially Drs. Ellison and Sorett who have been a fraternal community of encouragement throughout this process.

These days Princeton Theological Seminary fuels my intellectual and spiritual formation; it has been a joy to teach there these past few years. I am surrounded by a supportive earthly cloud of witnesses in the Practical Theology Department. I am particularly grateful for my colleagues in preaching, speech communication in ministry, and worship—Charles L. Bartow (now emeritus), Michael A. Brothers, Sally A. Brown, Nancy Lammers Gross, James F. Kay, Cleophus J. LaRue, and Martin Tel. They have encouraged this young scholar day in and day out and I am truly thankful. Also, Marija Diviaio, our faculty administrative assistant, was a great support during the process. In this list of "PTS witnesses," I must include Brian K. Blount, Geddes W. Hanson, Peter J. Paris, and my "godfather" Adrian Backus; along with others, I stand on their shoulders during the journey of life. They have fought the good fight and are winning. In addition, I thank President Iain R. Torrance and Dean of Academic Affairs, Darrell L. Guder, for their warm welcome to this esteemed faculty and their support for the work that I do.

The ideas in this book have been tested in the patient ears of many audiences who were gracious enough to ask wise questions and provide constructive feedback. I am grateful to the following institutions, organizations and groups: Atlantic School of Theology in Halifax, Nova Scotia, who invited me to give the 2008 Nicholson Lectures; 2008 Christian Scholars' Conference at Lipscomb University; Worship and Preaching work group at the annual meeting of the Academy of Homiletics in 2008; 2009 Calvin Symposium on Worship at Calvin College and Calvin Theological Seminary; American Baptist College in Nashville, who invited me to participate in the 2009 Garnett-Nabrit Lecture Series; 2009 Princeton Forum on Youth Ministry; students in my "Preaching, Passion, and the Spirit" course in Fall 2008; and, the 2007–2009 Engle fellows at the Joe R. Engle Institute of Preaching held at Princeton Seminary. These entities left traces of the Spirit indelibly marked on me and my work. Other homiletics conversation partners were kind enough to listen to my working out of these ideas during the process: my "brother" Kenyatta R. Gilbert, who has been on the journey with me for quite a while, Martha J. Simmons, and Brad R. Braxton. These ideas have also been tested through the wise editorial advice of Robert A. Ratcliff, Senior Editor at Abingdon Press. His excitement for preaching and my work excites me; this book is better and more accessible because of him.

I would be remiss if I did not thank those in the "trenches of ministry," the congregations that have nurtured my spirit throughout the years, showing me not only the signs of the Spirit, but the fruit of the Spirit. I am grateful for the Greater Miami Church of God in Miami, Florida, and Union Baptist Church in Trenton, New Jersey. Black Church at Stanford University led by the Reverend Floyd Thompkins was a crucial lifeline for me during my Stanford years. Last but not least, the International Protestant Church of Zürich in Switzerland, first as an intern, second as their associate pastor, nudged me towards the beautiful work of the Spirit across cultures and denominational lines. Without these ministries enriching my soul, I would not be who I am today so I am grateful to them.

However, I end this linguistic eucharist at the beginning, in my first church home, where it all started, in the loving arms of my parents, the Reverend W. Byron Powery and Emittie V. Powery. To them, "Brother Byron" and "Sister Mitty," I owe more than words can articulate. They nurtured in me a love for song, word, and spirit; their home was the "school of the Spirit." Without them, none of this would be possible. They have loved their "baby" endlessly and tirelessly. One could not ask for better parents who walk in the Spirit of love. They have cheered me on in every endeavor and this one is no exception. Alongside them are the rest of the Powery posse— my brothers, Calron, Dwight, and Emerson, and my sister, Monique, with all of their families. Particularly, Emerson, a New Testament scholar, provided critical support and assistance with Paul Wilson, at a "midnight hour" juncture in the manuscript process. Without them, the book would be much longer!

My gratitude reaches a celebratory climax when I think of my loving wife, Gail, and our children, Moriah and Zachary. I am because they are. They keep me grounded and fill my life with joy, laughter, and fun. In particular, Gail ("G") is a patient cheerleader, who embodies the Spirit in ways she will never realize; her spirit touches me. Christiana, to whom this book is dedicated, left two final prayerful words of intercession on the pages of her hospital journal—"also touch." Those words preach to me and remind me what the teaching and writing ministry are all about. This book is in the spirit of those two intercessory words in hope that this work would "also touch" the reader in ways too deep for words, sighs only the Spirit will know.

INTRODUCTION

Where Was the Spirit? An Unhealthy Situation

It was December 20, 2005 in San Jose, California. Five days before Christmas. The mall parking lots were full of people doing last-minute shopping. Churches were getting ready for an overflow crowd at Christmas Eve and Christmas Day services. Pastors were putting their best foot forward in their sermon preparations in anticipation of those who only attend church services once a year. People were excited for the Advent of Christ. A party mood filled the air. I, on the other hand, was getting ready for something else—not the celebration of the birth of Jesus Christ, but the lament of the death of my ten-year-old niece, Christiana, who died from a rare disease that shortens the life of three out of one million children. There I was, a minister of the gospel and "Uncle Luke," preparing to officiate the graveside ceremony of my niece. Like Jesus, who wept at the tomb of Lazarus causing onlookers to say, "See how he loved him!" (John 11:36), we wept at the tomb of Christiana as a sign of our love for her, for as Nicholas Wolterstorff says in his book, *Lament for a Son*, "Every lament is a love-song."[1] However, it appeared that not everyone present at the cemetery sang this same song of the Spirit.

There were those, even ordained ministers and preachers of the gospel, who appeared to be afraid to lament and allow the Spirit to groan through them, evidenced by their overemphasis on celebrating the fact that my niece was now in glory, in heaven, with God. They highlighted the hope of the Resurrection and Easter but ignored the lament of the Good Friday crucifixion. There were pleas for personal salvation to be heaven-bound through a sermonic "altar call." In front of my niece's casket, I wept not only over losing her but also over the loss of lament, the Spirit's song. There was no sense that the Spirit also manifests itself through laments and not solely through celebrations. The depth of expression found in the Spirit was absent. There was no sign of lament in this sermon. The sermon was disturbingly overwhelmed with celebrations for those who raised their hands to take the heaven-bound train. It was as if Christiana's life of love did not even matter and was not going to be missed. Why, even at a graveside service, are some Christian preachers afraid to lament and engage in the sighs of the Spirit? I left that graveside wondering, "Where was the Holy Spirit in that proclamation?" I began a discerning process about the signs of the Spirit in preaching that continues in this academic project.

Where Is the Spirit in Sermons?
A Homiletical Problem

Preaching is a theological act of worship rooted in the triune God. As worship, preaching necessarily needs the presence and power of the Spirit to be effective. The early church demonstrates this essential knowledge of dependence on the Spirit with its emphasis on Pentecost and *epiclesis* in the liturgy.[2] One early theologian, Basil the Great, says, "If you remain outside the Spirit, you cannot worship at all."[3] In fact, the entire life of the church is one long *epiclesis*, according to Yves Congar.[4] The theological assertion of the essential presence of the Spirit for the worship life of faith communities is difficult to refute in the Christian church; yet, James Forbes is only one of a few homileticians who speaks about the Holy Spirit in preaching in substantial ways. He argues that, "The preaching event itself...is a living, breathing, flesh-and-blood expression of the theology of the Holy Spirit."[5] But even his work leaves one wondering, "Where is the Spirit in the actual sermon?" Homiletical theorists traditionally assume the significance of the Holy Spirit but do not seem to adequately articulate how the Spirit is concretely at work in the preaching event through sermon language, content, and structure.

Discerning the Spirit in Sermons: A Hopeful Purpose

This book proposes constructive theological ways to recognize and describe the manifestations of the Spirit in preaching. Pneumatology is a difficult subject to address when considered in the abstract. Therefore, for the purposes of a homiletical discussion about the Spirit, it is pertinent to search for concrete avenues that may foster such a dialogue. In homiletics, celebration as a sermonic form has been recognized as one of the manifestations of the Spirit, at least in some expressions of African American preaching;[6] thus, it may serve as one approach to make concrete a pneumatological discussion in homiletics. However, on its own, celebration, though deeply rooted in African cultures, seems inadequate for a robust exploration of the Spirit in preaching. The biblical witness demonstrates individuals and communities approaching God, not only in joy, but also in sorrow. Celebration, therefore, needs to be paired with lament, another faithful response of worship to God who should be praised in the midst of both joyful and sorrowful occasions. This giving of worship itself is only possible through the Spirit's operation.[7] Lament, stemming from the Spirit, can be an appropriate way of addressing human failure or loss before God; and celebration, sparked by the Spirit, is an appropriate way of acknowledging God's ongoing care. In fact, just as celebration has been called a "nonmaterial African cultural survival,"[8] it has been noted that "for African peoples everywhere the experience of lamentation is as ancient as their days of existence."[9] Thus, the counterparts of lamentation and celebration are embedded in the cultural fabric of the experience of many African Americans.

Some homileticians bring lament to the fore, such as Mary Catherine Hilkert, in *Naming Grace: Preaching and the Sacramental Imagination,* and Sally Brown, in a more recent essay, "When Lament Shapes the Sermon"; but this focus has not been developed substantially in African American homiletics because celebration has been the main attraction.[10] This book posits lament as with a manifestation of the Spirit and a sermonic form, in conjunction both celebration; therefore, lament is also a helpful avenue in establishing a pneumatological discussion for homiletics. Furthermore, properly balanced and harnessed, lament and celebration may be conceived as doxology, two postures that should be united in giving praise and honor to God, indicating that homiletical worship is not limited to celebration nor is it tainted by lament.[11] Doxology, which will be discussed later, is a helpful concept with which to address homiletical literature because it is tensive and relates easily to other aspects of tensive language in homiletical theory, for instance, metaphor, law, and gospel.[12] As such, it offers signs or markers of its presence in sermon language, content, and structure.

Moreover, the consideration of lament and celebration as manifestations of the Spirit in preaching needs to be complemented by a holistic understanding of the work of the Spirit. Hence, both homiletical postures should be understood in terms of a communal act of worship that fosters individual experience of grace, ecclesial unity, and social fellowship or outreach by a congregation, for all of these are also manifestations of the Spirit, which will become clearer as this study progresses. These five manifestations of the Spirit—lament, celebration, grace, unity, and fellowship—will form a theological-hermeneutical lens for discerning the presence of the Spirit in preaching while providing a theological language for speaking about the Spirit in relation to sermons.

In particular, Christian preaching traditions within African American culture will be highlighted as cultural case studies that reveal the manifestations of the Spirit under discussion. Throughout this work, the term "African American" will be used to refer to people of African descent living in the United States of America. For the purposes of this study, other cultural expressions such as "blacks," "black people," or "African peoples" will refer to those in the United States. It is possible that these same terms may be used to speak of African diasporan people in other parts of the world, but this project attempts to focus its theological lens on the Christian religious experience of blacks in the United States. It is important to clarify the approach to this issue of cultural nomenclature because naming black people is still an unsettled issue in various parts of the world, including the United States. Historically, naming blackness has been connected to societal status; thus, naming the black race is mired with political connotations. Geneva Smitherman notes, "The status of Blacks remains unsettled. Name changes and debates over names reflect our uncertain status."[13]

Furthermore, any reference to "African American Christianity," "black Christianity," the "black church" or "African American church" in this study refers to the various black expressions and interpretations of Christianity within the United States. I should note that no agreement exists on what the "black church" means. A traditional understanding of the black church, espoused by C. Eric Lincoln and Lawrence Mamiya in *The Black Church in African American Experience*, "refers to the Protestant denominational sects (groups), dating back to enslavement that fused African styles of worship and beliefs with European American tenets of Christianity"; thus, it is not a replication of the white religious experience. In this perspective, the black church refers to the historically black denominations (AME, AMEZ, CME, National and Progressive Baptists, COGIC, and so on) that have been a "critical institutional force" for the liberation, survival, and daily life of black people. Many scholars recognize that there are predominantly black local churches in white denominations such as The United Methodist or the Episcopal Church but still assert that the "black church" refers to the previously mentioned historic and "totally black controlled denominations."[14]

On the other hand, there are those who speak of the black church in broader terms that are more congruent with my own viewpoint. For instance, womanist scholar Delores Williams makes a distinction between the black church and African American denominational churches. She says, "Contrary to the nomenclature in current black theological, historical, and sociological works... the *black church* is not used to name *both* the invisible black church and the African American denominational churches. To speak of the African American denominational churches as the black church suggests a unity among the denominations that does not consistently exist."[15] Instead, the black church, in the words of Barbara Holmes, is "a dynamic religious entity forged in oppression and sustained by practices that were often covert and intuitive."[16] The black church extends beyond an actual form but is "meta-actual." It permeates the imaginations of black people and "embodies a spiritual idea," an idea rooted not only in history but in the narratives and myths of an oppressed people.[17] Regardless of one's understanding of the black church, it is agreed upon that the black church is a spiritual wellspring of life from the times of its origins in the hush arbors during slavery to being an impetus for the civil rights movement. The black church is a safe place in an unsafe world—even a "virtual" space created by its particular worship practices and ethos.[18]

African American preaching expressions are the homiletical foci in this inquiry for several reasons. First, this study addresses African American Christian communities of which I am a part as a black Christian, indicating a biased inquisitive interest in black cultures. Second, the African American church has traditionally placed a great emphasis on the proclamation of the Word and the experience of the Holy Spirit in the worship life of the Christian community. As one scholar writes, "There is so much love of the Spirit in black churches."[19] These cultural expressions of preaching, therefore, represent a potential oasis for exploring the intersection of pneumatology and preaching. Third, as noted, the sermon forms of lament and celebration poignant in African American preaching are helpful avenues in grounding a pneumatological discussion for homiletics, though lament has not been adequately explored as of yet. The signs of the Spirit expressed in this cultural context will reveal that these manifestations of the Spirit are culturally dependent and yet can be discerned in sermon language, content, and structure. This means that lament and celebration, for instance, may be found in other cultures and similarly discerned to be of the Spirit, though they may be expressed differently.

Through this exploration of pneumatology for homiletics, it will be argued that the presence of the Spirit can be discerned in sermon language, content, and structure. Lament and celebration are particular manifestations of the Spirit in preaching and the juxtaposition and unity of the two is necessary for fulsome praise. Additional signs of the Spirit in such preaching are expressions of the experience of individual grace, ecclesial unity, and social fellowship or outreach by the community of faith. With this overarching argument guiding this study, the distinct contributions of this work to homiletics are the following: (1) the assertion that manifestations of the Spirit may be discerned in sermon language, content, and structure; (2) the naming of lament as a manifestation of the Spirit and sermon form in preaching; (3) the linking of lament and celebration—homileticians, if they even speak of lament or celebration, usually only focus on one or the other; (4) the focus of their union as doxology; and (5) the claim that these sermonic forms as manifestations of the Spirit in preaching are complemented by other manifestations of the Spirit expressed as the embrace of individual grace, the fostering of ecclesial unity, and the encouraging of social fellowship or outreach by a congregation.

Searching for the Spirit in Preaching:
A Helpful Method

This study will proceed dialogically by integrating traditional biblical and theological sources with African American Christianity, culture, and homiletical theory and practice. The Spirit is not confined to specific cultures or traditions, and neither is this study as it relates to the sources used to develop a theological-hermeneutical lens for "reading" preaching events pneumatologically. Chapter 1 presents the sociocultural context of African American preaching and worship with the aim of revealing the importance of holistic and outward manifestations of the Spirit in this setting. Chapter 2 will continue to explore pneumatology in relation to preaching by pursuing the Spirit's presence in human language, specifically in the relationship between the Spirit and the expressions of *lament and celebration*. Chapter 3 will be a dialogue about the work of the Spirit as *grace* in the personal realm, particularly justification and sanctification in the life of the believer nurtured through preaching. Chapter 4 will discuss the work of the Spirit as *unity* in the ecclesial realm, specifically the work of the Spirit to unify a church through preaching. Chapter 5 will stress the work of the Spirit as *fellowship*, particularly of the sort that stresses social outreach in preaching. Out of these previous chapters will emerge a theological-hermeneutical lens for discerning or "reading" the presence of the Spirit in sermonic moments—lament, celebration, grace, unity, and fellowship. Using this lens, chapter 6 will describe the presence of the Spirit in the sermon language, content, and structure of two African American sermons. The final chapter, chapter 7, will work for enhancing the practice of preaching in the Spirit through a further study of the rhetorical form and theological content of lament and celebration, that is, the aim of this chapter will be to foster stronger Spirit-filled preaching in local congregations.

Though this work is primarily a theological investigation into the relationship between pneumatology and homiletical theory and practice, the ideas presented in this study can also serve as markers of a life lived in the Spirit. Thus, this project begins with the desire that this discussion of the Spirit would not only change preaching, but also change our way of living. I am influenced by Saint Augustine, who believed that the grand style of speaking could affect how people live. Augustine writes, "There are many other experiences through which we have learned what effect the grand style of a wise speaker may have on men. They do not show it through applause but rather through their groans, sometimes even through tears, and finally through a change of their way of life."[20] This potential impact on a person's life is also possible through preaching in the Spirit.

Chapter One

Toward a Pneumatology for Preaching

If you got religion, show some sign.
—Geneva Smitherman, *Talkin and Testifyin*

There is so much love of the Spirit in black churches.
—Karen Baker-Fletcher, *Sisters of Dust, Sisters of Spirit*

A *Spiritual* People

Near the conclusion of *The Souls of Black Folk*, W. E. B. Dubois proudly proclaims that African people brought "three gifts" to America—the "gift of story and song," "the gift of sweat and brawn," and the "gift of the Spirit."[1] Similarly, Karen Baker-Fletcher says, "Spirit is not a gift of the White man. Spirit is for all in all, and our ancestors brought it with them from Africa."[2] The embrace of the Spirit in African diasporan cultures may be the reason Henry Mitchell boldly asserts with evident bias that African American culture is the "most responsive culture to the movement of the Holy Spirit" in the United States.[3] His stance breathes of cultural arrogance because he seems to suggest that other cultures are not as responsive to the Spirit as African Americans when in fact it may be that other cultures just respond differently to the Spirit. Even within a particular cultural milieu (for example, African American), response to the Spirit is not monolithic. Despite this critique of Mitchell, his statement does indicate the general importance of experiencing and manifesting the Spirit in African American religion.

The gift of the Spirit, a topic that is usually muted in most theological discussions, will be the focus of this chapter. It will present a sociocultural perspective on the work of the Holy Spirit as found in African American Christian cultural contexts in order to reveal the particular setting of African American preaching practices, which are the homiletical foci in this overall

1

project. Through this cultural perspective, the Spirit works materially and holistically in individual, communal, and social realms. This holistic material pneumatology forms a theological framework out of which the gospel is proclaimed and through which the presence of the Spirit in preaching may be discerned. Naturally, manifestations of the Spirit are culturally dependent, thus, what is revealed about the experience, expression, and manifestation of the Spirit in African American Christian religion is distinctive. African American Christianity asserts, more than other traditions, that the Spirit must be embodied in word and deed for genuine, robust worship to occur. As many African Americans assert, "if you got religion, show some sign."[4] For African American Christians, outward signs of the Spirit are vital for authentic spirituality to be discerned in a person or community's life.

This chapter will deal with a brief history of the spirit of suffering that African peoples have endured; the belief in and experience of the Spirit's real, sustaining presence; and the embodied expressions and outward manifestations of the Spirit through the human body, language, and hospitality. It will become clear that the holistic work of the Spirit in many African American settings is not primarily cerebral, but material, and can and should be expressed and discerned through human beings in action, including the act of preaching.

The Spirit of Suffering: A Lament

James Cone, the esteemed Black theologian, notes, "There is no truth for and about black people that does not emerge out of the context of their experience. Truth in this sense is black truth, a truth disclosed in the history and culture of black people. This means that there can be no Black Theology that does not take the black experience as a source for its starting point."[5] With this rationale, I begin this deliberation about the outward manifestations of the Spirit in every aspect of life by painting a picture of the historical experience of African peoples, an experience of lament. One can view the black religious experience as the "meeting of God in the depth of the despair and loneliness of slavery";[6] therefore, a study of the manifestation of the Spirit in African American preaching must begin with the pain of unjust historical subjugation, because these are the black spiritual roots of preaching. Howard Thurman truthfully declares that "suffering stalks man, never losing the scent, and soon or late seizes upon him to wreak its devastation."[7] Indeed, suffering's havoc is not limited to African Americans but is universal; yet, as African American homiletician Cleophus LaRue notes, the distinctive power of black preaching is not a matter of special techniques, but of "extraordinary experiences," experiences of marginalization and powerlessness stemming from the "school" of slavery. The "black church was born in slavery" and it was an "ungodly, unjust, undeserved" "burdensome context."[8] Black preaching expressions are historically rooted in lament.

This milieu of the oppression of African peoples in the Americas has been poignantly described as "terror" by Anthony Pinn. Africans endured the cruel "Middle Passage" of slavery to the so-called New World; this heinous voyage transpired in the belly of slave ships as human moans, shrieks, the smell of filth, and the stench of death prevailed. This terror is the history of struggle for survival as Africans in America, where "dehumanization" ruled through such devices as chattel slavery, causing a "social death," alienation from society. If this was not sufficient, blacks were also viewed as beasts, objects for study, property to be sold and stripped, and as "entertainers" who would at many times wear "rope neckties" (lynching).[9] Capturing the devastation and dehumanization experienced during the Middle Passage in poetical prose, Barbara Holmes argues that lament was the discourse of moans on the slave ships. She writes, "On the deck after evening rations, lament danced and swayed under the watchful eyes of the crew."[10] There was good reason to lament because as early as 1611, Africans were viewed not only as savages but also were considered "deformed" due to their blackness. These "savage" black bodies were the slave master's property. Being property polarized white and black bodies such that bonded Africans could be physically marked through branding (sign of possession) and whip-scarring (sign of punishment); these were signatures of slavery, naming blacks as *other* or even "bodiless" in a society of white privilege. African Americans, even today, are "scarred" because of this brutal history.[11]

The following account of the treatment of a Jamaican slave is representative of the experience of slavery across the diaspora and reveals the cause of the scar.

> Gave ["Port Royal"] a moderate whipping, pickled him well, made Hector shit in his mouth, immediately put a gag whilst his mouth was full and made him wear it 4 or 5 hours...Flogged...Quacoo well, and then washed salt pickle, lime juice and bird pepper; also whipped Hector for losing his hoe, made New Negro Joe piss in his eyes and mouth.[12]

It is not surprising then that the spirituals have been called "sorrow songs"[13] and that a black slave could sing and shout,

> No more auction block for me, No more, No more,
> No more auction block for me, Many thousand gone.

No more peck o' corn for me, No more, No more,
No more peck o' corn for me, Many thousand gone.
No more driver's lash for me . . .
No more pint o' salt for me . . .
No more hundred lash for me . . .
No more mistress' call for me. . . .
Many thousand gone.[14]

The slaves sang "Oh, freedom all over me . . . An' befo' I'd be a slave, I'll be buried in my grave . . ."[15] Sometimes they felt like a motherless child. Sometimes they felt like they were almos' gone, a long ways from home, because of their existential reality of suffering.[16] Death was better than life, so they sang, "Death, oh death, oh me Lawd, Death, oh death, oh me Lawd. When-a me body lay down in de grave, Den-a me soul gwine shout fo' joy."[17] Joy was hard to find in this context because lament was so prominent. Blacks lived the blues, the "black body fighting hard times."[18]

African peoples suffer not only at the hands of the broader society, but also because of the church. In the colonized West Indies,

> the missionaries assumed that their ethical rationalism was a mode of life accessible to all. Creole ideas . . . were understood by the missionaries only as corrupting superstition. Their practice of ethical rationalism with its disciplines of the body not only repudiated the world of play and its carnivalesque aesthetic, it also sought to stifle in Jamaica an intense eudemonic of freedom which both transformed and re-embodied an African sense of joy in the world.[19]

David Walker in his 1829 *Appeal* notes that "the white Americans having reduced us to the wretched state of slavery, treat us in that condition more cruel (they being an enlightened and Christian people), than any heathen nation did any people whom it had reduced to our condition."[20] The supposed "Christian" country propagated subjugation, not liberation, for the Christian masters of slaves prioritized the soul over the body. Riggins Earl calls this prioritization the "ideal Christian master type response," which leads to proslavery literature in which the slave of African origin is in theory made in God's image, but "it was the unchangeable blackness of the slave's body, which signified the demonic."[21] The black slave was viewed only as a body and the black body had only one worth—to work for the slavemaster. Enslaved blacks questioned whether their blackness was the creation of the devil as was preached to them. Blackness was a sin and the embodiment of evil. Blacks "became not simply strangers and aliens unfamiliar with Western ways but black devils who cavorted with minions from the underworld."[22] Due to the propagation of a false, distorted, prejudiced gospel, some

Africans even accepted the color symbolism of their white Christian enslavers. Blacks could sing "Wash me...and I shall be whiter, whiter than snow!"[23] thereby unconsciously singing this petition to a white god. By doing so, they implicitly acknowledged "how much separates them from their adopted deity."[24] God, who was white, wanted them to be white also because white was pure, beautiful, and godly.

This spiritualized color symbolism spills over into some African Americans' self-image of embodied blackness. African American writer James Baldwin, reveals his own struggle with self-loathing due to his father's impact on his life. Baldwin thought his father's "deep blackness" was beautiful but his father did not. He had succumbed to the society of white preference. His father believed that "black is ugly." Baldwin says of his father, "Because I was black, because I was little, because I was ugly. He made me ugly."[25] This self-belief in black ugliness is not limited to Baldwin but represents a plague that pervades African American communities to this day. "Self-hatred may be one of the deepest sources of conflict and turmoil *within* the African-American community. This may be especially true concerning women and their bodies." There is such a "history of ambivalence" about the physical appearance of African peoples, in general, but black women in particular, that self-hatred and cultural humiliation "assaults" African American women by undermining their capacity for "self-love."[26] Their inner vision can be tainted and scarred because of the paradoxical "home" in which they live.

Cheryl Townsend Gilkes insightfully analyzes this paradox with the following observation:

> In spite of the high premium placed on culturally exalted images of white female beauty and the comedic exploitation that surrounds the large Black woman, many African-American women know that the most respected physical image of Black women, within and outside of the community, is that of the large woman. Although it is respected, it is a culturally deviant image that is not necessarily loved. It is an image of power in a community where women need to be fortified and empowered. Yet some of the most powerless women in the community struggle with being overweight and its unhealthy consequences. It is an asexual image that sometimes permits escape from the constant harassment and sexual aggression, accurately called "hitting on," that disproportionately pervade the lives of those Black women who most approximate white cultural ideals. In the era of "fitness and health" that same image is officially labeled "obese" and makes every large Black woman an immediately suspected case of bulimia.[27]

Black bodies, male or female, may be disdained due to a historical consciousness that perpetuates black as ugly, evil, and even bodiless. This gospel of prejudice attempts to break the bodies and spirits of African Americans.

Even aesthetically, blacks have been portrayed as a "grim aesthetic" of monstrous-looking, thick-lipped, large-nosed, deviant sexual beings.[28] Lynne Westfield captures the suffering and brokenness, within and without, of African Americans, when she writes poetically,

> *so many parts are missing faded damaged*
> *it is difficult*
> > *to re-member my whole*
> > *danceable self* [29]

Westfield believes that the loss of body parts is due to the past and present oppression that African Americans have endured during their existence, thus she laments; it is "difficult to re-member" wholeness. Not only is the black body broken, but also it may even be missing or whitewashed. The African slaves had a right to moan, "I've been 'buked an' I've been scorned...Dere is trouble all over dis worl'...."[30] The trouble of discrimination and dehumanization created a situation of suffering that stemmed from the outside world that led to suffering on the inside (for example, self-image). This horrible scenario is an "exile" experience, not only historically but also in contemporary times. In her book *Saints in Exile: The Holiness-Pentecostal Experience in African American Religion and Culture* Cheryl Sanders describes the lives of African Americans, particularly those in the Sanctified Church, as one of an "exilic dialectic." Sanders's metaphor of "exile" is appropriate because African American people have not been at "home" for centuries, ever since the Middle Passage. Within this exilic existence, blacks have been rejected by the landlords of the Americas, yearn for home, and seek to learn how to sing the Lord's song in a strange land. Many times, the "Lord's song," the spirituals, was a lament due to injustice. Moreover, not only does the external locale create an estrangement from home, but also an internal tension or dialectic is present. Sanctified African Americans struggle with negotiating their identity, the "both-and" identity—African American in the world but not of it, static-ecstatic expressions of worship, protest-cooperation methods in education and religious institutions, sacred-secular music.[31] It is a continual "betwixt and between" existence where one is never at home in one of the dialectical poles. In fact, they are a "long ways from home" as the spiritual says because there is a constant negotiation of social reality and identity. Despite living in "exile," African American Christians, in general, have held on to their God and to their Christian religion, declaring, "Ain' gwine lay my 'ligion down."[32]

The spirit of suffering and lament endured by African Americans throughout history still influences the present situation in stereotypes propagated about African Americans in the larger society. It is evident when one considers the prison system within the United States, in which a disproportionate number of African American males are imprisoned compared to other racial groups. This has led to distorted self-images pervading the lives of many African Americans even today. However, there has been a profound sense of endurance and faith in the midst of it all. There are many reasons for this, but one main reason is theological and experiential—the Holy Spirit. In what follows, the belief in the presence of the Spirit and the actual experience of the Spirit in the midst of suffering will be detailed as a tremendous sustaining and sacramental source of hope, a reason for celebration.

The Experience of the Spirit in Suffering: A Celebration

Since slavery, African Americans have been sustained in life by the Spirit of God, who has been a wellspring of freedom, sparking celebration in the midst of lament. In his study of religious ceremonies in the African diaspora, *Working the Spirit*, Joseph Murphy argues that "the Spirit is a real and irreducible force uplifting communities throughout the African diaspora."[33] Enslaved Africans survived cruel oppression because of the Spirit's power. George Cummings notes that:

> the lives of black slaves, according to their testimonies, were filled with the consequences of the presence of the Spirit: secret meetings, which are an expression of independence; disobeying their masters in order to serve God in prayer and worship; getting practical tools to help with confronting life; hope; visions of freedom; and physical manifestations of being possessed by the Spirit.[34]

The Spirit instilled courage and hope, leading to celebration. Even the intoned spirituals can be viewed as the voice of the Spirit breaking through melody and crying out for freedom. These songs were tunes of the Spirit sustaining and empowering African peoples to endure suffering. James Cone asserts, "The spiritual . . . is the Spirit of the people struggling to be free."[35] In the midst of suffering, African Americans have never been alone, though some may have felt estranged from God due to enduring cruelty at the hands of other human beings. In pain, they could still celebrate God and sing "glory hallelujah" or "there is a balm in Gilead."[36]

Paule Marshall presents a wonderful example of the power of the Spirit in this context in her novel about African diasporic life, *Praisesong for the Widow*. In it, she presents a scene where the Ibo people from Africa are brought as slaves to the coast of the United States on Tatem Island. After arriving on land, Aunt Cuney conveys that the Ibos turned around and began to walk on water back to their African homeland, singing songs of joy. Marshall writes that the "chains didn't stop those Ibos none. Neither iron" and as they began singing, it "sounded like they was having such a good time."[37] There was celebration because the Spirit sustained and sustains African Americans in concrete ways, not solely through interiorized means or in isolated sacred spaces.

The entire cosmos is sacred, thus a realm for divine intervention that includes the individual, communal, and social dimensions of human living. Melva Costen notes that the "sacred cosmos" permeates all of life such that "humans live in a religious universe, so that natural phenomena, objects, and all of life are associated with acts of God. Life is thus viewed holistically rather than in separate compartments as created by secular-sacred dichotomy."[38] Even while on the slave auction block, an enslaved black woman or man could be heard singing,

> Over my head I hear music in the air.... There must be a God somewhere.... Over my head I hear singing in the air. There must be a God somewhere. Over my head I see Jesus in the air. Over my head I see Jesus in the air. Over my head I see Jesus in the air.[39]

The slave was not alone, but heavenly music and Jesus himself were near, pervading the universe, "in the air." Another spiritual declares the desire and belief that Jesus can "walk with me" through all of life's circumstances.[40] African Americans knew and know that Jesus walks with them to the gallows or to the garbage dumpster. Anywhere and everywhere they travel, the Spirit is present, never leaving them alone, whether by themselves, in a church community, or at work in society. African thinker John Mbiti echoes this view when he says,

> Wherever the African is, there is his religion: he carries it to the fields where he is sowing seeds or harvesting a new crop; he takes it with him to the beer party or to attend a funeral ceremony; and if he is educated, he takes religion with him to the examination room at school or in the university; if he is a politician he takes it to the house of parliament. Although many African languages do not have a word for religion as such, it nevertheless accompanies the individual from long before his birth to long after his physical death.[41]

Furthermore, in some cultural forms of literature, one discovers representative artful expressions of this sense of sacramentality within black religion. In Paule Marshall's novel, Avey Johnson, the main protagonist, is married to Jay, who upon returning home from work perceives his jazz albums as sacred objects and each record as an "icon," so much that these "anointed words" can "work their magic, their special mojo on him," amazingly easing his face and body. In addition, as Avey enters a rum shop on a beach, she describes it as having the "hushed tone of a temple or church," and while on the boat for excursion, she views the women like "the presiding mothers of Mount Olivet Baptist."[42] Sacramentality is not limited to a local church but is pervasive in the larger context of the world. Even nature speaks a holy word when Avey dreams of her Aunt Cuney being an imploring Holiness preacher, the trees give voice to an old invitational hymn, "Come/Won't you come . . . ?"[43] Life is viewed as a context of encounter with the divine Spirit, thus, there is continuity between the spiritual and physical realms.

Diana Hayes is one of many scholars who points to the basic African belief that the ancestors are the living dead as an example of this continuity of spiritual and material contexts.[44] In addition, two works of the African diaspora that reveal with cultural, artful concreteness how the spirits act in the earthly realm are *Brown Girl in the Ring* by Nalo Hopkinson and *Mama Lola: A Vodou Priestess in Brooklyn* by Karen McCarthy Brown. In *Brown Girl in the Ring*, the character Mami Jeanne or Ti-Jeanne experiences spirit possessions and visions that shape, change, and anticipate earthly realities. At times, one sees the spirits take on human flesh for varied reasons. In *Mama Lola,* the Vodou spirits act in everyday life such that human beings can even "hug them." The spirits eat the food served for them and marry "normal" human beings. At one point, one of the black women is so frustrated in her relationship with "her man" that she says, "I will serve spirit . . . I don't need a man." The spirits are alive on the earth and even the descriptions of the particular spirits highlighted in this novel are "earthy." Azaka is the mountain man, reminding one of her or his roots. Ogou is the warrior spirit. Kouzinn is the market woman, representing the economic lives of women. Ezili is the female spirit representing woman and water power. Danbala is the serpent spirit. These spirits are connected with the physical realm and manifest through the corporeal and can be discerned. McCarthy Brown emphasizes the everydayness of the spirits, even by the structure of her work that interweaves chapters about the spirits with narratives about the human family and friends of Alourdes, a main character. The spirits are connected to what happens in *real* life, demonstrating what I call the "humanity of the spirits."[45] These cultural literary pieces point to the overarching belief in the sacramental presence and experience of the divine throughout the African diaspora. Through African American Christian eyes, the Holy Spirit materializes, not least in preaching.

Moreover, it is vital for the experience of the Spirit to be appropriated personally if the power of the Spirit is to be known. Howard Thurman views God as companion and presence and though the human spirit views God as transcendent, God is also personal and intimate. God is near in ordinary life, thus humanity is not alone in suffering.[46] African Americans, and all people, live under "the shadow of His Spirit."[47] This Spirit is not only without, but also within people, leading a "quiet ministry" that transforms.[48] "There is a Spirit in us that contains our spirit," says Thurman.[49] The presence of God through the Spirit is a reality through individual experience, though not limited to this realm. African Americans did not and do not survive and overcome suffering by talking about the Spirit's work. Experiencing the Spirit's work of liberty in suffering is what delivers oppressed peoples and what stirs any sign of celebration. African American spirituality entails being "familiar with" the Spirit.[50] This gives Melva Costen reason to declare that, in general, "Worship is more experiential than rationalistic" in African American church settings.[51] One can sing "every time I *feel* the Spirit moving in my heart" because the Spirit must be experienced in one's personal life and known to be a sustaining force and source of survival. Walter Pitts notes that Afro-Baptists frequently proclaim, "Don't give me no religion I can't *feel*."[52] Feeling the Spirit demonstrates that the Spirit is a divine reality moving within human beings. African Americans believe that the Spirit is a sustaining source in the midst of suffering, giving reasons to celebrate life in the midst of death. This personal knowledge of the Spirit cannot be contained in isolation and is not necessarily quiet but is expressed and manifested externally in the physical realm, including the event of preaching.

Embodied Expressions and Manifestations of the Spirit

In what follows, three embodied forms of the manifestation of the Spirit will be highlighted. First, the manifestation of the Spirit through the black human body will be discussed. Second, black language will be presented as another venue for the manifestation of the Spirit. Third, the liberating hospitality of African Americans will be shown to be another key manifestation of the Spirit in these cultural contexts. These manifestations occur in individual, communal, and social ways, such that the holistic aspect of the work of the Spirit is noticeable.

Spirit Manifestations through the Human Body

Some of the most salient manifestations of the Spirit throughout all of black religion happen in and through the human body. Cheryl Townsend Gilkes proclaims, "All human experience is embodied experience";[53] thus, the human experience of the Spirit is also embodied through the human body. Drawing on the African American sense of sacramentality, Lynne Westfield asserts that grace is embodied "not in abstraction like virtual reality, but in tangible things—in real bodies and real gatherings. Sacramental experiences are experiences of persons' bodies, emotions, intellect, and will coming to deeper knowledge and love of God."[54] For many African Americans, "bodies are temples of the Holy Spirit," because in many African American churches, the Spirit is located in the body of the congregants.[55] In African diasporic religion, the ecstatic expressions of the body are believed to stem from the Spirit or spirits. Robert Hood argues that the Spirit is an "untidy, dynamic, and ecstatic power" in black American religion and within the larger context of African religion, immaterial, incorporeal spirits take on human shape.[56]

A primary avenue through which the Spirit of God takes on human flesh is spirit possession of the body. According to Cheryl Sanders, the "ultimate objective of worship in the Sanctified church tradition" is any form of spirit possession.[57] If a person becomes possessed by the Spirit, he or she is "caught up in the spirit," which means that he or she is "completely subject to a force outside of himself or herself."[58] It is known that the African slaves had a proclivity for "bodily exercises," movements influenced by the African heritage of dance. Albert Raboteau, in *Slave Religion*, highlights a particular woman, who could represent any African American body, when he says that she danced, threw back her head, threw her arms, tossed herself, gasping, sinking to the floor on which she gyrated "as if acting a death struggle."[59] In the "brush harbor" meetings, the Spirit "gotta hold of" slaves; there they felt the Spirit, were excited, and could "collapse from exhaustion while under its power."[60] The Spirit took hold of the bodies of black peoples to such an extent that those possessed by the Spirit could not remain voiceless but gave voice to the spiritual ecstasy through shouts.

Closely intertwined with spirit possession is the shout, which is also a physical expression of the human at worship in the Spirit. The "regular" shout, as some scholars call it, is what happens when the Holy Spirit fills a person to such an extent that he or she cannot remain still. There is religious ecstasy, uncontrollable physical movements; some call it "getting happy."[61] The "regular" shout is distinct from the ring shout that was a ritualized group activity prevalent in the praise houses of the South in the United States. In *Praisesong for the Widow*, Avey Johnson remembers the ring shout on Tatem Island while with her Aunt Cuney and describes it as the following:

> They were propelling themselves forward at a curious gliding shuffle which did not permit the soles of the heavy work shoes they had on to ever once lift from

the floor. Only their heels rose and then fell with each step, striking the worn pineboard with a beat that was as precise and intricate as a drum's, and which as the night wore on and the Shout became more animated could be heard all over Tatem. They sang *"Who's that riding the chariot?/Well well well . . . .";* used their hands as racing tambourines, slapped their knees and thighs and chest in dazzling syncopated rhythm. They worked their shoulders; even succeeded at times in giving a mean roll of their aged hips. They allowed their failing bodies every liberty, yet their feet never once left the floor or, worse, crossed each other in a dance step. Arms shot up, hands arched back like wings . . . singing in quavering atonal voices as they glided and stamped one behind the other within the larger circle of their shadows cast by the lamplight on the walls. Even when the Spirit took hold and their souls and writhing bodies seemed about to soar off into the night, their feet remained planted firm. *I shall not be moved.*[62]

"Regular" shouting, on the other hand, is believed to stem from the Spirit who is like a fire on the inside of a person.[63] When this fire of the Spirit ignites within an entire community and a whole gathering is immersed in the ecstasy and exuberance of spirit-possessed shouting, this may be referred to as the "frenzy."[64] The bodies of entire communities become free vessels of the Spirit at praise. This is why Zora Neale Hurston observes that individuals may shout, but it is still a "community thing. It thrives in concert."[65] Within African American Christian religion, it is important to recognize that though the Spirit is experienced and expressed individually, community expression of the Spirit is not negated. The Spirit, who plays melodies through human bodily instruments, aims to manifest through everyone.

The frenzy is inclusive. Wallace Best reveals this when he cites an article about the manifestations of the Spirit at All Nations Pentecostal Church in Chicago, founded in the late 1920s by Lucy Smith. The ecstatic praise, exuberant music, and "holy dancing" were evidence that the Holy Spirit was present in that congregation. The article from the periodical *Pentecostal Ensign* describes the presence of the Spirit within a community as the following:

> The power fell while Sister Holmes sang "Jesus is Mine." The Holy Ghost had his way for 20 minutes as the young and the old danced under the mighty power of God. When the Holy Spirit "had his way" members became overcome with religious emotion and enthusiasm, clapped their hands, threw their hands over their heads, and shouted "thank you, Jesus." Some would dance to the point of frenzy.[66]

This kind of outward expression and manifestation of the Spirit through the body in African American worship leads C. Eric Lincoln and Lawrence Mamiya to call the African American Church the "first theater in the black community."[67] These two scholars depict the "frenzy" of bodily Spirit mani-festation like this:

> Some worshipers "got the Spirit" and were propelled into a paroxysm shouting. While others "fell out" and rolled on the floor in a shaking, trance-like state, possessed by the Holy Ghost. Some people stood up in the pews and waved their hands over their heads, while others clapped their hands in time with the music.... The highlight of the service was to worship and glorify God by achiev-ing the experience of mass catharsis; a purifying explosion of emotions that eclipses the harshness of reality for a season and leaves both the preacher and the congregation drained in a moment of spiritual ecstasy.[68]

When the Spirit manifests through the human body, this indicates that the body is a site for the Spirit and a ritual space, an eventful place for creative ritual activity. Through the Spirit, the body "speaks" a word and becomes a "text" that one can "read." The black body is a cultural artifact conveying messages about African Americans, according to Anthony Pinn.[69] In the same vein, Clifford Geertz believes that a text is an object of interpretation that says something about a culture and is not limited to written or verbal texts; thus, cultural forms are texts. In his case, cockfighting in Bali is a text, "saying something if something."[70] This perspective opens the field of homiletics to not only read written sermon manuscripts but also to begin to read preaching bodies as sermonic texts. Communication theory teaches, "texts are not always printed on pages or chiseled in stone—though some-times they are. Usually, they are texts of public utterance or shaped behav-ior."[71] The black body behaving under the power of the Spirit not only says something about black culture but also says something about the Spirit's rela-tionship to African American Christians.

Spirit manifestations through the body also indicate that the Spirit accepts African American Christians despite any ongoing rejection in society. The manifestation of the Spirit through the body is important not only as a way of knowing the reality of God but also knowing that God welcomes African peo-ples into a spiritual relationship. In a racist society, "the incarnated Spirit heals the split between who people really are, and who America has said they are."[72] Because of this movement of the Spirit, there can be celebration in the midst of lament. The lively quality of African American spirituality resists the debasement of their personhood, because as Zora Neale Hurston notes in *Sanctified Church*, any sign of the Spirit in the body exemplifies "the sign of special favor from the spirit that it chooses to drive out the individual con-sciousness temporarily and use the body for its expression."[73] The belief that the manifestation of the Spirit is a sign of divine favor is probably one of the most important effects of the Spirit's generous work among the African

American community. Even during slavery, "the black body as ugly and important only as a tool of labor was signified during church gatherings, and it was transformed into a ritual device through which the glory of God and the beauty of human movement were celebrated."[74] Black bodies that were wrecked under slavery and oppression were "redeemed" through bodily rituals of Spirit manifestation and signified an eventual triumph over terror.[75] Similarly, Black theologian Will Coleman depicts the importance of spirit possession in the life of the enslaved as the following: "Under the sway of its power they could be transported beyond present oppressions while receiving the courage and strength to both endure and resist the absolute enslavement of body and spirit. For them, this meant psychological and emotional liberation where physical freedom was not immanent."[76]

Basically, bodily redemption by the Holy Spirit kept enslaved African peoples alive by providing a means of hope and celebration. If the Spirit manifests through a black human body by possession, shouting, or any other ecstatic form of worship, it means that the person is somebody in a world where many say that he or she is a nobody. The Spirit welcomes African Americans through these manifestations of the body and demonstrates her love and care for black peoples, contrary to the perpetuated subtle or overt discriminatory practices in society. The human body is not the only space where signs of the Spirit come to expression and manifest themselves. The discourse of African Americans also has the potential to embody the Spirit's presence in distinct ways.

Spirit Manifestations through Human Language

African Americans generally believe that the Spirit manifests in "preaching rhetoric"[77] despite the lack of reflection on these manifestations in the actual sermon. Zilpha Elaw, a nineteenth-century evangelist, describes her preaching as the Holy Spirit moving through her while William H. Pipes in *Say Amen, Brother!* mentions a black folk preacher who says "The Lord say, 'Open yer mouth and I'll speak fer you.' See what the Spirit gwine do."[78] These perspectives demonstrate the historical continuity in the belief that the Spirit speaks through the language of African American preachers in some form. In *God Struck Me Dead: Voices of Ex-Slaves*, the sermon is noted to be in three parts. The third part of the sermon is known as "the coming of the spirit," when the Spirit "envelops" and "strikes" the preacher. An ex-slave depicts the Spirit's manifestation as the following:

When this happens, the speaker's entire demeanor changes. He now launches into a type of discourse that borders on hysteria. His voice, changed in pitch, takes on a mournful, singing quality, and words flow from his lips in such a manner as to make an understanding of them almost impossible.[79]

This description of the coming of the Spirit on the preacher seems to be what is known as celebration and "whooping" in some contemporary African American preaching expressions, which will be discussed later.

The emotive expressions, engaged bodily performance, and sermonic language of a preacher are seen as stemming from the Spirit. This is a basic pneumatology underlying African American preaching discourse. There is no word or effective sermon without the Spirit. Henry Mitchell notes that in a theology of black preaching there is always assumed as in black folk theology that there is a third "personal presence in the process, even the Holy Spirit."[80] This point is reiterated by James Harris, who says, "preaching in the black church tradition is indeed dependent upon the Holy Spirit as the anointing power that makes prophetic utterance possible."[81] Preaching in many of these cultural contexts is participatory through the action of the Spirit, involving entire congregations as proclaimers. The Spirit works with individuals but also communities. The Word "becomes embodied in the rhythm and the emotions of language as the people respond bodily to the Spirit in their midst."[82] The Spirit leads worshipers to carry on a dialogue with the preacher "by shouting approval and agreement with ejaculations like 'Amen!' or 'Preach it!' or 'Tell it like it is!' At other times they encourage the preacher to work harder to reach that precipitating point of cathartic climax by calling out, 'Well?'... 'Well?'"[83] Through the Spirit, the sermon becomes a community's sermon and not the sole property of the preacher in the pulpit.

Other aspects of ecclesial discourse that may be linked to the Spirit and expressed individually and communally are the practices of singing and glossolalia. Not only are sermonic climaxes, shouts, or celebrations viewed as manifestations of the Spirit, but also when a soloist or instrumentalist leads a congregation to the brink of ecstasy, this is also a "witness of the Spirit."[84] Jon Michael Spencer studies singing in tongues and claims that these heavenly songs are new songs in the "color and culture of the Holy Spirit."[85] Elder Charles Mason, the founder of the Church of God in Christ, describes his experience of the manifestation of the Spirit through tongues in the following testimony:

> The Spirit came upon the saints and upon me.... So there came a wave of glory into me, and all of my being was filled with the glory of the lord.... When I opened my mouth to say Glory, a flame touched my tongue which ran down to me. My language changed and no word could I speak in my own tongue. Oh! I was filled with the Glory of the Lord. My soul was then satisfied.[86]

The various expressions of language in the African American church are usually considered to be pregnant with the potential of manifesting the Spirit of God. The congregational setting is assumed to be an open space for the Spirit to breathe in and through the worship participants. In many African American churches, it is no surprise when the Spirit-sparked frenzy manifests through the black body and language in the liturgical setting. It may be more of a surprise to ponder the possibility of the Spirit manifesting through the ordinary use of language in the wider society.

The Spirit continues to manifest in African American cultural discourse outside of the ecclesial context and in the social realm to further accent the point that the Spirit reveals herself and can be discerned in language. Riggins Earl, in *Dark Salutations: Ritual, God, and Greetings in the African American Community*, performs an insightful study of how black peoples use language to support and embrace one another and resist the demonizing metaphors of racism that were and are used to depict African Americans. Earl claims that black ancestors used "salutatory metaphors" that resisted oppression and affirmed that God was for and with blacks in political and spiritual ways and blacks were for and with one another. Instead of being named incorrectly as "boy" and "nigger," African American males redefine themselves and their relationship to one another with salutatory metaphors such as "soul brother," "brotherman," and "blackman," terms that are a creative attempt to maintain control over their social beings while reflecting a spirit of ethnic kinship. "Soul brother," for instance, is a response to the white denial that blacks had souls; it affirms that God is for and with them and that they can be trustfully for and with one another. These salutatory metaphors, as ritualistic acts of socially re-creating themselves, restore humanness and wholeness to African American males. The same is true for African American women who use salutatory metaphors of womanhood, sisterhood, and friendship such as "girlfriend" and "sistergirl" instead of denigrating terms like "mammy," "matriarch," "Jezebel," or "welfare mother."[87] Interestingly, Geneva Smitherman insightfully details how expressions and semantic concepts in African American English vocabulary, such as the ones mentioned, have a religious base rooted in the traditional black church. For instance, the linguistic concepts of "sister" and "brother," which are extended by the terms "soul brother" or "sistergirl," stem from the black church.[88] These salutations (for example, "brotherman," "sistergirl") are a spiritual reclamation of the human worth and dignity of a people who were deemed worthless. Through these salutations, blacks celebrate one another as part of the human family.

These life-giving salutatory metaphors of language are ultimately rooted in the life-giving Holy Spirit who specializes in welcoming the *other*, making these salutations particular social-linguistic manifestations of the Spirit. African Americans, or any people, cannot speak a word of truth without the Spirit. Human breath stems from the breath of the Spirit and in this culture, the Spirit or spirits must manifest outwardly through materiality and even humanity, in a variety of realms and ways. With this view, one can deduce that the Spirit does speak a language and that Spirit-language manifests through the means of human language. It is not an-*other* tongue of angels, but within this cultural milieu, the Spirit's language funnels through the vernacular of African peoples in the world, though not exclusively. The Spirit takes on flesh and becomes embodied in the language of salutations. Particularly, in the context of the African American church and culture, Spirit language is a tongue that resists violence to blackness and embraces blackness with all of its beauty and creativity. The demonizing metaphors used by white oppressors were not a Spirit language, because they were inhospitable and opposed life, perpetuating the denigration of a particular people. As African Americans use salutatory metaphors with one another, the Spirit is welcoming each person while at the same time opposing the inhospitable ways of racists, as the language of the Spirit resists dehumanization of any kind. A clue to discerning whether the Spirit is speaking through someone is to determine the salutatory nature of that person's language. If a person denigrates another person through his or her tongue, it is reasonable to believe that the Spirit is not speaking; for the Spirit brings life, not death, brings wholeness, not brokenness through human language, including sermonic discourse.

The Spirit manifests through language, individually, communally, and socially. Within local churches, the Spirit manifests through linguistic forms such as preaching, singing, and speaking in tongues, and not to the exclusion of other possible linguistic avenues of the Spirit (for example, prayer). In addition, the Spirit can manifest through language use outside of church confines, particularly through greetings of welcome or "salutatory metaphors" that are used within African American communities. This holistic material pneumatology is the theological framework for preaching in the Spirit and discerning the presence of the Spirit in sermons.

Spirit Manifestations through Liberating Hospitality

With the African American sense of pervasive sacramentality, the Spirit cannot be confined to a specific place or time but envelops and breathes through all of human life, including human relationships. The Spirit's touch is not limited to the body or language but can be perceived through loving human encounters. African slaves revealed that "it is in historical human relationships that the power of the Spirit is manifested concretely."[89] The shared communal experience of the Spirit is significant. When Howard Thurman thinks of the movement of the Spirit, he considers "the Spirit of God Without-Within," indicating that the Spirit mingles one's personal needs with the needs of others.[90] If one is in the Spirit, it is not possible to neglect another because the Spirit draws people together in reconciliatory relationships. As Thurman boldly proclaims, "No man can be happy in Heaven if he left his brother in Hell."[91] In fact, it is a "miracle in the Spirit" when one discovers that the "Covenant of Brotherhood" is the witness of the Spirit's work in a person's life and "the hymn of praise offered to [God] as Thanksgiving and Glory!"[92]

From this same deep sense of care for the *other*, Lynne Westfield writes about womanist practices of hospitality evident in the "concealed" home gatherings of resilience in African American women. She asserts that these women are put in touch with God through these interpersonal relationships because these gatherings are "thresholds for the God within African American women to be revealed."[93] She explicitly connects the Spirit to these gatherings when she writes, "In receiving our guests, coming together as strangers in the world that does not rightly know them, African American women, as strangers, invoke the power of the Holy Spirit."[94] Welcoming an-*other* is an *epiclesis*, implying that the Spirit is one of welcome and reveals herself through hospitality. Hospitality, welcoming an-*other*, is a valid sign of being possessed by the Spirit in African American contexts. Geneva Smitherman notes, "The preacher's job as leader of his flock is to make churchgoers feel at home and to deal with the problems and realities confronting his people as they cope with the demands and stresses of daily living."[95]

However, manifestations of the Spirit or sacramental encounters are not limited to church altars or sanctuaries because "the mystery of God dares to break forth in church and out of church, with church officials and in their absence, but always for the blessing of the people of God."[96] Experiencing the Spirit embodied in genuine hospitality makes one feel at "home" and leads to celebration; this is why the African American women gatherings are like "down home" prayer meetings.[97] African American women can "have church" outside of the traditional church setting because the Spirit creates an atmosphere for hospitality and divine knowledge through these relationships. This hospitality, which is a manifestation of the Spirit, allows the participation of every member and welcomes the rhythmic expressive word of each member because there is "No Shhhhhh! Here."[98] Expressions of lament and celebration are welcome. In the context of real hospitality, African Americans have a free space of cultural expression to be who they are and where every perspective matters. In African American hospitality, there is freedom[99] that is often connected with concrete social liberation, which is also a form of hospitality to the oppressed other.

Working for the liberation of anyone is a posture of hospitality toward the one who is enslaved and manifests the liberating Spirit of God.[100] African American liberation theologians view the Spirit's work as extremely connected with the work of liberation for oppressed people. J. Deotis Roberts argues that the Spirit, who is present in the gathered community, sends African Americans out to "claim their humanity" in a society that dehumanizes them. He says, "The Spirit that comforts and heals in Black worship, renews and empowers us as we oppose the evils in the society which would humiliate and destroy us."[101] Justice in the social order, along with joy and peace within the heart, is the Spirit's work, affirming the holistic understanding of the Spirit being demonstrated in this chapter. Albert Cleage taught that Black churches "waste the Holy Spirit" on Sundays if they fail to tie the Spirit to any "real down-to-earth" program.[102] He believed that "The Holy Spirit is the revolutionary power which comes to an exploited people as they struggle to escape from powerlessness and to end the institutional oppression forced upon them by an enemy."[103]

Cleage clearly represents the desire of African American Christians to see the Spirit at work concretely in the material realm. Hospitality reveals the importance of human relationships as a potential context for the manifestation of the Spirit. Individual experience and expression of the Spirit cannot replace the manifestation of the Spirit in communal and social ways and vice versa. Whether individual, communal, or social, the manifestation of the Spirit happens in concrete, tangible ways that are expressed uniquely in African American Christianity. This holistic, material pneumatology is the beginning framework for a constructive theological discussion about preaching in relation to the Spirit. Manifestations of the Spirit through black bodies, language, and hospitality demonstrate that the Spirit accepts and embraces the humanity of African Americans, despite the historical oppression of this people. This is a reason to celebrate and not lament.

A Holistic Manifestation of the Spirit

Ideally, African American Christians are not satisfied with an inward religiosity void of outward relevance or significance in the world; they strive for a spiritual congruency between inner pneumatological experience and outer pneumatological expression. Howard Thurman demonstrates this when he says, "I determine to live the outer life in the inward sanctuary. . . . What I do in the outer will be blessed by the holiness of the inward sanctuary; for indeed it shall all be one."[104] In this cultural context, the life of the Spirit is ultimately authenticated by the evaluation of one's life in the world. The aim is to show some sign that one is possessed by the Spirit. Intellectual theological speculation about the Spirit is insufficient by itself for African American Christians, because for them knowledge of God comes primarily through experience of God; this experience translates into outward expressions and manifestations of the Spirit through individuals, communities, and societies.

Many so-called Christians, who were supposedly in the Spirit, propagated evils against African Americans in their history of suffering. Thinking about the Spirit alone was insufficient to convince oppressed African Americans that these Christians manifested the Spirit. Outward manifestations of the Spirit can be a critical means for authenticating a life in the Spirit, and can reveal a mutual acceptance of one another in African American communities. Embodied manifestations of the Spirit represent a spirit of welcome, divinely and humanly speaking, which sustains people. This material presence of the Spirit is complemented by the pervasive and holistic work of the Spirit.

In an article, "The Black Christian Experience and the Holy Spirit," Edward Wimberly notes, "Indeed, there is a linking of the personal, communal, and social dimensions in the conception of the work of the Holy Spirit within black church tradition."[105] Likewise, Thurman argues that it is important to have a "sense of Presence" on the personal, social, and cosmic levels of life because "the God of life in all its parts and the God of the human heart are one and the same."[106] This holistic material pneumatology, the belief that manifestations of the Spirit occur individually, communally, and socially and can be discerned, will serve as a theological lens to further probe preaching in the subsequent chapters.

Chapter Two

The Spirit of Lament and Celebration

Through speech . . . we are invited to share in the
fellowship and communion of the Holy Spirit.
—Walter Brueggemann, *Finally Comes the Poet*

Nobody knows the trouble I see . . . glory Hallelujah!
—Traditional Spiritual

T he Spirit's influence is felt in all domains of life and the Spirit manifests concretely and outwardly in the physical realm through people,
demonstrating that the Spirit can be discerned and is not a "numinous
entity."[1] From a cultural perspective, the manifestation of the Spirit may
occur through human language, including *lament* and *celebration* in preaching. This chapter will cement the theological relationship between the Holy
Spirit and the expressions of lament and celebration.

It begins with an overview of the lament Psalms. In the second section of
this chapter, the groans of the Spirit, particularly expressed in Romans 8, will
be presented as a way of viewing the Spirit's presence in suffering and hope.
These groans implicitly link to the Psalms, specifically the lament genre, and
its overall movement from plea to praise. The intimate connection between
the Spirit and the work of Christ in the suffering of the Crucifixion and the
hope of the Resurrection will be revealed in the third section. The final section will actually introduce the Spirit manifestations of lament and celebration such that the Spirit's work can be shown to materialize in actual sermon
forms and expressions. Any sign of these emphases within sermons may be
discerned to be a manifestation of the Spirit.

Lament Psalms as Voice of the Spirit

A discussion about the expressions of lament and celebration through
humanity should necessarily begin with the lament Psalms, a vital portion

of the hymnal of the church. Biblical lament acknowledges "pain is present . . . and can be articulated with candor" to God because "dysfunction" is viewed as "God's proper business."[2] For instance, in Psalm 39:1-12, once the psalmist's "distress grew worse," he cries out to God, "And now, O Lord, what do I wait for? / My hope is in you. / Deliver me from all my transgressions. / Do not make me the scorn of the fool." According to Stephen Breck Reid, "The crucible of the laments is to trust in God even in the face of the apparent absence of God and the presence of the enemies."[3] The psalter presupposes a conversation between the psalmist and God even while in conflict because "loyalty to God remains essential for life" within the psalms.[4] The "conflictual self"[5] of the psalmist does not relinquish God but embraces God, because as Walter Brueggemann says: "The faith expressed in the lament is nerve—it is a faith that knows that honest facing of distress can be done effectively only in dialogue with God who acts in transforming ways."[6] These psalms "cannot be prayed to a god who does nothing."[7] Therefore, the biblical genre of lament is dialogic, addressed to Someone, therefore, the use of "I" for the speaker and "You" for God is frequent in these psalms (for example, Ps. 55).[8] It is important to note that in talking to God ("You"), one may be speaking against an enemy or even against God, but in either instance, the language is direct and in the imperative (for example, Psalm 88).[9] In addition, as implied already, God and the lamenter are key subjects in the lament psalms, but there is also a third subject that dominates this genre along with God and the lamenter: the enemy.[10] The "plot" of lament incorporates all three subjects by including the reality of the psalmist's alienation, conflict with others, and sense of the absence of God.[11] Biblical laments assert honestly that life is burdened by hurt, which causes "disorientation,"[12] leading to rhetorical questions such as "why?" (Pss. 2, 22) and "how long?" (Ps. 13).

Lament psalms express real-life experiences that may be individual (for example, Ps. 13), or communal (for example, Ps. 80), dealing with a variety of issues. The contexts for laments are varied and may be personal conflict expressing piety in terms of situations of persecution where the antagonist sees the psalmist as other and enemy or corporate royal and cultic concerns as expressing official maintenance of the institution of the royal household. The conflict may be internal turmoil or external turmoil due to enemies.[13] Whether individual or communal lamentation, there is an experience of alienation in relationships with God and others (Pss. 60, 74, 83). There are adversarial psalms dealing with enemies (Pss. 3, 13, 30, 31, 102, 143) and the wicked (Pss. 12, 26, 28, 141), psalms of sickness (Pss. 6, 35, 41, 86) and even lament psalms about public national disasters (Pss. 44, 58, 74, 79, 80), to name a few themes. In all of these, the psalmists feel marginalized, yet cry out to God to interrogate God about life. The scope of the lament psalms is vast and wide, as the above suggests, but biblical scholars still assert that there are certain recognizable characteristics that reveal a particular movement within psalmic lament.

Claus Westermann, in *The Praise of God in the Psalms*, notes the characteristic components of the lament psalm to be *address* (Pss. 4:1; 5:1; 12:1; 16:1; 17:1) *complaint petition* (Pss. 6:2; 22:11; 22:20; 41:4); *motivation* (Pss. 22:4-5, 22); *vow of offering* (Ps. 26:12); and *assurance of being heard* (Ps. 13:5-6).[14] The address is to God, indicating a divine-human relationship. The complaint describes the situation of trouble, whether it be sickness (Pss. 6:2, 13:3; 22:14-15; 38:5-6; 39:4-6), loneliness and sense of abandonment (Pss. 3:11; 38:11), danger before enemies (Pss. 6:8; 7:1-4, 13; 17:9,13; 35:4; 38:12; 55:3; 56:2; 64:1-6), shame (Pss. 4:2; 22:6-7), or death (Pss. 28:1; 59:3; 88:3-9). The petition asks God to act decisively. The motivation presents the reasons that God should right the wrong. The vow of offering asserts that the speaker will give or pay something as an offering to God in response to deliverance. The assurance of being heard presents the psalmist's confidence that God has heard the lament. The complaints or petitions "do not function as the end of a process."[15] Rather, the components suggest a certain movement and form that shifts from plea to praise, with the plea encompassing the first four traits and the praise including the last two (for example, Pss. 3, 13).

This plea-praise form of the lament suggests that the lament psalms are "no longer mere petition but petition that has been heard. They are no longer mere lament, but lament that has been turned to praise."[16] For example, Psalm 22 begins with "My God, my God, why have you forsaken me? / Why are you so far from helping me, from the words of my groaning?" but shifts to "You who fear the LORD, praise him! / All you offspring of Jacob, glorify him; / stand in awe of him all you offspring of Israel... before him shall bow all who go down to the dust, / and I shall live for him" (Ps. 22:23, 29). This biblical genre begins with the realization that something is not right but moves in faith toward a God who can make things right; thus, there is praise as a response to God's intervention. These voices of plea and praise, which also demonstrate a general movement within the Psalms, represent the dynamic modes of lament and celebration discussed in homiletics. For the Psalms, it is important to remember "what concludes in praise does not begin in praise. It begins rather in hurt, rage, need, indignation, isolation, and abandonment," suggesting that the "proper setting of praise is as lament resolved."[17] This is not to suggest that *all* lament psalms move toward praise or resolution, but many do.

For instance, Psalm 88 is an example, in the words of Brueggemann, of an "unanswered complaint in the psalter." He says,

> In this psalm, there is no hint of answer, response, or resolution from God. The speaker addresses what is apparently an empty sky and an indifferent throne.

> This psalm is a witness to Israel's theological realism. There are unanswered prayers. There are unresolved situations. There are times when Yahweh's *hesed* is not mobilized and is not operative.[18]

However, in general, the psalmic lament form moves from plea toward praise. Also, one must note that "no single psalm follows exactly the ideal form, but the form provides a way of noticing how the psalm proceeds. That form has a dramatic movement."[19] The drama of lament, whether one contains each of the traits listed above or not, "enables the faithful to read situations of hurt as situations of potential transformation."[20] This is at the core of the lament psalms and indicates the "heart of the prayer for help." Patrick Miller views the "heart" of this prayer to be the "distinctive conjoining of question and trust, of protest and acceptance, of fear and confidence."[21] Lament psalms are "not uni-focal, but bi-focal";[22] thus, "one moment is not less faithful than the other.... In the full relationship, the season of plea must be taken as seriously as the season of praise."[23] Westermann affirms this understanding of the bifocal makeup of biblical worship when he says, "Something must be amiss if praise of God has a place in Christian worship but lamentation does not. Praise can retain its authenticity... only in polarity with lamentation."[24] Whether in the form of plea or praise, lament as a genre essentially asserts that "the Lord reigns," the fundamental theology of the Psalms[25] and the fundamental theology of many African American Christians, who can sing: "God is a God! God don't never change! God is a God an' He always will be God!"[26]

The truthfulness and bare honesty of these lament psalms represent what one might call "the voice of the Spirit" in Scripture. One might even say these words of human prayer, whether in the mode of plea or praise, are expressions of the Spirit crying out of God's creation before God. One scholar goes as far as calling the Psalms, "the songs of the Holy Spirit."[27] With this perspective, one may view the voice and movement of the Spirit to include the bifocal expressions of plea and praise or lament and celebration. In this way, the totality of human existence and worship before God is already a part of the person and work of the Holy Spirit. These psalmic expressions of lament and celebration are true to the groans of the Spirit articulated through the entirety of God's creation. The nature, work, and voice of the Spirit are not only embedded in the Psalms but also can be found in the experience of suffering and hope, permeating all of creation.

Groans of the Spirit

Romans 8 presents a compelling portrait of how the Spirit is linked to hope-filled suffering through the groans of creation. The Spirit does not avoid suffering or pain but actually causes a believer to suffer with Christ in anticipation of eventually being glorified with him (v. 17). Thomas Hoyt writes:

> The Spirit does not bring release from present suffering but propels believers into it. Present suffering prevents confidence for the future from becoming triumphalistic. But if the Spirit does not nullify suffering, neither does suffering nullify the confidence that the community may have for the future. In Paul's mind the Spirit is connected with a universal yearning to experience the fulfillment of God's purposes.[28]

The Christian community yearns for God's future, but they are not alone "for the creation waits with eager longing for the revealing of the children of God" (v. 19). The creation is in "bondage to decay," and the whole created order groans in labor pains (v. 22), indicating the presence of pain in the present even while it longs for a brighter future from God. But the creation is not alone in its groaning, because as Paul writes "and not only the creation, but we ourselves, who have the first fruits of the Spirit, groan inwardly while we wait for adoption" (v. 23). The Spirit engages believers, preachers, in honest groans and lament. Gordon Fee argues that "inwardly" may mean "within ourselves," but he questions the use of the word "inwardly" as if the groans are not expressed outwardly. He declares:

> the phrase does not ordinarily function as a mere synonym for inaudible, as over against aloud. When used with verbs of speaking it generally means "to oneself," as over against "to others" which may be audible or not. The phrase therefore probably does not refer to whether or not such groaning is expressed, but that it is not expressed in the context of others. [29]

What is important here is the possibility that these groans are voiced. One cannot endure suffering and always be silent because even the Spirit speaks through Christians, those who have the first fruits of the Spirit.

Yet creation's groans and human groans are not enough. There is a clear sense that the Spirit, too, groans because of the travail of the world. The Spirit "intercedes with sighs too deep for words" (v. 26). Once again, the work of Fee is insightful, because he translates "sighs too deep for words" to "inarticulate groanings," not "silent" or "inexpressible" sounds, but more to do with words that we cannot understand with our own minds.[30] This translation provides the opportunity to speak of the Spirit's sighs also as groanings, joining the whole creation, including human beings, in yearning for the full redemption of God. The Spirit articulates groans of suffering, that is, "the Spirit participates in the yearning by assisting the believer who hardly knows how to prepare in anticipation of the future restoration. The Spirit puts a meaning into human sighs that they would themselves not have. Thus, God, too, participates in the yearning for renewal that God is now accomplishing."[31] Creation and humanity are not isolated from God during these groans of suffering, but God actually fosters such truthful groaning as part of what it means to be God's creation. One scholar says "groans are enlivened by the Spirit (of God) who groans through humans. Such groans recognize, by the Spirit, the incompleteness of justice and righteousness in the land."[32] Martin Luther King, Jr. understood and decried the injustice of the bombing of the Sixteenth Street Baptist Church in Birmingham, Alabama, in 1963, in which four little girls were killed as they attended Sunday school; thus he groaned, "These children—unoffending, innocent and beautiful—were the victims of one of the most vicious, heinous crimes ever perpetrated against humanity."[33]

These groans of the Spirit also suggest a working toward a future in hope. In a context of much groaning and acknowledgment of "the sufferings of this present time" (v. 18), Paul is adamant that there is a "glory about to be revealed to us" (v. 18). This is why creation longs "for the revealing of the children of God...in hope that the creation itself will be set free from its bondage to decay and will obtain the freedom of the glory of the children of God" (vv. 19-21). There is present suffering and decay but a hope for a future glory and freedom. In like manner, humans, who have the "first fruits of the Spirit," groan for the "redemption of our bodies" in hope, waiting for it "with patience," (vv. 23-25). As Paul notes earlier in the letter, "hope does not disappoint us, because God's love has been poured into our hearts through the Holy Spirit that has been given to us" (5:5). This same Spirit fills King with hope even though it is a moment of great suffering. Because of the Spirit, he declares in his eulogy for the four little girls:

> At times, life is hard, as hard as crucible steel. It has its bleak and painful moments. Like the ever-flowing waters of a river, life has its moments of drought and its moments of flood. Like the ever-changing cycle of the seasons, life has the soothing warmth of the summers and the piercing chill of its winters. But through it all, God walks with us. Never forget that God is able to lift you from fatigue of despair to the buoyancy of hope, and transform dark and desolate valleys into sunlit paths of inner peace.[34]

For Paul, the groans are not just full of suffering but are also full of hope, even if it is just because "the Spirit helps us in our weakness" (Rom. 8:26).

The relationship between the Spirit of suffering and the Spirit of hope can be best understood within an eschatological perspective. The "first fruits of the Spirit" within believers indicate a divine pledge that will eventually be fulfilled. The first fruits is a metaphor derived from giving the first fruits of a crop to God in confidence that God will bring an abundant harvest. First fruits imply that there is a guarantee from God in the present about the final redemption.[35] Through the Spirit, a new age has begun but it has yet to be fully realized. Because the Spirit is involved in both the suffering and hope, the groans of the Spirit within individuals express suffering and hope simultaneously.

These groans of the Spirit represent the eschatological "already-not yet" tension of the Christian "between what we are and what we shall be."[36] In the present, God's people suffer like the Lord, the "not yet," but there is the belief that Christians will identify with Christ in his glory too. "There is no truly Christian life that does not so identify with Christ," in both suffering and hope for glory.[37] The Spirit is involved in both the suffering of the cross and glory of the Resurrection. Thus, Christian groans express these sentiments through the Spirit; this will become clearer in the following section with the discussion about the relationship of the Spirit to Christ's work. In Romans 8, the groans of creation, Christians, and the Spirit, voice present suffering and future hope; therefore, these groans are an active yearning for full redemption. The Spirit keeps believers rooted in the present but hopeful for the future; this is why Paul speaks about both the suffering and glory of Christ (vv. 17-18). Suffering and glory are both evident when the enslaved would sing, "Soon-a will done-a with the troubles of the world. Goin' home to live with God."[38] The suffering is real, but the glory to be revealed is real as well, which gives Paul reason to boast in the hope of sharing in Christ's glory and also in Christ's sufferings (5:2-3).

The groans of the Spirit indicate that suffering will not have the final word. The victory of hope through the Spirit is even evident as Paul concludes his discussion of groaning with a celebratory doxology (8:31-39). The Spirit reaches this height of doxology and celebration because she first engages the depths of human despair, pain, and lament. The Spirit makes room for celebratory worship because, although these groans of the Spirit acknowledge "nobody know the troubles I see," they still declare in the end, "Glory hallelujah."[39]

Crucifixion and Resurrection in the Spirit

The entire history of Christ, his suffering and glory, is the history of the Spirit because their histories are "indivisibly bound."[40] In *The Spirit of Life*, Jürgen Moltmann declares, "Both chronologically and theologically, the operation of the divine Spirit is the precondition or premise for the history of Jesus of Nazareth."[41] In other words, if the Spirit is not active, then Jesus is impotent in history, because the power and life of Jesus Christ flows in and from the divine Spirit. In the lament of the Crucifixion and celebration of the Resurrection, the Spirit is present. Indeed, "there was no time and no period of his life when Jesus was not filled with the Holy Spirit,"[42] but the Spirit does not make Jesus Christ a "superman."[43] Jesus endures the shame of the cross like a common criminal and even laments "my God, my God, why have you forsaken me?" while on the cross (Mark 15:34; cf. Psalm 22). Throughout his life, Jesus weeps, and on the cross he sweats drops of blood, suffers, and eventually dies.

In particular for African Americans, "Jesus' death by crucifixion is a prototype of African Americans' death by circumscription."[44] Traditionally, black people have identified with the story of Jesus' suffering as their story of suffering to such an extent that theologians like James Cone speak of the relationship between the cross and the lynching tree. In a lecture titled "Strange Fruit: The Cross and the Lynching Tree," he argues that "the lynched black victim experienced the same fate as the crucified Christ."[45] For him, Christ was a "lynched black body."[46] This lynching creates lament from the "lynching tree" that is the cross. Preaching, therefore, that is supposed to be in the Spirit cries out from this tree, for the way to the cross is the way the Spirit leads Jesus. The Spirit accompanies Jesus in his suffering. In Jesus' very own weakness, persecution, pain, and groans, the Spirit resides and even laments. It is no wonder then that the enslaved lamented in songs of the Spirit with words such as "Were you there when they crucified my Lord? Were you there when they nailed him to the tree? Were you there when they pierced him in the side? Were you there when the sun refused to shine? Were you there when they laid him in the tomb?"[47] The Spirit was there when "they crucified my Lord an' he nevuh said a mumbalin' word."[48] Through the perspective of the cross, pneumatology connects our lives to the real suffering of God's creation and to the suffering experienced within the triune God. This suffering of the cross should give preachers reason enough to lament. Many times, African American preachers can be heard voicing lament because of the agony of the cross. Carla A. Jones laments the cross when she declares, "Hanging...exposed...naked...stripped of his clothes...nailed to the cross. I was there, I heard the sound of his bones being crushed when they drove those nails into his hands and feet. I heard it! I heard it! All I can do is see him. I see the sweat. I see his tears. I see his tears and I can't even cry."[49]

It is at the cross where we remember God's passionate love as suffering love and voluntary fellow-suffering that suffers in solidarity with the suffering, groaning creation, even the groaning Spirit.[50]

Jesus, my darling Jesus,
Groaning as the Roman spear plunged in his side;
Jesus, my darling Jesus,
Groaning as the blood came spurting from his wound.
Oh, look how they done my Jesus.[51]

The suffering love of the passion of Jesus flows through the Spirit and continues in the sighs of the Spirit, yet the Spirit also opens up a hope for new life through the future of the coming of God to the world. This love of the Spirit allows all of creation to fellowship with the sufferings of Christ as well as experience the new life to come because the death of Christ was not the end of the Spirit's story. "Death is not a period that ends the great sentence of life, but a comma that punctuates it to more lofty significance."[52] Lament, cries, and the pain of the cross is in the Spirit, but the joy of the new life through the Resurrection is too. As the Spirit is the first breath of life in God, the Spirit is also the pledge or first fruits of the future redemption. In terms of suffering, one could say the Holy Spirit is the "Spirit of the cross," or lament; but the Holy Spirit is also the "Spirit of the resurrection," or celebration, who is present in the experiences of "the shadow of the cross."[53] The lament of Christ in the Spirit does not end in suffering or despair but is very much like the biblical genre of lament in moving toward praise, hope, and celebration because of the Resurrection. As enslaved Africans sang, "They crucified my savior . . . [but] He 'rose.'"[54] This rising movement flows in the Spirit.

The same Spirit who does not prevent Jesus from death on a cross is the same One who raises him from the dead (Rom. 8:11). This act of the Resurrection and the hope and new life it promises is the foundation for celebration in preaching. The "Spirit of the resurrection" is symbolically eschatological, because raising the dead means that in the crucified Christ, the future of resurrection and eternal life, the annihilation of death, and the new creation has already begun. The Spirit is the bridge between the history of the risen crucified Christ and the eschatological transformation of the world. The Holy Spirit mediates the past and future, suffering and hope, in the present. As a pledge of the future through the resurrection of Christ, the future kingdom of God through the Spirit can be anticipated and a foretaste of the new creation in the present can be experienced; thus, we can celebrate in our preaching because the Spirit breathes hope within us.[55] The message of preaching is not all bad news, because there is also good news to proclaim, the good news of the Resurrection and life eternal. The divine joyous future of God may be experienced in the face of present suffering through the Spirit because "God is able."[56]

The world is not yet what God desires, but the promise of the future seen in the act of raising Jesus to new life is a new creation for this world, not some other world, thus opening up possibilities for earthly anticipations of the future kingdom of God. This means that in this world there are glimpses of God's kingdom, signs of new life and resurrection, or in the words of Mary Catherine Hilkert, an "echo of the gospel."[57] Christian hope for the future coming of God already affects the world such that even the church can act for change in the present world in the direction of God's future.[58] Through the Spirit of resurrection and hope, the church is empowered to act in the world, celebrating not only what God has done but also what God is doing and will do. The Spirit speaks hope and life and sparks celebratory preaching because of it. One sermon example celebrating the hope of the Resurrection while not ignoring the awful crucifixion is clearly articulated by Henry Mitchell. He says:

> At the name of him who went from crying and complaining "if it be possible let this cup pass from me," but ended up declaring, "Nevertheless not as I will but as thou wilt." Because of his nevertheless, His name is above every name.
>
> Because of his nevertheless, his name is the only name given under the heavens by which men, women, boys, and girls must be saved. Because of his nevertheless, he suffered the humiliation of the Cross. Nevertheless, he got up from the grave on Easter Sunday morning. Nevertheless, he ascended into heaven and sitteth at the right hand of the Father. Nevertheless he's coming back again. Nevertheless, eyes have not seen, ears have not heard, nor hath it entered into the hearts of men what the Lord has in store for those that love his appearing. Amen.[59]

Mitchell demonstrates that preachers can celebrate the new life of the Resurrection in sermons while still holding to honest lament and the Crucifixion of Christ and the pain of the world.

Through the Spirit, the suffering and hope of Jesus become a living reality for the Christian preacher and community.[60] The Spirit is a mediator, shaping individuals and sermons into the pattern of Christ, crucifixion and resurrection, lament and celebration. It is as Paul says, the "Spirit of him who raised Jesus from the dead dwells in you" (Rom. 8:11) and "the Spirit is life" (Rom. 8:10). Celebration due to the Resurrection does not negate the experience and reality of death expressed through lament. Talk of resurrection and celebration or hope must be tempered with talk of crucifixion and lament and vice versa, because both are manifestations of the Spirit in preaching, reflecting the "plea-praise" and "bi-focal" mode of the lament psalms and groans of the Spirit. Both aspects of the pattern of Christ, crucifixion and resurrection, are faithful and true to human existence in the Spirit. The groaning Spirit gives sermons depth and height by leading preachers to descend into hell through the Crucifixion and to ascend into heaven through the Resurrection.[61] Through the Spirit, the manifestations of lament and celebration provide depth and height to preaching while remaining grounded in the work of Jesus Christ, the "epitome of liturgy."[62]

Lament and Celebration in Homiletics: An Introduction

There is a shortage of homiletical literature that substantially discusses the Spirit in relation to preaching. James Forbes is one of a few contemporary homileticians who focuses *explicitly* on the integral connection between the work of the Spirit and preaching. Many homileticians believe that the Holy Spirit is absolutely essential for preaching, but this is not fleshed out in relation to the actual language, content, and structure of a sermon. All would agree that the negation or suppression of the life of the Spirit is the death of Christian preaching, but teaching about the Spirit in homiletics up to this point has not been integrated with the practice of preaching. If one were to read the history of homiletics in the twentieth century pneumatologically, there would be four main trajectories of thought in relation to the Spirit. These themes are revelation, grace, community, and ethics, yet history reveals that these important ideas about the Spirit and preaching do not speak to the Spirit's movement in sermon language, content, and structure.[63] For a homiletical discussion about the Spirit of crucifixion and resurrection, it is essential to explore the conversation about lament and celebration in preaching. I begin with celebration in preaching because it is the manifestation and form that is most prominent in contemporary homiletics.

Preaching as Celebration

African American Christians generally believe that the Spirit manifests through the language of preaching. African American homiletics has made considerable contributions in the area of celebration and its link to the Spirit's work in preaching. Celebration is believed to be a "nonmaterial African cultural survival."[64] This is not to say that other homileticians have not made mention of preaching as celebration but that African Americans have emphasized it and boldly expressed it in worship settings. Evans Crawford says that the ultimate goal in preaching is communion and celebration and praise moving from the supplication of "Help 'em Lord" to "Glory Hallelujah!" representative of celebration.[65] Celebration is not emotionalism where emotion is the end, but as Olin Moyd says, "it is one form of the means by which joy and ecstasy and glory and praise are uttered to God out of the overflow of gratitude of persons who are experiencing the full reality of being."[66] The experience of the gospel and the assurance of grace lead to this exciting praise of God. Whenever good news is received and appropriated, celebration is the natural response.[67] As part of a community of celebration, preaching serves to help the church receive and celebrate the good news. Because sermons enable others to celebrate, some homileticians teach students methods of sermonic celebration.

Foremost in teaching sermonic celebration as a method is Henry Mitchell. Celebration is "high art, as well as universal emotional logic," he says.[68] In *Celebration and Experience in Preaching*, Mitchell teaches that the gospel is good news, and thus the sermon should demonstrate a contagious joy about the gospel through a celebratory sermonic end. He writes:

> The Word audiences seek must mean so much to the preacher that he or she is manifestly glad about it. Public jubilation should not be reserved for touchdowns and home runs. Authentic gospel feasting begets its own irresistible celebration; to hold it back or inhibit it is to lose the joy itself, along with the whole message.[69]

Mitchell teaches a particular method of emotional logic while not negating reason. Most important, he emphasizes that the sermon should end on an affirmative note since the end is celebration, an "ecstatic reinforcement" of the total sermon content.[70] Emotional knowledge through an emotive, holistic encounter between the preacher and congregation called celebration reinforces the good news to the end of intensifying one's core belief or inner assurance of victory regardless of tragic circumstances.[71] Frank Thomas defines celebration as "the culmination of the sermonic design, where a moment is created in which the remembrance of a redemptive past or the conviction of a liberated future transforms the events immediately experienced."[72] Some scholars disagree with the idea that celebration is only present at the sermonic end. Instead, they see the whole sermon itself as the celebration of God.[73] Furthermore, celebration is taught to be contagious through a preacher's spirit, facial expressions, and tonal qualities.[74] It is viewed not as a "quaint cultural habit" but as essential to all faithful preaching, not only in African American denominations.[75]

At a first reading, it might appear that Mitchell and others are speaking about celebration in terms of human agency only, but a closer study reveals that the Holy Spirit propels the celebration. Despite the great methodological focus on what we do as preachers to foster celebration, Mitchell concludes his book, *Celebration and Experience in Preaching*, with a word about the Holy Spirit. He says, "At best, the preacher is only an instrument in the hands of God, who saves all the souls that are saved, and who stimulates living faith using the catalyst called preachers, who are guided by the Holy Spirit." He continues and declares, "We human beings must pray, prepare, and preach as if the whole responsibility were on the preacher, but trust, knowing that ultimately the responsibility is God's, no matter how useful or useless our best efforts may appear."[76]

True worship as celebration is not something humans create, but rather celebration is a "method and vehicle the Holy Spirit effectively utilizes to bring the assurance of grace to the core belief of people."[77] Through celebration, the Spirit transforms the present lives of people. Celebration is truly a gift of the Spirit who brings hope and causes resurrection.[78] The Spirit sparks celebration to such a level that some African American preachers even begin to intone or whoop, what William Turner calls "singing in the spirit."[79] Practicing celebration in such a way instills hope in the hearers and leads to concrete living in the world and is not limited to the corporate experience of worship. Real celebration connects with situations of human suffering, and sermonic celebration will only glorify God if it does not avoid "God's plan to uplift humanity."[80] This is because the Spirit of celebration is also the Spirit of suffering and lament. Authentic celebration of God must overflow into just participation in the world, for participation in the Spirit is to move from celebration to mission.[81] The Spirit is the One who gathers a community and sends a community into the world through celebratory preaching. This movement into mission can also occur through the sermonic lament of the Spirit.

Preaching as Lament

Participating in the groaning Spirit of suffering and crucifixion also entails preaching that laments, if it is to be truthful. However, this area of homiletics is underdeveloped and has not been viewed as a significant area for pneumatological explorations as of yet, although the Spirit is the source of sermonic lament as she groans through preaching. A few scholars have highlighted lament in preaching, yet these important contributions rarely mention the Spirit in conjunction with this expression, missing an opportunity to bolster study of the Spirit in homiletics. Nonetheless, just recognition of lament as a voice in preaching represents progress in the field.

Marjorie Suchocki says that preaching is truly worship when it honestly explores the breadth of human emotions in the light of God in Christ;[82] this necessarily includes lament as an aspect of worshipful proclamation.[83] Black homileticians view preaching as relevant in the highs and lows of life; thus,

celebration is not the only worshipful preaching that may occur, though it
may be presented as such. Lament, too, is a viable homiletical option and
some African Americans note this. James Harris is one homiletician who recognizes the interplay of lament and celebration in preaching and connects
this to the Holy Spirit. Harris cites lament (or as he says, "sad") in relation to
the Spirit's work. He writes:

> Black preaching is indeed exciting and jubilant, but it is also sad and reflective. It
> represents the ebb and flow of the Holy Spirit that correlates with the ups and
> downs of life. It reflects the reality of context and experience. Additionally, it is a
> creative interplay between joy and sorrow, freedom and oppression, justice and
> injustice.... It reflects the power of the church in the presence of the Holy Spirit. [84]

This cultural interplay of joy and sorrow is parallel to and closely aligned with
the trouble-grace homiletical theory of Paul Scott Wilson. In fact, Wilson
views African American preaching as part of the "trouble-grace" homiletical
school of thought.[85] What this cultural dialectic in preaching suggests is that
if preaching is in the Spirit, then preaching must flow with the Spirit in times
of hope and celebration and in times of suffering and lament, being true to
the crucifixion and resurrection of Christ.

Rudolf Bohren makes this explicit when he writes:

> Preaching inspired by the Spirit looses the tongue not only to praise but also
> protest and lament. The Holy Spirit is the Spirit of joy in the sense that he
> deludes himself about things. He knows very well about sadness; he can waken
> the ability to mourn since he teaches not only the exaltation of Pentecost but
> also lamentation and even perhaps the psalms of vengeance.... Joy and sorrow
> are named here as two forms of "inspiration" with which the Spirit opposes the
> new against the most widespread Anti-spirit-indifference. The new establishes
> itself as freedom and brings itself to articulation in laments and praise.[86]

Bohren connects the Spirit to the expression of lament, validating lament in
preaching as a sign of the work of the Spirit of groans. A liberation perspective
may even be helpful in exploring the fruitful potential of lament in preaching.
Justo González and Catherine González embrace groans as the place where
the gospel of God may be heard. They argue passionately, "The word of the
gospel today, as in the times of Jesus, as ever, comes to us most clearly in the
painful groans of the oppressed. We must listen to those groans. We must join
the struggle to the point where we too must groan. Or we may choose the
other alternative, which is not to hear the gospel at all." They urge preachers
to groan or lament, for the gospel is found in the groans [87] This perspective
may mute celebration, but it is helpful in challenging homiletics to explore

lament further. The image of groans may also serve as a connecting point to the work of the Spirit, though this is not the Gonzálezes' focus. Mary Catherine Hilkert also maintains the breadth of expression in preaching, particularly by embracing the value of lament for proclamation.[88] She calls for the retrieval of lament which she defines as "grace at the edges" of existence. She teaches preachers to name "situations of impasse and 'dis-grace' or sin that confront creation and call out for redemption."[89] Not fearful of lament, she sees anger as a "mode of relatedness" to God; therefore, she warns preachers not to move too quickly to hope or celebration because this does not do justice to the paschal mystery.[90] Also, rushing to celebration does not do justice to the depth of expression found in the Spirit of the Crucifixion. Lament is a manifestation of the Spirit in preaching; thus, it should be valued as an effective manner of preaching the gospel. "Good news is to be found already in the language of lament and tears. Naming pain and claiming forgotten memories are parts of a larger journey toward healing, wholeness, and joy, although that future hope cannot be seen at every step on the journey."[91] Expressing anger or lament over situations implicitly expresses hope that the present will change and give way to a future that will be different.

Furthermore, lament remains rooted in everyday experiences, keeping preaching honest. Sally Brown, in thinking about how lament shapes sermons, notes that "news of grace and resurrection rings hollow disconnected from daily realities of loss, dispossession, and yearning for justice. Testifying to the God of Easter requires the language of lament."[92] Lament is "nonoptional" for life and preaching.[93] Lament cries out to God in faith during trouble. It is a "rhetoric that wails and rages, protests and interrogates, and finally whispers its hope."[94] This hope is grounded in the promise of God in Jesus Christ to wipe away tears and establish a new creation.[95] This new creation is the work of God through the Spirit of the Resurrection.

Summary

The Holy Spirit is integrally connected with expressions of suffering and hope, crucifixion and resurrection, and lament and celebration. Homiletics has recognized celebration as a work of the Spirit in preaching, but the same has not been true for lament, though it has been discussed without reference to the Spirit. One can argue that the presence of the Spirit can be discerned to be lament and celebration in sermons, giving depth (crucifixion) and height (resurrection) to preaching in the Spirit. The "Spirit of lament and celebration" will be helpful for reading sermons pneumatologically, along with other manifestations of the Spirit, such as grace, which the next chapter will discuss.

Chapter Three

The Spirit of Grace

We cannot live without Thy grace and benediction.
—Howard Thurman, *The Centering Moment*

Another manifestation of the Spirit is the individual experience of *grace*, particularly expressing itself in preaching as the embracing of existential grace. I will first explore the importance of experience of the Spirit in the life of faith, followed by a discussion of the work of the Spirit in relation to grace and how individuals experience the Spirit in this manner. Then I will discuss some implications of this understanding of the Spirit for homiletics. It will become clear that grace is a necessary manifestation of the Spirit in sermons, and it also contributes to the range of individual issues that one may lament or celebrate in preaching.

Experience (of the Spirit) as a Way of Knowing God

Howard Thurman notes, "Religious experience is interpreted to mean the conscious and direct exposure of the individual to God."[1] To know that God is with us happens through the human experience of divine grace. To say that African people brought a "*gift* of the Spirit" to America, as W. E. B. Dubois declares, already suggests the experience of the grace of God at work in human lives.[2] The African American ideal of the sacramentality of life emphasizes human experience of the divine such that one can say "God is with me."[3] This experience of God does not negate the communal and social realms, but it is highly personal and individual. Through grace, God is known immanently because "there is a Spirit in us that contains our spirit."[4] Elsewhere, Thurman teaches that a person can find a "home *within* by locating in his own spirit the trysting place where he and God may meet."[5] This possibility of the experience of God is a manifestation of divine grace. The experience of God and grace is only possible through the presence of the Spirit, most visibly through ecstatic expressions of the Spirit such as the shout when one is "caught up in the spirit," though it is not limited to this kind of outward expression.

Regardless of the nature of a sign of the Spirit, the Spirit is the One who allows humanity to experience and participate in the gracious life of God.

God cannot be experienced without the Holy Spirit. Also, divine revelation occurs because God takes the initiative through the Spirit to make the divine self known. John Wesley asserts:

> Every good gift is from God, and is given to man by the Holy Ghost.... "The natural man discerneth not the things of the Spirit of God," so that we never can discern them until "God reveals them unto us by his Spirit." "Reveals," that is unveils, uncovers; gives us to know what we did not know before. Have we love? It is "shed abroad in our hearts by the Holy Ghost which is given unto us." He inspires, breathes, infuses into our soul, what of ourselves we could not have. Does our spirit rejoice in God our Savior? It is "joy in (or by) the Holy Ghost." Have we true inward peace? It is "The peace of God" wrought in us by the same Spirit.... We have an inward experience of them, which we cannot find any fitter word to express.[6]

The Spirit "gives us to know what we did not know before" in regards to the things of God. This knowledge incorporates an inward experience of the Spirit of God through such fruit as love, joy, and peace. The Holy Spirit is the means of revelation, particularly important in preaching. The Holy Spirit is the One who makes God known through human experience of the Spirit and a Christian experience then is only possible within the framework of the Spirit of the triune God.

Martin Luther King, Jr. comes to know and to experience God in a deeper way one late night in his home after receiving a threatening phone call. He tells the story in his sermon "Our God Is Able."

> I hung up, but I could not sleep. It seemed that all of my fears had come down on me at once. I had reached the saturation point.
>
> I got out of bed and began to walk the floor. Finally, I went to the kitchen and heated a pot of coffee. I was ready to give up. I tried to think of a way to move out of the picture without appearing to be a coward. In this state of exhaustion, when my courage had almost gone, I determined to take my problem to God. My head in my hands, I bowed over the kitchen table and prayed aloud. The words I spoke to God that midnight are still vivid in my memory. "I am here taking a stand for what I believe is right. But now I am afraid. The people are looking to me for leadership, and if I stand before them without strength and courage, they too will falter. I am at the end of my powers. I have nothing left. I've come to the point where I can't face it alone."
>
> At that moment I experienced the presence of the Divine as I had never before experienced him. It seemed as though I could hear the quiet assurance of an inner voice, saying, "Stand up for righteousness, stand up for truth. God will be at your side forever." Almost at once my fears began to pass from me. My uncertainty disappeared. I was ready to face anything. The outer situation remained the same, but God had given me inner calm.

Three nights later, our home was bombed. Strangely enough, I accepted the word of the bombing calmly. My experience with God had given me a new strength and trust. I knew now that God is able to give us the interior resources to face the storms and problems of life.[7]

King demonstrates the importance of the inner relationship with God through which one can live the outer life. King knew that God was trust-worthy and "able," and thus he could be calm and celebrate the assuring presence of God. Along with the traditional avenues of scripture, reason, and tradition, experience is a reliable source of knowledge. One scholar notes "experience is the medium through which religious reality is transmitted. If the reality of the spiritual is to register on us, it must do so through our experience."[8] The Spirit combines various epistemological sources to foster a person's relationship with God. Furthermore, sources such as experience and scripture are void without the gracious initiative of God desiring to be known.

Grace as the Experience of the Work of the Spirit

In a sermon titled "The Grace of God," Howard Thurman describes grace in a helpful way by speaking of an act of kindness. He says, "The kind act is one in which the individual bestows upon another human being something that in a thousand years the other human being could not really merit."[9] Grace, divine favor extended, can never be repaid nor is it deserved, but God, through the Spirit, continues to grant it to individuals. Grace is God's pardon of sin, but grace is also the power of the Holy Spirit. In a sermon by John Wesley, "The Witness of Our Own Spirit," he says:

> By "the grace of God" is sometimes to be understood that free love, that unmer-ited mercy, by which I a sinner, through the merits of Christ am now reconciled to God. But in this place it rather means that power of God the Holy Ghost which "worketh in us both to will and to do of His good pleasure." As soon as ever the grace of God in the former sense, his pardoning love, is manifested to our souls, the grace of God in the latter sense, the power of his Spirit, takes place therein. And now we can perform, through God, what to man was impossible.[10]

The power of the Holy Spirit is vital for humans trying to "perform" or live out the life of Christ. In fact, the Christian life cannot be lived without the grace that is the power of the Spirit "enabling us to believe and love and serve God" because it "reigns" in human hearts.[11]

The Holy Spirit gives people the power to live the Christian life throughout a lifetime, not just at one particular moment in time. Grace, which is the work of the Holy Spirit, is an ongoing process through which we are shaped more into the image of Christ by the power of God. The grace of which I am speaking and that is essential for the preaching task is in relation to Jesus Christ. The pardon and power of grace leads one to sing like the spiritual "Give Me Jesus."[12] Moreover, the power of the Spirit as grace takes various forms throughout the Christian journey. For instance, when the nineteenth-century preacher Jarena Lee struggles with thoughts of suicide, she claims God saved her from suicide. She writes in her spiritual autobiography: "It was the unseen arm of God which saved me from self murder."[13] Her experience of God in her desperate moment of need was an act of grace in the Spirit. God's salvific love and grace is also evident in our creation, God's forgiveness, our transformation, and the means to this transformative end.[14]

Creation Grace

This first aspect of grace is closely linked with a sacramental understanding of the presence of God in human creation. Humans are not just bodies but also spirit because the breath of God moves within all of humanity. In the human spirit, there is the "crucial nexus that connects him with the Creator of Life, the Spirit of the Living God."[15] Grace is present before human beings are ever conscious of God at work in them.[16] God's gracious action "comes before" (pre-venio) any human response. This type of grace is the universal presence of the Spirit that gives an initial knowledge of God even to those who have not heard of Christ; and, it is an expression of God's grace epitomized in the revelation of Christ. There is a "small degree of light" or grace given to all people, even those who do not confess Christ, because God's grace cannot be confined to explicit religious circles.[17] Grace does not necessitate a person being Christian. Rather, this work of the Spirit stresses the primacy of God's loving initiative in salvation, and it asserts, "Thou hast not left us alone in the living of our lives."[18] The divine breath of God ebbs and flows through all human beings as the creation story accounts such that "man became a living soul."[19] Humanity lives because God does not leave us alone by graciously providing breath to live, implying that "every [human] is somebody because he is a child of God."[20] This generosity of God gives good reason to celebrate.

God makes the first move of grace through the subtle work of the Holy Spirit. Where the Spirit is, grace is; but, if the Spirit is absent, grace is also absent, for "There is no [one], unless he has quenched the Spirit, that is wholly void of the grace of God."[21] Humanity could not experience divine grace without the work of the Spirit, even in our consciences.[22]

Forgiving Grace

A second crucial aspect of grace in the salvation process of the Spirit has to do with God's justification and forgiveness of human sin. Justification is God's grace of pardon or forgiveness of human sin through the person and work of Jesus Christ. James Weldon Johnson captures this in "The Crucifixion":

> Oh, I tremble, yes, I tremble,
> It causes me to tremble, tremble,
> When I think how Jesus died;
> Died on the steeps of Calvary,
> How Jesus died for sinners,
> Sinners like you and me.[23]

One trembles and laments "how Jesus died," yet his death stirs relief and celebration for the life Christ gives through God's grace. "For by grace you have been saved through faith, and this is not your own doing; it is the gift of God" (Eph. 2:8). Christian theology "teaches that the crowning, dramatic expression of the grace of God is manifest in the giving of the only Son of God as the living sacrifice for all men."[24] This divine pardon is "not by any power, wisdom, or strength, which is in you, or in any other creature; but merely through the grace or power of the Holy Ghost, which worketh all in all."[25] Justification is the work of the Spirit experienced as free grace in the life of a person. It includes regeneration or what some traditions call being "born again." This regenerating and forgiving grace is "midwifed by the Spirit."[26]

Faith as Spiritual Sense

One experience of forgiving grace is the awakening of faith or the spiritual senses.[27] Faith is the divine evidence through which spiritual people discern God and the things of God. The Spirit of God opens and enlightens the eyes of the soul, allowing human beings to see (that is, have faith).[28] The Holy Spirit awakens individual faith, causing people to become conscious of God. The Spirit convinces people that God in Christ reconciled the world to the divine. Furthermore, the Spirit witnesses to our spirit that we are truly pardoned. "When we cry 'Abba! Father!' it is that very Spirit bearing witness with our spirit that we are children of God" (Rom. 8:15-16). Thurman affirms this scripture by asserting that "God has not left himself without a witness in our spirits"[29] and in our lives. Because God witnesses to our spirits through the Spirit, it is possible to say, "My feets is tired, but my soul is rested." These words of Mother Pollard, an older adult active in the civil rights movement, point to the sense of believing that God is present in one's soul regardless of the circumstances of life. Mother Pollard, this faith-filled woman, approached Dr. King one evening after he spoke at a mass meeting and discerned his weariness in well-doing. To encourage him, she told him, "But even if we ain't with you, God's gonna take care of you." King says, "as she spoke these consoling words, everything in me quivered and quickened with the pulsing tremor of raw energy."[30] The energy King felt was due to God's grace, a grace that was reawakening his faith such that he could sense and know the care of God on his journey. Through Mother Pollard, God was graciously witnessing to King's spirit so that he could testify and celebrate that "God's gonna take care of me."

Personal Testimony of Faith

It is not enough to have one's faith awakened to the fact of God's love, but one must actually experience God's love and be assured of God's presence such that one may be able to testify or witness to the work of the Spirit in her life.[31] Particularly in African American settings, the practice of testimony is central and has been called "one of the most cherished practices of the Black Church."[32] Faith is more than assent or understanding of God's love, but it is a confidence that one is indeed forgiven and can say something about that spiritual experience.[33] The Spirit testifies to the human spirit that one is loved by God. Because of this, a person should know if they are justified and be able to testify about this grace.[34] In reference to his famous Aldersgate experience, John Wesley says, "I felt my heart strangely warmed. I felt I did trust in Christ, Christ alone for salvation; and an assurance was given me that he had taken away my sins, even mine, and saved me from the law of sin and death."[35] Wesley had personal assurance or confidence that he was indeed saved and could testify to this experience. In another cultural context, nineteenth-century preacher Julia Foote testifies about her conversion when she says:

> Something within me kept saying, "Such a sinner as you are can never sing that new song." No tongue can tell the agony I suffered.... I thought God was driving me on to hell. In great terror I cried: "Lord, have mercy on me, a poor sinner!" The voice which had been crying in my ears ceased at once, and a ray of light flashed across my eyes, accompanied by a sound of far distant singing; the light grew brighter and brighter, and the song more distinct, and soon I caught the words: "This is the new song—redeemed, redeemed!" I at once sprang from the bed where I had been lying for twenty hours, without meat or drink, and

commenced singing: "Redeemed! Redeemed! Glory! Glory!" Such joy and peace as filled my heart, when I felt that I was redeemed and could sing the new song. Thus was I wonderfully saved from eternal burning.[36]

Foote laments her sin but celebrates her salvation. Though a person has a testimony of faith demonstrating an assurance, the Spirit is the One who initiates it. Thomas Hoyt is accurate when he says, "The testimony of the Black Church receives its power from the presence of the Holy Spirit."[37] The entire salvation process is the work of the Spirit, who takes the initiative in witnessing directly to our spirit. The witness of the Spirit occurs *before* the witness of the human spirit that assures one of God's love. In his sermon "Witness of the Spirit, Discourse I" Wesley proclaims:

> This testimony of the Spirit of God must needs, in the very nature of things, be antecedent to the testimony of our own spirit..."We love him, because he first loved us." And we cannot know his pardoning love to us, till his Spirit witnesses it to our spirit.[38]

Also, the Spirit's witness is direct to the human spirit, though a person may be unsure exactly how the Spirit's testimony is communicated to the heart.[39] Despite this uncertainty about the Spirit's method, an individual can be certain that the Spirit gives one a testimony of divine adoption.[40]

One is conscious of having received the spirit of adoption and testifies to this boldly. Inward assurance of faith stems from a consciousness of the inward proof or "self-evidence" that one is a child of God.[41] The witness of the Spirit to our spirit can be perceived.[42] A person perceives the effects of the Spirit, confirming the witness of the Spirit that one is saved by grace. One is aware of God at work internally and this only happens through the Spirit. This self-evidence of the work of God in one's life is part of the indirect testimony of the Spirit that is called more properly the fruit of the Spirit. Without the fruit of the Spirit, the testimony of the Spirit that one is a child of God is null and void, because a significant result of the witness of the Spirit is the fruit of the Spirit. Through experience, one knows if one possesses the fruit, signifying the children of God.[43]

Transforming Grace

Transforming grace is a third vital part in the process of salvation through the Spirit. Many refer to it as *sanctification*. Wesley's definition of sanctification is helpful to our conception of this grace. He defines sanctification as "the life of God in the soul of man; a participation of the divine nature (2 Pet.

1:4); the mind that was in Christ (Phil. 2:5); or the renewal of our heart after the image of him that created us (Col. 3:10)."[44] This form of grace allows a "recovery" of the likeness or image of God or in other words, holiness.[45] Sanctification, therefore, is the process of becoming holy and the grace which propels this process is the power of the Holy Spirit.

The Spirit is "not only perfectly holy in himself, but the immediate cause of all holiness in us."[46] The grace that causes one to become more like God stems from the Spirit, and it is an experience of the Spirit that allows increasing participation in the very life of God. There is no holiness without the *Holy* Spirit. The experience of the Spirit as transforming grace implies a gradual process of transformation in the believer that causes a believer to reflect the image of God in an increasing fashion as she participates more in the life of God, affirming the message of Thurman that "I become like Him, when I respond to His movement in me."[47] Furthermore, as the Spirit sanctifies an individual, the witness of the Spirit's work should eventually be perceivable through the fruit of the Spirit.

Fruit of the Spirit

The Holy Spirit as transforming grace, not only mortifies the deeds of the flesh, but also creates fruit for reflecting the divine life. The fruit of the Spirit—love, joy, peace, patience, kindness, generosity, faithfulness, gentleness, self-control—are not pure emotions, but are what some have called "holy tempers" or affections that are an impetus for action.[48] The power of the Holy Spirit as grace renews the image of God within a person so that his or her life reflects the nature of God in word and deed. The Spirit was working in the life of Jarena Lee to reflect the nonviolent nature of God, "Glory be to God for his redeeming power, which saved me from the violence of my own hands, from the malice of Satan, and from eternal death."[49] Lee was fashioned to bear more fruit of the Spirit in her own personal life. These fruits are not solely inward or individualistic because the life of God in the hearts of people reveals itself in "outward fruits" such as "the doing good to all men; the doing no evil to any; and the walking in the light, a zealous, uniform obedience to all the commandments of God."[50] Individual transformation should impact wider social settings. This may be referred to as "the fruits of the inner life."[51]

Actions of Love

Thurman says, "We see grace most effectively and simply expressed in an ordinary act of human kindness."[52] An act of love is physical evidence of

God's grace at work in a person's life because "faith...worketh by love" (Gal. 5:6 KJV). This notion urges King to preach, "I want you to be first in love. I want you to be first in moral excellence. I want you to be first in generosity. That is what I want you to do."[53] Transforming grace leads people "to do." Spirit-induced faith is a means to love; thus, the fruit of the Spirit developed by the sanctifying Spirit naturally evolves into social acts of love. Albert Outler argues, "Faith that justifies bears its fruits in the faith that works by love."[54] One's works demonstrate one's faith, because good works flow out of faith. These works produced by faith are loving acts toward others, because faith is the "handmaid of love."[55]

The Spirit always aims at right relation to God and neighbor, leading to a "synthesis of mystical and prophetic piety."[56] King represents this synthesis in the last sermon he preached.

> It's alright to talk about "long white robes over yonder," in all of its symbolism. But ultimately people want some suits and dresses and shoes to wear down here. It's alright to talk about "streets flowing milk and honey," but God has commanded us to be concerned about the slums down here, and his children who can't eat three square meals a day.[57]

One may desire union with God but not at the expense of others. Even though grace has an individual and personal emphasis, there remains a great sense of social responsibility that calls for reform in the sociopolitical realm on numerous levels. Sanctification, transforming grace, is linked to social liberation, because "it is not the intent of the love 'which is shed abroad in our hearts' to draw human love to itself in the heavenly sphere but to spend itself in the world in outpoured service," even fighting social injustices such as slavery and other forms of oppression.[58] Katie Cannon argues that God's grace "enables us to resist the forces of death and degradation arrayed against us and to affirm our dignity as beloved persons created in the image of God."[59]

Ultimately, all actions have to be guided by the principle of love because "love is the end of all the commandments of God."[60] Love is "the greatest of these" (1 Cor. 13:13). The mark of a Christian is the love of God and love of one's neighbor, according to Jesus (cf. Luke 10:27). When one is "spiritually empowered" due to being "caught up in the spirit" through a shout, for instance, if this empowerment does not lead to actions of love, one necessarily can question what the shout was all about and whether it was indeed the transforming grace of God at work.[61] The believer has the love of God shed abroad in his or her heart by the Holy Spirit (Rom. 5:5), the "Holy Spirit of Love."[62] Transformative grace produces individuals who share love unconditionally.[63] These actions of love could be as concrete as the secret brush harbor meetings, the underground railroad, or other avenues toward freedom, which aided the enslaved to survive cruel oppression. These speak to the fact that Christian faith without loving works is dead and may not even be Christian.

Sacramental Grace

A fourth component in an individual's experience of the Spirit is sacramental grace or "means of grace."[64] These means are outward signs of an inward grace, the usual definition of a sacrament.[65] These sacramental actions possess no power without the presence of the Holy Spirit. The true means of grace is the Spirit of God. Wesley is clearly helpful in making this pneumatological connection with these means of grace, whatever they may be.

> We allow, likewise, that all outward means whatever, if separate from the Spirit of God, cannot profit at all, cannot conduce, in any degree, either to the knowledge or love of God . . . and all outward things, unless He work in them and by them, are mere weak and beggarly elements. . . . We know that there is no inherent power in the words that are spoken in prayer, in the letter of Scripture read, the sound thereof heard, or the bread and wine received in the Lord's supper; but that it is God alone who is the Giver of every good gift, the Author of all grace.[66]

Through these means, the Spirit nurtures and sustains the Christian faith of individuals through grace received personally. These means have no inherent power to save and merit cannot be gained by partaking in them, for there is only one "Author of all grace." Sacramental grace receives its sacramental nature from the Holy Spirit. The Spirit is not limited to the direct, immediate conveying of grace to the heart of an individual but can also use an indirect path through the physical creation of God such as these means, including preaching. Yet, regardless of the directness or indirectness of the work of the Spirit, it is clear that the above-mentioned forms of grace—creation, forgiving, transforming, sacramental—are experiences of the Holy Spirit's internal and external work in the life of a person. Any work of God, particularly salvation, cannot be experienced by humanity unless the Holy Spirit is vitally present and active.

Preaching and Grace

Gift and Empowerment

Preaching itself is an expression of the grace of God as a gift given from above for the benefit of others, especially if one conceives preaching to be the "ministry of raising the dead."[67] The Spirit of grace allows the preacher to preach with power in conjunction with proper preparation. Grace allows preachers to perform for God and witness to divine action in the world. Jarena Lee testifies to divine empowerment for preaching when she declares, "My tongue was cut loose, the stammerer spoke freely."[68] Preachers must be dependent on grace for every single sermon, because without it, there can be no preaching and experience of God. Grace as a manifestation of the Spirit affirms what has been taught by many homileticians like James Harris, who declares, "The preacher cannot preach without the Holy Spirit. Regardless of one's ability, strength, or study habits, the sermon is ultimately a product of the power of the Holy Spirit, which enables us to utter 'what thus saith the Lord.' "[69]

Revelation in preaching is also an act of grace because revelation provides the power in preaching. Experience of God through the Spirit happens because revelation occurs through preaching. This revelation is God speaking through sermons; this is an act of unmerited favor toward humanity. To receive a word from God is a gift that no one deserves. Preaching is an act of grace because God in Christ comes willingly to the hearers through the Spirit without coercion. The coming of Christ as the Word through preaching is possible because of grace at work, for there is no encounter with the divine unless the Spirit is present.

Salvation

To speak of grace in relation to preaching points to the primary purpose of preaching—salvation. In many ways, grace is the individual experience of the Spirit's work of salvation and the goal of preaching is the salvation of all involved in the event. The Spirit produces the salvific effect of the gospel message. In his lecture, "Conversion as our Aim," Charles Spurgeon teaches that "for the most part, the work of preaching is intended to save the hearers."[70] In terms of justification, even Henry Mitchell, who establishes a human strategy for over-recording "tapes" of human intuition through experiential encounter, asserts that it is the Spirit who begets and nourishes faith through preaching.[71] This faith is not confined to the hearers alone, because salvation through the Spirit, both justification and sanctification, is also for preachers.

To preach in the Spirit of grace suggests that preachers must themselves be people of faith. Preachers should experience grace for themselves before they even preach. In fact, a presupposition of any preaching activity is that the preacher should have already experienced the grace of God through the Holy Spirit, especially since this grace is what he or she proclaims. Some homileticians put great emphasis on connecting the hearer to the grace of God while neglecting the importance of the preacher experiencing God's grace firsthand. This does not negate the communal and social dimensions of salvation, which are also evidence of the Spirit's work, but it stresses that the preacher should personally experience grace. Herbert H. Farmer argues that through preaching, God's saving activity encounters listening humans in challenge and succour, yet it "is that activity focusing on you, the preacher, also, for no man has truly preached who has not tremblingly felt the sermon penetrating of his own soul also."[72] The preacher must experience the grace of the Spirit and be able to make preaching an act of testimony, declaring what one has seen, heard, and experienced.[73] Jarena Lee testifies to her own conversion, revealing that she has heard about God's grace, experienced it, and then shares it with others. In her autobiography, she tells of how under the preaching of AME Bishop Richard Allen she is "gloriously converted to God."

> The text was barely pronounced, which was: "I perceive thy heart is not right in the sight of God" [Acts 8:21], when there appeared to *my* view, in the centre of the heart *one* sin; and this was *malice*, against one particular individual, who had strove deeply to injure me, which I resented. At this discovery, I said, *Lord* I forgive *every* creature. That instant, it appeared to me, as if a garment, which had entirely enveloped my whole person, even to my fingers ends, split at the crown of my head, and was stripped away from me, passing like a shadow, from my sight—when the glory of God seemed to cover me in its stead.
>
> That moment, though hundreds were present, I did leap to my feet, and declare that God, for Christ's sake, had pardoned the sins of my soul. Great was the ecstasy of my mind, for I felt that not only the sin of *malice* was pardoned, but all other sins were swept away together. That day was the first when my heart had believed, and my tongue had made confession unto salvation—the first words uttered, a part of that song, which shall fill eternity with its sound, was *glory to God*. For a few moments I had power to exhort sinners, and to tell of the wonders and of the goodness of him who had clothed me with *his* salvation. During this, the minister was silent, until my soul felt its duty had been performed, when he declared another witness of the power of Christ to forgive sins on earth, was manifest in my conversion.[74]

Lee experiences salvific grace and then testifies to it by exhorting others, pointing to the evangelical mission of preaching that leads others to Christ, who will then offer them "the fresh bread of forgiveness."[75]

This testimony is not only that individuals are forgiven but also that they can be transformed by the grace of God through the Spirit. The preacher is saved, but the people in the pew can also be saved by grace, forgiven, and transformed. A sermon's impact does not finish after the benediction of a service, but the Word continues to move in the lives of the hearers throughout each day such that fruit of the Spirit is born and nurtured, leading to actions of love in the world. King was concerned with the phenomenon of worship as entertainment that would consist of "more religion in their hands and feet than in their hearts and souls."[76] Through preaching, individuals, churches, and the world can be changed, because preaching is an "agency of the grace of God."[77] If preaching is not in the Spirit, there can be no salvific grace; but in the Spirit of grace, the potential of preaching is limitless, because grace is what allows preaching to be effective.

Openness to the Spirit

A sign of the Spirit at work in preaching is when a preacher embraces existential grace by being vulnerable to the Spirit or the "anointing," which is also a "yielding" through prayer.[78] Yielding to God is a sign that one desires the grace of God and reveals one's reliance on the presence of the Spirit. Underlying this openness is the conviction that "there is no true preaching without epiclesis."[79] Invoking the Spirit of God for preaching is an embrace of grace. Henry Mitchell writes, "The use of a dedicated mind and the openness of a spirit to *the* Spirit can, thus, be expected to yield conditions which appear best to be used of God toward the wholeness and growth of persons."[80] One's openness to the Spirit is also about putting forth one's best efforts and skills in the homiletical task.

Preachers assist and collaborate with the Holy Spirit through their skills and efforts.[81] Sermon preparation reveals one's trust in the grace of God to develop an effective sermon and as such is an embrace of grace. Preachers are "farmhands of the Spirit,"[82] and by doing the necessary work for preaching invite the power and grace of the Spirit to come. Preparing a sermon is an act of faith because preachers know that it is God who makes preaching effective, yet humans are needed to preach the Word.[83] It is a step of faith to enter the pulpit to preach because only the grace of God can make preaching powerful. Preachers know this; thus to step into the pulpit is a prayer for grace, an embrace of existential grace. This embrace makes all the difference in preaching because it suggests the presence of the Holy Spirit at work in imperfect sermons.

Summary

Grace is the experience and work of the Spirit whether it manifests as creation, forgiving, transforming, or sacramental grace. Without grace through the Spirit, there would be no preacher, no power, and no salvation, suggesting that preaching is a gift of grace and as such any impact preaching may have on individuals is solely due to the power of the Spirit. Without grace, preaching dies. With grace, preaching can live and stir salvation in all hearers, including the preacher. Because of the significance of grace for preaching, it is vital that preachers embrace this grace for their lives and for the preaching moment. The embrace of existential grace by lamenting the absence of grace or celebrating the presence of grace is a sign of the Spirit in sermons, as will be shown later, as the Spirit leads one to experience the grace of God personally. The "Spirit of grace" will be helpful for reading sermons pneumatologically. The next chapter discusses the ecclesial work of the Spirit as another aspect of the holistic manifestation of the Spirit.

The Spirit of Unity

Long before the Spirit was a theme of doctrine,
he was a fact in the experience of the community.
—Edward Schweizer, *"Pneuma,"* TDNT

No one ever wins a fight.
—Howard Thurman, *Deep Is the Hunger*

T he mark of *unity* emphasizes the communal dimension of the Spirit's work, and specifically the fostering of ecclesial unity may be deemed to be a sign of the Spirit in preaching. This trait of the Spirit, ecclesial unity, is another way of grounding the pneumatological discussion for homiletics developing in this work. It also contributes to the range of ecclesial issues that may be lamented or celebrated in a sermon. The Spirit fosters unity within the faith community, guiding Christians to do the same; thus, any sign of this emphasis within sermons may be discerned to be a manifestation of the Spirit.

To help explore the presence of the Holy Spirit within an ecclesial setting, I will converse mainly with Pauline scriptural thought (though this is problematic in some ways given the sometimes-ambivalent relationship between Paul's writings and the history of African Americans). A common narrative within African American religion is the story told by Howard Thurman about his grandmother, who refused to listen to the Pauline letters, except 1 Corinthians 13, because during the time of slavery, the white ministers used Paul to preach and justify slavery. Renita Weems, in "Reading *Her Way* through the Struggle: African-American Women and the Bible," uses this story as an example of how African American women struggle with the Bible, at times using hermeneutical strategies of resistance toward biblical texts.[1] Despite the African American struggle with Pauline material, C. Michelle Venable-Ridley strives to reclaim the writings of Paul as a religious source for African Americans by demonstrating how the "good news of Paul was very different from the *euangelion* of the slavocracy."[2]

Furthermore, Pauline material may be problematic for women preachers in particular because in some theological camps Paul is viewed as a patriarchal misogynist whose writings have been used by some church groups as a basis for opposing the call to women to preach. In some cases, Paul seems to be supportive of women in public ministry (Acts 18:18, 26; Rom. 16:1; 1 Cor. 11:5; Phil. 4:2-3); while at other times, he appears to mute women's voices and lower the social standing of women in the church (1 Cor. 11:5-6; 1 Cor. 14:34-35). Elsewhere, Paul seems to suggest that gender hierarchy has been dissolved through baptism (Gal. 3:27-28). Thus, what is presented in the scriptural witness about Paul's views on the role of women in the church is complex. In my own appropriation of the writings of Paul and in light of the unity of the Spirit that is epitomized in mutual Christ-like love, women, as human beings, are gifted individuals, who if called by the Spirit of God to preach, are fully capable of practicing an effective public ministry in the pulpit, regardless of contrary opinions.

Despite these ongoing cultural tensions with Pauline thought, his writings are a constructive conversation partner in furthering discussions about the Spirit. The church community in Corinth, as revealed in Paul's First Epistle to the Corinthians, is familiar with experiences of the Spirit, which is one reason for dealing with this biblical book here. The experience of the Spirit is a "fact" for this believing Corinthian community and presents a particular perspective on the work of the Spirit in the life of a Christian congregation, though, according to Paul, the active life of this community is not congruent with an understanding of the Holy Spirit's communal work. This is mainly due to the apparent conflicts that are present in the church at Corinth that are inconsistent with a particular concept of a Spirit-directed life. The Corinthians, however, view themselves as *pneumatikoi*, spiritual, despite their evident conflicts. Thus, Paul and the Corinthian church are at odds over the role of the Spirit in the life of the Christian community, leading to his letter of 1 Corinthians being "full of Spirit concerns."[3]

A study of this church in conflict that is "full of Spirit" will demonstrate that a key mark of the Holy Spirit in the life of a congregation is unity. The first portion of this chapter, the study of the church in 1 Corinthians, will express how the Spirit relates to ecclesial unity. The second section will tease out the homiletical implications of this concept of the Spirit's presence. The Spirit is the divine resolution to the Corinthian congregation's conflicts because the Spirit aims to unify people rather than divide them, making unity a necessary manifestation of the Spirit in sermons.

Division and Conflict in the Corinthian Church

The church at Corinth reflects the heterogeneous makeup of the city of Corinth, particularly in relation to social standing.[4] The congregation's socioeconomic diversity eventually leads to social stratification, which contributes to the church's conflicts. Paul writes his letter to the Corinthian church after receiving correspondence about the dissension and conflict in their community. Early in his letter, he makes an appeal to them to "be in agreement and that there be no divisions among you, but that you be united in the same mind and the same purpose" (1:10; cf. 11:18). Richard Hays calls this statement the fundamental theme of Paul's letter—a call for unity to a divided people.[5] In *Paul and the Rhetoric of Reconciliation*, Margaret Mitchell asserts that "Paul's rhetorical stance throughout 1 Corinthians is to argue that Christian unity is the theological and sociological expectation from which the Christians have fallen short, and to which they must return."[6] Mitchell believes that the innate cause and further result of *all* of the problems in the Corinthian congregation is "factionalism," which she deems to be the topic of the entire letter, not only the first portion of it (that is, chapters 1–4).[7] Factionalism, according to Mitchell, is the "division of persons within the confines of community ranks."[8] This definition fits the divided state of the Corinthian church, which demonstrates its "fledgling" and "refractory" qualities through its internal behavior.[9]

This community is torn in many ways, but two key issues of discord involve Paul's authority and his understanding of the gospel.[10] To some scholars, the major conflict in 1 Corinthians is between Paul and the church and not between individual members. To some, the rhetoric of Paul is "combative," "attacking," and "challenging with all the weapons in his literary arsenal" because his apostolic authority has been attacked.[11] Paul does not have to say, "This is my defense to those who would examine me" (9:3; cf. 4:3) if he is not being questioned as a pastoral leader. There are "quarrels" in the community regarding leadership indicated by Paul when he writes that some say "'I belong to Paul,' or 'I belong to Apollos,' or 'I belong to Cephas,' or 'I belong to Christ.' Has Christ been divided? Was Paul crucified for you? Or were you baptized in the name of Paul?"(1:11-13). He exhorts the church to find their source of life in Christ rather than in a human leader (1:30; 3:21) because they are *God's* field, building, and temple (ch. 3). Yet the Corinthians continue to "magnify the messenger and miss the message."[12] Paul tries to assert his authority over this community by naming himself their "father through the gospel" (4:15), but he is unsuccessful because his leadership is mistrusted (cf. 4:3, 6, 18-20).

Gerd Theissen believes that the group divisions and arguments are due to various missionaries gaining influence in the community creating "tussles over prestige" in the congregation.[13] Particularly, through his sociological lens, Theissen argues that the main problem involves the theological issue of apostolic legitimacy that is connected with the material question of the apostle's subsistence. The two types of itinerant preachers are the itinerant charismatic and the community organizer. The charismatic missionary begs for subsistence and believes that he will be voluntarily supported for his ministry. In contrast, the community organizer, represented by Paul, renounces the privilege of being supported (9:3-15) in this manner and is economically self-sufficient. Because of the approach of Paul, his apostolic legitimacy is suspect in the minds of some in the Corinthian church.[14]

The other salient divisive issue has to do with Paul's conception of the gospel. The main theological tension over the gospel message has to do with what it means to be "spiritual" (*pneumatikos*), or a Spirit-person. The Corinthians embrace an "overspiritualized eschatology" through which they view themselves as angels because many of them practice glossolalia, the dialect of heaven.[15] In *The Corinthian Body*, Dale Martin says that 1 Corinthians 12–14 is "built on the assumption that the practice of speaking in tongues has ruptured the Corinthian church precisely because glossolalia carries status implications."[16] Tongues, in this setting, are a high-status indicator,[17] revealing the reason Paul stresses the value of every gift based on the same Spirit, who gives each gift "for the common good" (12:7). Paul emphasizes the oneness of the community and the importance of each member and gift for the maintenance of the unity of the body (12:12-30), because speaking in tongues has apparently caused division in the community. Mutual empathy in suffering and rejoicing (12:26) is vital, because the weak, most likely those without the higher status gift of tongues, are most often forgotten. Paul thus urges the "more excellent way" of love because the congregation is going another way that actually opposes the way of the Spirit.

This "spiritual" issue leads Paul to question early in his letter, "What do you have that you did not receive? And if you received it, why do you boast as if it were not a gift?"(4:7). In his thanksgiving (1:4-9), Paul teaches that it is because of the grace, or *charis*, of God that people "are not lacking in any spiritual gift"(*charisma* or manifestation of grace). Paul wants to show them that God's grace is the source of their gifts and "not expressions of the Corinthians' own autonomous spiritual capacity or brilliance."[18] The Corinthians, however, seem to practice glossolalia at the expense of loving behavior and care for the community (13:1), indicating a lack of acknowledgment of the divine source of this speech gift. They are overly enthusiastic for tongues even though this does not aid the community in any way. This is why Paul stresses that tongues must be interpreted in order to build up the community and that these gifts must be practiced in a decent and orderly fashion in worship (14:1-40). Paul would not have to give this instruction if community worship was functioning properly. Instead, he constantly urges the community to be built up because it has broken down. With the obsession over "angelic speech" comes the Corinthian belief that they have already arrived at an ultimate spiritual existence (except that they still possess bodies). They believe that they already experience the fullness of the future world; thus, they are superior to the happenings of the present world and can neglect "bodily" and ethical matters.

It is not surprising, then, that most of the concerns Paul discusses are behavioral and ethical in nature. The Corinthians do not walk in love toward one another nor do they build up one another, at least not in Paul's mind (cf. chapters 12-14). Paul and the church at Corinth may have their disputes, but it is also clear that *within* the community there are struggles and rivalries. The "Corinthians are quite right about the importance of the Spirit as the key for Christian life; but they are wrong as to what that life looks like and how such people live and behave in the present world."[19] Basically, their tensions relate to matters of "practical ecclesiology."[20] These ecclesiological tensions include the previously discussed matters but are further fueled by other conflicts that will be discussed subsequently.

Some in the Corinthian church have what Victor Furnish calls a "proto-gnostic spirituality,"[21] a belief that they are enabled with special wisdom and knowledge (cf. 4:7, 8, 18-21; 3:18; 5:2, 6; 8:1, 11). This is one of the main problems in the community, because this kind of spirituality privileges certain members over other members; most likely the privileged members are those of the upper strata. A community cannot flourish with the propagation of Gnostic tendencies, because "the wisdom of the world is the set of values and norms which divide persons of higher and lower status into separate groups, a wisdom which prefers dissension to unity, superiority to cooperation."[22] "Knowledge puffs up," and therefore Paul constantly tells the church to "build up" one another (8:1; cf. 10:23; 14:5, 12), especially those who are weaker (12:22-24). Paul encourages this because he sees the church being destroyed while Corinthians boast (5:6).

In addition, sexual immorality tears the community apart, which is why Paul calls for corporate responsibility in this matter (5:1-13; 6:12-20). The church at Corinth does not realize that the conduct of individuals affects the entire community. Moreover, the community is split when believers pursue litigation against one another in pagan civil courts. Paul calls these legal disputes a "defeat" for the church and a means of wronging and defrauding fellow Christians (6:1-11). Even in regard to issues of food, Paul urges the community as a whole not to flaunt their freedom (8:1-13; 10:23-33). They are told to "take care that this liberty of yours does not somehow become a stumbling block to the weak" (8:9). Paul focuses on what benefits the entire community because this congregation has demonstrated a pattern that breaks down the community. The solidarity of the community has been betrayed by human wisdom and the church has failed to be the church.[23]

This failure is even evident in the conflict that arises when they "come together" for worship. The irony of this can be found in the Corinthian practice of the Lord's Supper (11:17-33). When they come together they do not "come together" in unity (11:17, 18, 20, 33, 34) but in disunity with schisms (11:18; cf. 1:10). The sacrament of unity has become one of disunity. "For when the time comes to eat, each of you goes ahead with your own supper, and one goes hungry and another becomes drunk . . . do you show contempt for the church of God and humiliate whose who have nothing?" (11:21-22) The major conflict is between the "haves" and "have-nots," the rich and the poor, revealing the socioeconomic problem at the Corinthian table.

Some believe that the conflict was sparked by a habit of the rich.[24] Perhaps they took part in the meal by themselves, maybe physically separated from others, or began eating before the commencement of the meal. The Corinthians' conventional social mores "require distinctions of rank and status to be recognized at table: the more privileged members expect to receive more and better food than the others. Paul regards this as a humiliation for the community and as an abuse of the Supper of the Lord, whose own example contradicts such status divisions."[25] "Those who have nothing"[26] are treated like nothing, showing that the Corinthian Christians "demonstrate an odd amnesia about Jesus' death."[27] The selfish actions and proliferation of social privilege at the table disrupts this community. The Corinthians prize their spirituality, especially their wisdom, knowledge, and angelic speech of tongues, but as a result, the spiritual growth of the congregation suffers.

The condition of the Corinthian congregation is one of diversity, division, and tremendous conflict. Paul is dissatisfied with such a sad state of affairs in the community that he founded; thus he writes to them as their caring "father" (4:15). He believes he knows the theological solution to their problems. For these particular ecclesial circumstances in Corinth, the theological solution is the Holy Spirit. In the following, I will examine Paul's teaching on the Spirit in response to this congregation in conflict as a way of demonstrating the Spirit's work of unity that also can be discerned in preaching.

Pastoral Teaching on the Spirit in 1 Corinthians

The Holy Spirit is vital in Paul's response to the Corinthian conflicts because the Spirit is the effective means toward unity within this local congregation. Though some may say that "there is no considered doctrine of the Spirit in 1 Corinthians,"[28] one cannot argue that the Spirit is unimportant, especially in 1 Corinthians. The congregational problems may not be based in theological ideas, but Paul frames the issues theologically, and specifically, pneumatologically. His pastoral task is community formation and his strategy is to reframe the Corinthians' pneumatological thinking in order to alter their behavior as a community.[29] Community is so critical for Paul because "deep within himself he knows that if he settles for anything less than this, he denies the profound intent of his own spirit, which is one with the intent of the Creator."[30] Community is a fundamental human aspiration, especially if one believes in humanity's "elemental grounding in unity."[31] Community is also inspired by the Spirit, which is the reason for Paul's concentration on the work of the Spirit in this crisis situation. Paul's pastoral theological response to this congregation necessarily includes the work of the unifying Spirit because "there is no aspect of his theology—at least what is fundamental to his theology—in which the Spirit does not play a leading role."[32] Paul, there-fore, teaches about three crucial ways in which the Spirit fosters unity, rather than disunity, in this community, in an attempt to resolve their conflicts.

Spirit and Revelation (2:1-16)

The first pedagogical focus for Paul that is crucial in viewing the Spirit as a unifying source for the Corinthian division relates to the Spirit's role in reve-lation. The apparent controversy over "wisdom" (chapters 1–3) sparked by the Corinthians' prideful boasting (1:29-31; 3:21; 4:7) and "puffed up" nature (4:6, 18-19) is rooted in a form of human wisdom. In reaction to the Corinthians' wayward perspective, Paul teaches about God's true wisdom that is contradictory to their conceited human wisdom. He argues that the nature of the gospel (1:18-25), the congregation's experience of it (1:26-31), and Paul's preaching that leads to their Christian existence (2:1-5), are based on God's wisdom rather than human wisdom.

In God's wisdom, knowledge of God and salvation comes through "the foolishness of our proclamation" (1:21), not through human wisdom or feats. This foolish preaching is not performed "with eloquent wisdom" (1:17) or "in lofty words or wisdom" (2:1; cf. 2:4) like the popular Greek orators of the day. Rather, the word of the cross of the crucified Christ, the content of the gospel, comes "with a demonstration of the Spirit and of power, so that your faith might rest not on human wisdom but on the power of God" (2:4-5). Paul attempts to convince this church that their faith is not based on his or their abilities but on the power of God through the Spirit, for conversion begins with Spirit-empowered proclamation.[33] Paul distances himself from accepting any credit for conversion. Instead, Paul gives rhetorical proof ulti-mately to the Spirit as power and renounces any status as rhetorician.[34] Fee notes that "In every possible way Paul has tried to show them the folly of their present fascination with wisdom, which has inherent within it the folly of self-sufficiency and self-congratulation. Even the preacher whom God used to bring them to faith had to reject self-reliance."[35]

Paul uses this argument because he believes that they cannot know God in Christ without the Spirit. It is the Spirit through preaching who creates a gospel community. The formation of a Christian *community* is primarily the work of the Spirit; therefore none of them has reason to boast in humanity. They, on the other hand, should walk in a humility that nurtures a unified church established by the Spirit. Boasting in themselves disregards the Spirit and creates a hierarchical division in the community.

Divinity deserves to be the object of boasting (1:31) for "No one can say 'Jesus is Lord' except by the Holy Spirit" (12:3). The Spirit creates the Christian community through the word of the cross, hopefully leading God's people to recognize that their Christian identity is a gift from God. They have "received . . . the Spirit that is from God" (2:12) to act in ways that are congruent with the crucified Christ. The Spirit is the source of salvation, calling for humility in the community that has seemingly lost its way because of pride. Through the power of God, the Spirit births Christians on an equal spiritual plane, not on a spiritual hierarchy as some of the Corinthians have practiced. This is why Paul does not "parade himself." Instead, he "resolves to provide a transparent window onto the cross" because that is where the Spirit leads believers. "Hence *any* 'self-preservation' on the part of *any* 'leader or name' has no place in a community founded by and on the gospel."[36] Only the power and wisdom of God, Jesus Christ crucified (1:24), has primary place in the community, for the heart of the church is Jesus and this can only be discovered through the Spirit, who reveals God's wisdom and the way of the cross.

The Spirit leads to conversion through her revelation of the content of God's wisdom. Paul says, "We do speak wisdom . . . we speak God's wisdom, secret and hidden, which God decreed before the ages for our glory. None of the rulers of this age understood this . . . these things God has revealed to us through the Spirit" (2:6-10). The human wisdom purported by the Corinthian church does not grasp God's wisdom. God's hidden wisdom is only revealed through the Spirit, who "searches everything, even the depths of God" (2:10). This wisdom of God, as opposed to the Corinthians' "wisdom of this age" (2:6), is none other than the crucified Christ and the way of the cross. The Spirit "discloses that the word of the cross is the truth about God."[37]

In this section of his teaching, revelation is stressed as God's action through the Spirit and not a human spiritual capacity because "no one comprehends what is truly God's except the Spirit of God" (2:11); thus, one must first receive the Spirit in order to understand God's wisdom of the cross. "Like is only known by like," demonstrating our human inability to know God without God's assistance. Paul even declares that he is taught the revelation of God's wisdom by the Spirit (2:13). Furthermore, this Christian congregation should understand God's wisdom and way because they have "received not the spirit of the world, but the Spirit that is from God, so that we may understand." (2:12). Proper understanding stems from the Spirit; however, they act as if they do not have the Spirit of God in their lives.

Paul attempts to "retool their understanding of the Spirit and spirituality"[38] because they have obviously gone astray and espouse a wisdom "of the rulers of this age," which is coming to nothing (2:6). To those who are "spiritual," true wisdom, God's wisdom, is the gospel of the crucified Messiah (2:13-14). The Corinthian church thinks they are "spiritual," but, "by pursuing _sophia_ they are acting just like those without the Spirit who are likewise pursuing wisdom but see the cross as foolishness. The net result—and the irony—is that they are 'spiritual,' yet 'unspiritual'; they are pursuing 'wisdom,' yet missing the very wisdom of God."[39] They are acting like "people of the flesh" (3:1) because they use "wisdom" for status and human achievement rather than real "wisdom as a sheer gift of God given in and through Christ" in the Spirit.[40] The Spirit reveals a wisdom defined by the salvific cross of Christ and this is the wisdom that should be guiding their lives as Christians. Paul wants the Corinthians "to understand who they are—in terms of the cross—and to stop acting as non-Spirit people."[41] They have the Spirit; therefore, they have "primary and immediate resources for reckoning proper behavior,"[42] but ironically their behavior does not exemplify those who have received the Spirit.

The way of the Spirit is the way of the cross of Christ for Paul. Those who have the Spirit "have the mind of Christ" (2:16) because the Spirit appropriates the way of Christ to the life of the believer and community. Furnish declares that the "mind of Christ" means "critical thought and reasoned action are informed and guided by wisdom of the cross."[43] The way of the crucified Christ, the wisdom of God, is antithetical to the human wisdom and way propagated by the Corinthians. Paul urges them to follow another way and pattern of life, one that would unify a community rather than divide it. Their problem stems from the fact that they "exchanged the theology of the cross for a false triumphalism that went beyond, or excluded, the cross," thus negating the way of the Spirit.[44]

Through a crucified Messiah, God overturns expectations and turns the tables on the pattern of wisdom followed in the world.[45] Through the cross, the Spirit reveals that power is found in weakness and wisdom in foolishness;

God choosing the foolish, weak, and lowly is the way and wisdom of the cross (1:26-31). The Corinthians boast in wisdom, knowledge, and spirituality, but Paul insists "the word of the cross brings all boasting in such qualities to nothing."[46] These qualities have been the source of division and conflict in the community. The cross levels the spiritual field such that there is no room for boasting in any human trait or ability and only space for boasting in the Lord who unites a community with one spiritual focus. Salvation comes to all through the same avenue of the crucified Christ and not through some other creative way devised by human beings.

The Spirit "is to be measured by the cross"[47] and the cross destroys spiritual elitism; thus, the Spirit as revealer teaches how one should follow the humble way of Christ. Paul presents the act of God in Christ on the cross as the foundation and criterion of authentic wisdom and the reverse of human evaluations of status, achievement, and success.[48] The cross is "the great divine contradiction to our merely human ways of doing things."[49] The prideful way the church at Corinth has done things causes tremendous problems in their community, but the way of the cross taught by the Spirit leads to a humility that unites a people. The Spirit focuses the church on Christ crucified, the one Messiah, resulting in a unified way for the congregation; the Spirit unites the church in Christ. God's wisdom revealed by the Spirit gives life to a community. The Christian community is marked by the cross through the Spirit giving the church a central focus and pattern to follow in faithful discipleship. If the Spirit is the only revealer of God's wisdom and power exemplified in the crucified Christ without any human assistance, there is no reason for congregational conflict, because the Spirit forms a humble community rooted in the one crucified and risen Lord and Messiah, Jesus Christ.

Spirit and Embodiment (6:12-20; 3:9-17)

The second pedagogical focus that is crucial in viewing the Spirit as a unifying force in the midst of Corinthian conflicts relates to the Spirit and embodiment. "Embodiment" is not only the physical body of a person but also the relationships of that person within a larger corporate and social whole. Embodiment implies how one relates to a larger social system. James Dunn notes that *soma*, the word Paul uses for body, has a wide spectrum of meaning and includes physical, relational, social, and ecological dimensions; in fact, the word *body* implies embodiment within a wider social setting.[50] In two sections of 1 Corinthians (3:9-17; 6:12-20), the image of temple is used to represent embodiment in all of its meanings.

Spirit and Physical Body as Temple (6:12-20)

In one instance, Paul asserts, "do you not know that your body is a temple of the Holy Spirit within you, which you have from God, and that you are not your own?" (6:19). Here, a person's physical body is equated with the temple. The temple (*naos*) is the actual sanctuary and place of a deity's dwelling. This temple imagery reflects the Old Testament people of God because they were those among whom God chose to dwell by tabernacling in their midst (Ps. 114:2). The term may even have eschatological overtones (Isa. 28:16; Ezek. 40–48). Nonetheless, the point is clear—"you are not your own" because God's Spirit is within you; thus, the Corinthians cannot behave in any way they choose. The Spirit within them leads them to "glorify God in your body" (6:20) in ways that are "beneficial" (cf. 6:12). "In the same way that the temple in Jerusalem 'housed' the presence of the living God, so the Spirit of God is 'housed' in the believer's body."[51] The Corinthians are familiar with pagan temples and shrines (*naoi*) in their city. But there is only one temple of the Holy Spirit "which you have from God" and it is their physical body; therefore, one should shun fornication because it hurts the body that is supposed to be united with Christ (6:15-18).

Paul focuses on the body because, as John A. T. Robinson says in his work, *The Body: A Study in Pauline Theology*, "the body for the Hebrew, like the flesh, is what ties men up with each other, rather than what separates them as individuals.... The body is that which joins all people, irrespective of individual differences, in life's bundle together."[52] One's physical acts have larger ramifications for one's community. Therefore, the Spirit is linked with the body in order to move this congregation in the direction of unity and healthy relationships with humanity and God. This affirms the notion that "the profoundest disclosure in the religious experience is the awareness that the individual is not alone....What is disclosed in his religious experience he must define in community."[53] This is true because of the interrelatedness of humanity. Martin Luther King, Jr. proclaims, "I can never be what I ought to be until you are what you ought to be. You can never be what you ought to be until I am what I ought to be. This is the way the world is made. I didn't make it that way, but this is the interrelated structure of reality."[54]

A person's spiritual journey occurs not solely in solitude but also in the context of community, implying that one's actions, including bodily acts, impact a community, for the Christian life is a communal life. For instance, if a body is united with a prostitute and this is sin against the body, then this action will prevent unity with Christ and ultimately unity in the church of Christ. The work of the Spirit in the body as temple keeps the body as a member of Christ and thus unified with the Lord, maintaining unity in the congregation. The body as a temple of the Spirit suggests that the body in relation to Christ should be pure and holy because the "name of Christ and the pneuma of God are cleansing agents" (6:11).[55] This perspective on the Spirit-body, affirming the body as the dwelling place of the Spirit and thus valuable for the Christian life, is in direct opposition to the behavior and beliefs of the Corinthians.

Dale Martin notes that a "general deprecation of the body enjoyed wide currency among the educated elite of Greco-Roman society" and the Corinthian church follows suit.[56] A Corinthian maxim was "All things are lawful for me" (6:12), and since they devalued the importance of the body for spirituality, they believed they could practice sexuality in any manner they desired. Sexual immorality and the body dominate this portion of Paul's letter because prostitution was prevalent, legal, and a normal cultural practice at the time. Corinthian men who used prostitutes were not asserting some unheard-of new freedom but were insisting on continuing in this widely accepted social convention.[57] Charles Talbert insightfully writes, "The sexual latitude allowed to men by Greek public opinion was virtually unrestricted. Sexual relations of males with both boys and harlots were generally tolerated."[58] Corinthian Christian men argue for the right to engage in this practice because "being people of the Spirit, they imply, has moved them to a higher plane, the realm of spirit, where they are unaffected by behavior that has merely to do with the body."[59] Being influenced by the Greeks' low view of the material realm, they believe that God will destroy the body (6:13); but Paul counters this perspective by affirming the body and saying, "The body is meant not for fornication but for the Lord, and the Lord for the body. And God raised the Lord and will also raise us by his power" (6:13-14). Paul teaches that the "presence of Spirit in their present bodily existence is God's affirmation of the body", not the negation of it.[60]

There is "the unity of the self," the physical and spiritual together,[61] affirmed by the bodily resurrection of Christ and humanity (6:14; cf. 1 Cor. 15), showing that the work of redemption includes the whole person, which in the Jewish view includes the body. One, therefore, needs to "shun fornication" because members of Christ should never become members of a prostitute (6:15, 18). This would destroy one's body and one's union of "spirit" with the Lord (6:15-17), defiling the entire community. The Spirit in the body works to keep a person joined to Christ and the body of Christ, leading to a separation from bodily actions that taint community life.

As noted earlier, some Corinthians' actions in the physical realm disrupt the unity of the church, even though they believe that they are spiritual just because they possess the Spirit. But true spirituality involves the work of the Spirit in the human body for the glory of God. The body is significant for life in the Spirit. "The body matters. To misuse the body is to hold the creator in contempt."[62] The body matters because the Spirit embraces it as a temple; thus, everyday ethics matter. The Spirit continues to guide Christians to the glorification of God in their bodies; thus, any embodied action that hurts any*body* hurts the community, brings shame to God, and is not of the Spirit. The Spirit works with individuals-in-community, not apart from community. The African American church is aligned with this understanding because it "is based on the African notion of 'self-in-community,'"[63] which is why Zora Neale Hurston observes that individuals may shout, but the work of the Spirit "thrives in concert."[64] The understanding of the physical body as temple reveals that the Spirit works in the human body toward what is beneficial for the community, demonstrating once again that the Spirit aims for unity rather than congregational division.

Spirit and Congregation as Temple (3:9-17)

In the earlier section where Paul uses the metaphor of temple, he speaks of the congregation, as a whole, being "God's temple" (3:16). Not only do individuals as temples embody the Spirit, as just discussed, but communities as temples also embody the Spirit. Paul tells the Corinthian congregation, "Do you not know that you are God's temple and that God's Spirit dwells in you?...God's temple is holy, and you are that temple" (3:16-17). Anthony Thiselton, in his commentary on 1 Corinthians, affirms this when he declares, "Here Paul is not saying that each individual Christian is a temple within which God's Spirit dwells, but rather that the Spirit of God dwells in the Christian community *corporately as a community* . . . whatever we conclude about 6:19, however, 3:16 refers to a corporate indwelling of the Spirit of God."[65] As a community, Corinthians are "God's field, God's building" (3:9), and more specifically, "God's temple" (3:16), the place where the Spirit of God resides. Paul emphasizes *God* as the owner of the field, building, and temple in an attempt to call the Corinthians back to being unified servants in God's kingdom. They are resources in the community God has created, but God is the only life source for their church. They should be a people built on the foundation of Jesus Christ (3:11) rather than on other human foundations that destroy the community.

The use of building metaphors is strategic because these metaphors are *topoi* in ancient literature, urging unity to divided groups. The temple metaphor is one of a particular building symbolizing peace and unity.[66] By associating the Spirit with the temple, the Spirit is connected to unity and peace; thus, this church that is supposedly indwelled by the Spirit should exemplify unity. "God's presence *constitutes* the temple status of his people, and without it they are no temple."[67] This temple that belongs to Christ

(3:23) should be an alternative temple in Corinth, but by boasting, worshiping wisdom, and stirring divisions, they "banish the Spirit" and destroy God's temple (3:17).[68] "God will destroy" (3:17) whomever destroys the temple because God the Spirit aims for unity, not disunity and destruction. "By sinning against the consecrated corporeity, some are sinning against God and committing sacrilege against the Spirit."[69] Humans "are made for each other, and any sustained denial of this elemental fact of life cannot stand,"[70] though it may stir much trouble within the community of faith. To deny community is to deny one's humanity and the presence of the Spirit.

Those who boast of being "spiritual" actually cut themselves off from the Spirit as their source of life by destroying the church community through their spiritless behavior. Paul is shocked that this community does not understand this fundamental connection with the Spirit and questions them, "Do you not know that?"(3:16).[71] Those who boast of knowing do not know that they are to be a "holy" temple (3:17), set apart for God, ritually, but also in the "moral-ethical sense."[72] What is exemplary of the Spirit-empowered gospel is not the flaunting of spiritual gymnastics but a holy life lived in accordance with the pattern of Christ, who is the foundation of the temple. The means to the holiness of the temple is the Spirit, who aims for peace within a unified community. Ultimately, it is the community's embodied witness in the Spirit that reveals the spiritual nature of it, because the "public embodied life of Christ's people" is "the instantiation of the gospel."[73]

Spirit and Community Worship (12:1–14:40)

In 1 Corinthians, there is a concern about the public, embodied life of Christians in the local assembly. The third and most prominent pedagogical focus in viewing the Spirit as a unifying source for the Corinthian church has to do with community worship. The question raised, "What should be done then, my friends?"(14:26) is addressed in 12:1–14:40 with Paul's insightful teaching about the Spirit in the community.[74] When the congregation comes together (11:18-19, 23, 26; 14:12, 23, 33, 40), the focus is to edify the community in worship though contrary to the belief of some members (cf. chapters 12–14). The emphasis is on the community because "Paul's anthropology is not a form of individualism; persons are social beings."[75] His "primary context for thinking about believers is the community. He labors assiduously to maintain and edify the communal fellowship. The community is, after all, the matrix within which individual lives of faith are nurtured and maintained."[76] The church consists of individuals-in-community, who search for common ground among themselves.

The life of the community is vital; thus, it must be maintained, despite the forces that may threaten it. As noted, some Christian Corinthians see themselves as "spiritual soloists," but worship is a corporate action of the community that requires complementary participation.[77] Community life is not to be snubbed or disregarded, because it is the work of the Holy Spirit. "The Spirit is the principle par excellence of *communitas*, of spontaneous, direct interaction apart from the roles and antinomies of 'the world.'"[78] The Spirit brings unity in the community through an equal distribution of spiritual empowerment. In the latter part of this letter, Paul continues to show that the Spirit fosters unity; thus, any action that divides the community is not of the Spirit.

Common Confession (12:1-3)

First, the Spirit gives every believer a common confession in the lordship of Jesus Christ, the heart of unity. Paul begins his teaching about the spiritual gifts by saying, "I want you to understand that no one speaking by the Spirit of God ever says, 'Let Jesus be cursed!' and no one can say 'Jesus is Lord' except by the Holy Spirit" (12:3). The foundation of the spiritual life is Jesus Christ; thus, authentic Christian spirituality is rooted in Jesus as Lord, not in the excess of spiritual gifts. The focus of this confession may even be heard in the words of the spiritual, "Give me Jesus, give me Jesus, you may have the world, give me Jesus."[79] The Spirit empowers this Christian confession; thus, anyone making this Christocentric statement is "ipso facto living in the sphere of the Holy Spirit's power" and should not be despised (cf. 12:12-13).[80] This confession is the fundamental criterion in determining whether one is possessed by the Spirit. "Jesus is Lord" is the "Spirit-inspired watchword" that separates the work of the Spirit from other spirits.[81] Also, those who make this confession are bound by one Spirit, regardless of the gifts they practice, because "there are varieties of gifts, but the same Spirit" (12:4).

The same Spirit received by all Christians exalts the same Jesus as Lord in the community. "Whatever takes away from that, even if they be legitimate expressions of the Spirit, begins to move away from Christ to a more pagan fascination with spiritual activity as an end in itself."[82] No spiritual gift can replace the confession of Jesus Christ as the true mark of the Spirit. Because of his Christocentric theology, "Paul relativizes all claims to greater or less spiritual attainment because of ecstatic gifts by saying that every Christian is indeed a spiritual person."[83] Even the pneumatics need to submit to the lordship of Christ; this is the unifying principle created by the Spirit for the Christian community. The Spirit unifies the church through the common confession in one Lord. This letter calls the fragmented congregation back to true comm*unity* under the leadership of Christ, empowered by the Spirit. This focus on a common confession does not imply a suppression of spiritual gifts but the regulation of them for the betterment of the community in the Spirit/spirit of love.[84]

Charismata from the Same Spirit (12:4-11)

When Paul begins to speak about the variety of "gifts" (12:4), he uses the term *charisma*, revealing that the gifts are due to the grace, or *charis*, of God (cf. 1:4). Those who have gifts have them because of God's grace, not because of a special human trait or ability. The Corinthians should concentrate on the Source of their life together, rather than on supernatural spiritual manifestations. This charismatic community has a variety of gifts, services, and activities, but it is the "same Spirit," "same Lord," and "the same God who activates all of them in everyone" (12:4-6). The "same" source of the gifts is emphasized in order to focus on the unity of the community. Despite a diversity of gifts, the Spirit maintains unity without establishing a hierarchy of gifts because it is the "same" and "one" Spirit who gives, activates, and "allots to each one individually just as the Spirit chooses" (12:8-11). Ralph Martin notes that "one Spirit" emphasizes unity and "since the Spirit is one, unity is of the essence of the church's life."[85]

The gifts may be varied, but all of the gifts are from the same Spirit, who gives and activates them according to God's purposes; hence, unity is in order. Indeed, the charismata are God's gifts, not personal property; therefore, all of the gifts are significant and important for the church. "Paul continually stresses unity in diversity in order to overcome divisiveness owing to different valuations being assigned to different gifts, with tongues as the implied higher-status gift."[86] "Each" is given a gift (12:7); thus, no one is left out of the Spirit's plan, making everyone "spiritual." Moreover, these diverse gifts are given to the church without discrimination, creating a heterogeneous community. Everyone does not have the same gift and individuation is not "shackled"[87] due to the communal ideal, but rather the Spirit does work for the good of the community (12:7).

Each person's gift is for building community. "To each is given the manifestation of the Spirit for the common good" (12:7). Not only is the source of the gifts (i.e., Holy Spirit) common, but the ultimate aim is the building community. The gifts are given to each person for the common good of the "community. The test of the *charism* is its benefit to the community.[88] The unifying Source of the gift has a unifying purpose despite the diversity of gifts. The purpose of the *charismata* is functional—"to promote the God-given unity of the church, made up of many parts."[89]

Unity and Diversity in the Body (12:12-30)

This theme of unity within diversity continues with the use of the body metaphor as an image of how the Spirit works in community. Paul stresses that the Spirit is the "one" who creates the unified community, an "organic unity," namely the body.[90] "For in the one Spirit, we were all baptized into one body—Jews or Greeks, slaves or free—and we were all made to drink of one Spirit" (12:13). The "one Spirit" incorporates people into the "one body." George Montague calls this a "spirit-body" ecclesiology in which the Spirit cannot be possessed apart from the body.[91] All drink of the same Spirit, revealing to the pneumatics that their gifts are no greater than others' gifts, because it is the same Spirit, who is not divided, that gives them their gifts; they have a common, shared experience of the Spirit out of which the one-ness grows. The emphasis on "one" is the language of unity, which is the intended focus for this congregation. "For just as the body is one and has many members, and all the members of the body, though many, are one body, so it is with Christ" (12:12). Within this vision, division and conflict do not exemplify the body of Christ.

To be a "body" means to be unified. Scholars have shown that the body metaphor stands for political unity in the *topos* of ancient political litera-ture.[92] This image is "used to combat factionalism" while promoting belong-ing, harmony, interdependence, and unity in diversity, based usually on a hierarchical political structure.[93] The body analogy is conservative rhetoric that urges order. Paul stands "squarely in the Greco-Roman rhetorical tradi-tion," as his teaching reveals, because it contains familiar elements of the *homonoia* (concord) speeches.[94] This letter urges unity and argues that it is the charismatic Spirit who creates this unity of the body of Christ.

At the same time, the body includes diverse members who do not destroy the oneness of the body (12:20). The "church as charismatic community means unity in and through diversity."[95] Paul says, "Indeed, the body does not consist of one member but of many" (12:14; cf. 12:12). Each member is important and part of the body; thus one should not say, "I do not belong to the body" (12:15-16). Also, the body needs every different part thus one part should not tell another, "I have no need of you" (12:21, 17). All members form a "vital part" of the community because "no member lacks a manifesta-tion of grace,"[96] suggesting that the Corinthians should not despise any member or gift because all are graced by the same Spirit. Even "the mem-bers of the body that seem to be weaker are indispensable" (12:22). Mem-bers are not ranked based on gifts but because each gift is important for the healthy function of the body. As humans, "We literally feed on each other; where this nourishment is not available, the human spirit and the human body—both—sicken and die."[97] The body of Christ will die too; thus the body is organized in such a way that each gift or part plays a vital role in the sustaining of the community, the body.

"God arranged the members in the body, each one of them, as he chose"

(12:18, 24); therefore, this is not a call for anarchy but unity based on mutual care and empathy for one another. God's arrangement is "that there may be no dissension within the body, but the members may have the same care for one another. If one member suffers, all suffer together with it; if one member is honored, all rejoice together with it" (12:25-26). The Spirit of God binds the lives of each member together, forming the one body. No member of the community can live isolated from the larger community. Isolation would mean the death of a person, because, as Thurman notes, "men, all men belong to each other, and he who shuts himself away diminishes himself, and he who shuts another away from him destroys himself."[98] As one body, "one does not belong to oneself" due to the "inescapable interdependence" of the gifted members.[99] The interdependence of humanity is summed up so effectively by Martin Luther King, Jr. in his sermon "A Christmas Sermon on Peace." King declares:

> Whatever affects one directly, affects all indirectly. We are made to live together because of the interrelated structure of reality. Did you ever stop to think that you can't leave for your job in the morning without being dependent on most of the world? You get up in the morning and go to the bathroom and reach over for the sponge, and that's handed to you by a Pacific Islander. You reach for a bar of soap, and that's given to you at the hands of the Frenchman. And then you go into the kitchen to drink your coffee for the morning, and that's poured into your cup by a Chinese. Or maybe you want tea: that's cocoa for breakfast, and that's poured into your cup by a West African. And then you reach over for your toast, and that's given to you at the hands of an English-speaking farmer, not to mention the baker. And before you finish eating breakfast in the morning, you've depended on more than half of the world. This is the way our universe is structured, this is its interrelated quality.[100]

This "interrelated quality" pertains to Christian congregations also, and it is through the Spirit that the body is maintained as each member aims to build up the community through love.

Primacy of Love

This teaching about the Spirit in community worship finishes with an emphasis on a love that builds up the community. Any observant reader cannot avoid the value placed on love in this letter, especially in the famous chapter 13 (cf. 4:21, 8:1-3, 12:31b–14:1a, 16:14). Love takes primacy as a combatant against the abuse of spiritual gifts because it functions as an "antidote to factionalism" leading to concord.[101] The Corinthians are to "strive for the greater gifts," but love is called a "more excellent way" (12:31; cf. 14:1). None of the gifts are negated, including the overemphasized glossolalia, but

Paul presents a "theological critique in the name of *agape*."[102] Love is the "necessary ingredient for the expression of all spiritual gifts."[103] Those who claim to speak in an angelic dialect (that is, tongues) through the Spirit are "nothing" without love (13:2-3).[104] Hays asserts, "The purpose of chapter 13 is to portray love as the sine qua non of the Christian life and to insist that love must govern the exercise of all the gifts of the Spirit."[105] Another scholar puts it this way: "The charisms are slaves, love is the master" in this context.[106] Love guides the gifts and does not debunk them as the criterion for all Christian action.[107] The Corinthians' overall behavior contradicts love, the true sign of one's spirituality; thus, they are not as spiritual as they assume.[108] "The Corinthian problem was not with their experience of the Spirit, but with their misunderstanding of what it meant to be Spirit people."[109] To be spiritual means to live a life of love no matter what, even in the face of violence. During the civil rights struggle, King declares,

> We will meet your physical force with soul force. Do to us what you will and we will still love you…throw us in jail and we will still love you. Bomb our homes and threaten our children, and, as difficult as it is, we will still love you. Send your hooded perpetrators of violence into our communities at the midnight hour and drag us out on some wayside road and leave us half-dead as you beat us, and we will still love you. Send your propaganda agents around the country, and make it appear that we are not fit, culturally and otherwise, for integration, and we'll still love you.[110]

King understood that love was primary as a human vocation and without it humanity would be ruined. Love is the force that unifies divided people, which is why King emphasized love as the guide for the nonviolent movement of resistance.

Furthermore, love is not a feeling or attitude but actions of costly service towards others; therefore it is ethical in nature (cf. 16:14).[111] The Corinthians' zeal for tongues is placed in a "broader ethical context that will ultimately disallow uninterpreted tongues in the assembly. That context is love for others over against self-interest; in chapter 14 such love will be specified in terms of 'building up' the church."[112] Fee adds that chapter 13 "is not a 'hymn to love,' as though 'love' were an abstraction, or worse, simply a beautiful sentiment. For Paul, just as in 8:2-3, this is ethical instruction, as the imperative in 14:1 makes plain. To miss the parenetic thrust of this chapter is to miss the point altogether."[113] Love follows the lead of the Spirit because it builds up community (8:1). Love "*is* behavior. To love is to act; anything short of action is not love at all…. Love is the *way* in which the gifts are to function. To desire earnestly expressions of the Spirit that will build up the community is *how* love acts in this context."[114]

The Spirit uses love as a means to unity within the Corinthian congregation. The gifts of the Spirit, "nurtured and normed by love,"[115] lead to building up the church (14:5, 12, 17, 26, 40; cf. 8:1; 10:23-24). Those who are overly enthusiastic about the gift of tongues (cf. 13.1; 14:23) without a care for their ethical behavior in the church are indicted by this teaching.[116] The excessive valuation and undisciplined practice of unintelligible tongues-speaking is counteracted by contrasting it with intelligible prophecy that aids the entire community. Paul "argues for *the absolute need for intelligibility* in the assembly" because this helps the entire community.[117] Those who speak in tongues only help themselves, because no one can understand them except God; whereas those who prophesy "speak to other people for their upbuilding and encouragement and consolation" and "build up the church"(14:1-25). Much of chapter 14 "concerns respect for the needs of *others*"; thus the emphasis on building up the community.[118]

This concern leads to worship being done "decently and in order" regardless of the gifts. Moreover, "God is a God not of disorder but of peace" (14:32), which calls the community to unity in their worship, empowered by the Spirit of order and peace. Because God is a God of peace, Paul says, "Let all things be done for building up" (14:26), because this will bring peace; this is the guiding principle of Paul's liturgical thought. The Spirit creates order and moves the church away from self-centered worship. The church is not discouraged from striving to excel in spiritual gifts but is encouraged to do so for "building up the church" (14:12), which is the way of the Spirit, who establishes the one body of Christ, accenting the belief that the Spirit's "gifts are for the service of the community, not the community for the gifts."[119] This kind of Spirit unifies a community and does not divide it; therefore, the Spirit is the unifying source that can prevent further division in the Corinthian church and in any community. This rich connection between the Spirit and ecclesial unity has several implications for preaching, especially if one desires preaching to be propelled by the Spirit.

Preaching and Unity

Context of Hurt

This study of unity as the work of the Spirit within the particular setting of the Corinthian church reveals the reality of the context for much of our preaching: hurting people. To use the words of Thurman, the church is "divided into dozens of splinters."[120] Though every congregation is different and has its own dynamics, one can be sure that there is probably some kind of division or conflict within the community because people are imperfect.

The presence of sin is implied through the weekly liturgical confession of sin in many churches. Humans are born into sin and thus are broken people. Preaching occurs within this context of hurting individuals within a community. The conditions may not be the exact situation of Corinth, where there was great diversity, social stratification, mistrust of leadership, and suspicion of the message, but there will be other issues that plague congregations, which will then be in dire need of unifying preaching. Christians are broken people, which frequently causes the entire community to divide; thus, in the Spirit, one of preaching's goals is to unify a church.

Attentiveness to a church's context is vital for a preacher because preaching in the Spirit involves the whole Church. God's revelation through preaching is not solely for one person but for an entire community. The Church needs a Word from the Lord, especially when its members are hurting. One should keep in mind Tom Long's insight that the preacher goes "from the pew to the pulpit," coming "from *within* the community of faith and not *to* it from the outside."[121] This implies that the preacher hurts as well and has need for the presence of a unifying Spirit. Preachers should assume that there is need in their congregations and address this need.[122] Without dealing with the actual hurt of the people, how will they ever know that there is a balm in Gilead? This balm is no other than Jesus Christ, who is the core message of any preacher who yearns to preach in the Spirit of unity.

Content of Christ

As a manifestation of the Spirit, unity is due to the central focus on Jesus Christ. Any preacher who wants to unify a people should search for this unity in Christ. Christ is our peace who has "broken down the dividing wall, that is, the hostility between us" (Ephesians 2:14). First Corinthians demonstrates that through Christ the different members find a unified body because the body of Christ cannot be divided and as such "does not consist of one member but of many" (1 Cor. 12:14). In Christ is found oneness. The gospel of unity can only be found in Christ and a Christocentric message is a clear sign that one is on "the way" in preaching. Preaching in the Spirit entails proclaiming "Jesus is Lord" (1 Cor. 12:3). Christians "proclaim the Lord's death until he comes" (1 Cor. 11:26) and not some other event of death, because right relations within a congregation happen through Christ and the proclamation of his life, death, and resurrection.

To view unity as a sign of the Spirit implies that individuals are unified around the person and work of Christ. In particular, preaching that aims to unify focuses on the word of the cross for the cross of Christ possesses power, the power of God to save. "For the message about the cross . . . is the power of God" (1 Cor. 1:18). Sermons that centralize their message on people or issues other than the triune God miss the power of the gospel and the potential of unity in the Spirit. Without Christ, preaching is powerless; thus, the examination of unity as a manifestation of the Spirit points preaching in the direction of Christ, the reason for unity and the one who breaks down divisions. This means that the content of the sermon message should ultimately be "Christ crucified" (1 Cor. 1:23).

Character of Humility

This particular focus on Christ as the core content of our preaching, as opposed to ourselves, calls for an approach of humility. Preaching is effective, not because of human power or wisdom, but because of God's power and wisdom found in the cross of Christ. No amount of eloquent "plausible words of wisdom" or "lofty words" can save (1 Cor. 2:1, 4); only preaching as a "demonstration of the Spirit and of power" can (1 Cor. 2:4). In this way, salvation can be viewed as an occurrence of God's power and wisdom, not any human feat. Only God "gives the growth" (1 Cor. 3:7). No human preacher can take credit for what only God can do through preaching. Preachers have no reason to boast in themselves, but "let the one who boasts, boast in the Lord" (1 Cor. 1:31). In knowing that the power of preaching comes from God, preachers should necessarily be humble in regard to their role in the preaching moment. In addition, God chooses the "foolish" and "weak" to engage in a foolish task with a foolish message (1 Cor. 1:18, 21, 27). In fact, God chooses morons to be his pulpit witnesses, which in and of itself should be a humbling notion.[123] An approach of humility toward the ministry of preaching can only foster the unity among a particular group, whereas pride or arrogance might disturb and divide a congregation. For the sake of unity, preachers are called to come "in weakness" (1 Cor. 2:3), not strength, so that the power of Christ may dwell in them (2 Cor. 12:9).

Homiletical humility is also a necessity when one realizes that revelation or knowledge of God is only possible through the Spirit (1 Cor. 2:10-11). Any knowledge gained through sermons is ultimately due to God, not the preacher, and any understanding that preachers have about the "gifts bestowed on us by God" is only through receiving the Spirit (1 Cor. 2:12). Reception implies that God gave the Spirit; thus Spirit-filled preaching is a gift of God. Churches do not deserve it, but God gives this ministry to the church. Even to understand how the foolishness of preaching is divine wisdom and how it functions requires the presence of the Spirit. The "mystery of God" (1 Cor. 2:1) preachers proclaim leaves no room for boasting. The way and the word of the cross inverts the normal human way of operating, even in the preaching life, "for God's foolishness is wiser than human wisdom, and God's weakness is stronger than human strength" (1 Cor. 1:25). This understanding of God's work in the world should extinguish any haughtiness a preacher possesses while nurturing a genuine humility.

This humility of understanding the divine purposes of God through preaching will reveal that we are not our own (1 Cor. 6:19). Preachers are "God's servants" (1 Cor. 3:9) and as such must glorify God even in the body (1 Cor. 6:20), in everyday ethics, because how one lives individually impacts the community's unity. Aiming for unity requires a humility through which one comprehends that one is a self-in-community, a part of a larger whole, the body of Christ. With this realization, preachers recognize that personal holiness in word and deed is linked with communal harmony; thus how one lives one's sermons matter, for preaching is a communal act. The call to preach, just like gifts of the Spirit, happens to an individual for the benefit of the community.[124] The gift of preaching is given to build up the community of faith. If preaching instead tears down a community, then one must question, "Where is the Spirit?" As James Forbes says, "The anointing in the pulpit is by the same Spirit effecting in the sense of 'bringing about' the anointing in the pews. If it is not happening in the congregation, even if it appears to be happening in the pulpit, it will not be the moment of preaching we anticipate in the power of the Spirit."[125]

A humble preacher knows that the word event is not the sole possession of the preacher but is the community's word; thus he or she is also a listener, not just a speaker. Preachers, filled with the Spirit, will look out "for the common good" (1 Cor. 12:7). One way of doing this will be to view the sermon as a dialogue in the manner of Henry Mitchell. Mitchell suggests that sermonic material should be familiar to the hearers and meet their "felt need," the biblical story should be viewed as "my story," and sermons should "make it plain" through vernacular proclamation or what he calls the "mother tongue of the Spirit."[126] In this way, preachers work within the culture of a congregation and take into account a congregation's particularities so that the gospel speaks to people's needs.[127]

Role of the Community

Paying attention to the common good will also reveal that those in the community also have gifts of the same Spirit to share and contribute to the fostering of unity. All members are indispensable because of the mutual interdependence of the body of Christ. Even in the preaching moment, "listeners are active participants."[128] This is most evident and nurtured during the call and response dynamic of many African American preaching moments. During this, preachers "converse" with the congregation, because the congregation also has something to say. Allowing for this "homiletical musicality" strengthens the unity of a church in which the audible and oral responses such as "Help 'em Lord," "Well?" "That's all right!" "Amen!" and "Glory Hallelujah!" are heard.[129] This is not only a manifestation of the priesthood of all believers but also can "represent the profoundest motions of the human heart, the Spirit's stirrings in the depths of the soul."[130] Preaching becomes "participant proclamation," indicating that the sermon belongs to both the preacher and the entire congregation. This musicality is more than method; it is God working through the community of the Spirit.[131] One speaks and another listens and responds verbally or nonverbally, or both. Some may wave their hands, clap, stand, run, cry, shake their heads, rock back and forth, moan, hum, kneel, or even throw items at the preacher in affirmation. There are "facial expressions, swaying bodies, nodding heads, raised hands, foot patting, shouting, tears, and hand clapping."[132] Mitchell claims that this "Congregational response is so important that without it, there could be no genuinely Black sermon."[133]

One instance of this united performance of the sermon occurs in the novel *Praisesong for the Widow*. Paule Marshall depicts the call and response like this:

"'This little light of m-i-n-e . . .'"
It was a hoarse, ecstatic song, torn raw and bleeding from his abraded throat.
"What're you gonna do with it?"
And the answer came in a great outpouring: "'Let it shine.'"
"Shine in all its glory! But you got to do like Jesus first. You got to raise up your voice and call on the Lord. Just call Him. What must you do beloved?"
And once again the tumultuous response: "Call Him."
"Call Him in the midnight hour."
"Call Him."
"Call Him in the stillness of dawn."
"Call Him."
"Ask Him to roll away the stone of unrighteousness."
"Ask Him."
"The stone of sin."
"Ask Him."
"Just ask Him beloved."
"Ask Him."
"Call on the Lord."
"Call Him."
Back and forth it went: the call, the thrilling response. Until after a time it seemed Reverend Morrissey ceased being merely God's messenger, a mortal charged with bringing the Word, and was God Himself.[134]

This congregational call and response is important, but true communal proclamation will be impossible if the preacher is not guided in his or her vocation by love. Seeking unity requires that everything the preacher does "be done in love" (1 Cor. 16:14). Love directs the humble approach of the preacher and looks out for the interests of others in the congregation. "Love builds up" (1 Cor. 8:1) and "love has no awareness of merit or demerit; it has no scale by which its portion may be weighed or measured. It does not seek to balance giving and receiving. Love loves; this is its nature."[135] A preacher follows the "more excellent way" (1 Cor. 12:31b) for the betterment of the church and its unity. Regardless of the preacher's talents or gifts in the pulpit, if he or she does not have love for the congregation, they are nothing (cf. 1 Cor. 13). God's love, *agape*, should be the master of every sermon and life because love is "the matchless virtue of the spiritual life."[136] Without it, disunity and hurt will prevail; with it, humility and unity will, for "*agape* is love seeking to preserve and create community. It is insistence on community even when one seeks to break it. *Agape* is a willingness to go to any length to restore community."[137] If love is present in and through the preacher, one can be assured that the Spirit is too and if the Spirit is present, the community of the preacher will be unified.

Summary

The Corinthians claim to be people of the Spirit, yet they do not seem to act in a manner congruent with the ways of the Spirit. The Spirit is a source of unity for the Corinthian situation in revealing the crucified Christ to form a Christian comm*unity*. Paul uses the metaphor of temple to teach that through the indwelling of the Spirit, God creates a holy people who by the very nature of being holy should not be enduring conflicts. Most clearly, the Spirit aims to unify this people in corporate worship. The Spirit leads to a common confession in the lordship of Jesus Christ, gives gifts for the "common good," and establishes the one body of Christ, which seeks the continual building up of the community through love. The genuine way of the Spirit is the way of unity. Preaching should necessarily foster unity within a community by centering on Christ as its content and by preachers possessing a spirit of humility. Promoting unity by lamenting disunity or celebrating unity is a sign of the Spirit in sermons. The "Spirit of unity" is helpful for discerning or "reading" the Spirit in preaching. The next chapter discusses the social work of the Spirit as another aspect of the holistic manifestation of the Spirit that may be present in sermons.

Chapter Five

The Spirit of Fellowship

Total lack of relationship is total death.
—Jürgen Moltmann, *The Spirit of Life*

What are you doing for others?
—Martin Luther King, Jr., *The Three Dimensions
of a Complete Life*

The Spirit works with persons in communities in a centripetal fashion, but the Spirit also moves in a centrifugal manner. This means that the Spirit aims for preaching to influence more than just congregational settings, because the Spirit gathers and sends communities of faith. The Spirit aims to reach the world through preaching by sending the church into the world propelled by the Word. Through the Spirit, preaching influences what happens both inside and outside of the church walls. Individual (grace) and ecclesial transformation (unity) by the Spirit is notable, but this is not sufficient when considering the entire role of the Spirit in preaching. The social realm must also be transformed. One scholar argues that the only appropriate response to the primary discourse of preaching (for example, "I love you") is confession, praise, prayer, and worship;[1] but there are many other thinkers, including myself, who would also see acts of social justice as an appropriate response to preaching in the Spirit.

In conjunction with lament, celebration, grace, and unity, the holistic work of the Spirit includes the societal realm, particularly expressing itself in preaching as the encouraging of social *fellowship*. This chapter will begin with a discussion that solidifies the relationship between the Holy Spirit and fellowship, followed by some implications of fellowship for homiletics. The Spirit encourages social engagement and service in the world, and any sign of this emphasis within sermons may be discerned to be a manifestation of the Spirit.

Fellowship as the Work of the Spirit

In the midst of the harsh historical realities of people of African descent, blacks experienced the fellowship of the Spirit as empowerment to endure, hope, and work toward freedom. The Spirit was viewed as a wellspring of freedom that sustained the oppressed as blacks yearned for true fellowship, home, and equality. The spiritual "Sometimes I feel like a motherless child"[2] could be heard in the brush harbors, expressing the feeling of estrangement. Inhospitality had "jagged tears ulcerated stomachs bent-over backs. . . . This inhospitality vomits sanity leaves insanity as nourishment."[3] To stay sane, they sang more songs like "I am a poor wayfaring stranger, while journeying through this world of woe."[4] But in the midst of this woe, the work of the Spirit was present, blessing them with hospitable fellowship. However, African Americans are not alone in suffering. For instance, Jürgen Moltmann, a twentieth-century white German Protestant theologian, discovers this aspect of the Spirit when he experiences God as a prisoner of war during World War II and the Holocaust.[5] While in prison, he experiences God in the dark night of his soul, which initiates his belief that God is one who suffers with us and is yearning to be in fellowship with us.

Enslaved African Americans could sing, "Nobody knows the troubles I see, nobody knows like Jesus" or "I want Jesus to walk with me"[6] because they had a deep sense of the fellowship and outreach of Jesus toward them. Jesus provided fellowship and a "joy divine" like no other because he served them and the rest of humanity. Paul declares, "The grace of the Lord Jesus Christ, the love of God, and the communion of the Holy Spirit be with all of you" (2 Cor. 13:13). Fellowship, or *koinonia,* is usually thought of as solely relating to the internal affairs of a church community; this is a form of parochialism, but true fellowship includes the interrelatedness of all of creation, including service towards all of creation. Fellowship is the Spirit's hospitality toward us, as well as mutual human hospitality. As noted earlier, welcoming an-*other* is an *epiclesis*, which implies that the Spirit is one of welcome and reveals herself through hospitality. Hospitality, welcoming an-*other*, is a valid sign of being possessed by the Spirit in African American Christian contexts.

A Trinitarian Way

Social fellowship, hospitality, service to another, is grounded in the nature of God the Spirit, and any human gesture of hospitality comes from God. In regard to working in the world, "All three Persons of the Trinity are always involved."[7] That means that none are subordinated to another, all are active in relating to the world and to each other, and all are in fellowship. The three persons of the Trinity are relational and hospitable to one another. They have communal collaboration and complementarity in their work in the world. Within the Trinity, the Spirit is the Person who acts to bring community or fellowship as the "unifying God."[8] Each divine Person has a particular role, but the Spirit of fellowship within the triune God reveals the divine nature to be one of interrelationship, mutuality, and hospitality.[9]

This fellowship has been called in Greek *perichoresis*, meaning the mutual indwelling of the divine Persons, who are community without uniformity and persons without individualism. There is a mutual reciprocal relationship of love between the Persons who because of this love are open to including the world in this trinitarian love. The triune God, who is the sociality, mutuality, and reciprocity of love, "*is* community . . . calls community into life and . . . invites men and women into sociality with him."[10] The God who is community or fellowship is not in isolation but is hospitably open to otherness. As Moltmann says, "God is not a solitary Lord of heaven."[11] According to the sermon in verse, "The Creation," when God "stepped out on space" and looked around, God said, "I'm lonely—I'll make me a world,"[12] indicating God's desire for fellowship. The triune God is an open, loving fellowship for the world that invites the *other* to experience this fellowship through the Spirit.

Through the Spirit, the triune God is not a closed circle, but an open fellowship of love, a "sending and seeking love."[13] God seeks fellowship with humanity. God "first loved us" (1 John 4:19), making room for us, demonstrating holy hospitality in the Spirit. Through the fellowship of the Holy Spirit, all of creation can experience God and is served by God. Fellowship with God happens through the fellowship of the Holy Spirit. This fellowship is a matter of life and death for creation because a "total lack of relationship is total death."[14] The life-giving Spirit welcomes fellowship to such an extent that God initiates relationship with us through Christ, who was the embodiment of fellowship and hospitality by his agenda of service.

A Christ(ian) Pattern of Service

Jesus Christ "came not to be served but to serve" (Mark 10:45) and his service possessed power because of his fellowship with the Spirit, who empowered his ministry. Jesus is able to act in the manner he does, and in fact is the Christ, because he was "filled with the power of the Spirit" (Luke 4:14). He says, "The Spirit of the Lord is upon me, / because he has anointed me / to bring good news to the poor. / He has sent me to proclaim release to the captives and recovery of sight to the blind, / to let the oppressed go free, to proclaim the year of the Lord's favor" (Luke 4:18-19). In what some call his first sermon, Jesus claims the anointing of the Spirit and it is this anointing that allows him to minister in the way he names. In *Jesus and the Disinherited*, Howard Thurman asserts, "Wherever his spirit appears, the oppressed gather fresh courage; for he announced the good news that fear, hypocrisy, and hatred, the three hounds of hell that track the trail of the disinherited, need have no dominion over them."[15] The disinherited are served and liberated because of the Spirit of Christ.

Jesus the Christ performs in a divine way because the whole history of Christ is the history of the fellowship of the Spirit.[16] If the Spirit was not active in him, then Jesus would have been impotent, because the power of Jesus Christ flows in and from the divine Spirit. Without the fellowship of the Spirit, Jesus cannot be the Messiah, the anointed one. Moltmann summarizes this understanding with these words:

> The efficacy of the divine Spirit is the first facet of the mystery of Jesus. . . . Jesus' history as the Christ does not begin with Jesus himself. It begins with the *ruach*/the Holy Spirit. It is the coming of the Spirit, the creative breath of God: in this Jesus comes forward as "the anointed one," proclaims the gospel of the kingdom of power, and convinces many with the signs of the new creation. It is the power of the creative Spirit: through this he brings health and liberty for enslaved men and women into this sick world.[17]

The fellowship of the Spirit, as evidenced in the life of Christ, leads to powerful service in the world. The service of Christ as the fellowship of the Spirit is rooted in the concept of love, *agape*, because "the religion of Jesus makes the love-ethic central."[18] Foremost is his sacrifice of love on the cross. He dies that we might live. God in Jesus Christ selflessly empties himself (*kenosis*) of divinity for the salvation of humanity (Phil. 2:6-11). The Wholly Other becomes an *other*, like us, through the incarnation. Jesus makes a point about the sacrificial nature of his hospitality, "No one has greater love than this, to lay down one's life for one's friends" (John 15:13). Jesus also teaches to love one's enemies (Matthew 5:44) and in fact, loves his betrayer, Judas, by washing his feet despite knowing that Judas was going to betray him (John 13). This is loving the neighbor as yourself, where *everyone* is the neighbor. In the Spirit, Jesus lived this kind of fellowship, even unto death. Judas could not reciprocate the love Jesus gave, but divine hospitality welcomes those who cannot even repay the hospitality given. This loving fellowship is unconditional and seeks no favors in return. It is as Thurman preaches, "I can love only when I meet you where you are, as you are, and treat you there as if you were where you ought to be," without any expectations of having love returned.[19] "Like Jesus, we ought to worry less about who needs compassion and more about how to get it to them."[20]

This Christ(ian) pattern of service demonstrating the social fellowship of the Spirit is artfully captured in Martin Luther King, Jr.'s sermon "The Drum Major Instinct." He declares:

> I know a man, and I just want to talk about him a minute, and maybe you will discover who I'm talking about as I go down the way, because he was a great one. And he just went about serving. He was born in an obscure village, the child of a poor peasant woman. And then he grew up in still another obscure village, where he worked as a carpenter until he was thirty years old. Then for three years, he just got on his feet, and he was an itinerant preacher. And then he went about doing some things. He didn't have much. He never wrote a book. He never held an office. He never had a family. He never owned a house. He never went to college. He never visited a big city. He never went two hundred miles from where he was born. He did none of the usual things that the world would associate with greatness. He had no credentials but himself. . . . Nineteen centuries have come and gone, and today, he stands as the most influential figure that ever entered human history. All of the armies that ever marched, all the navies that ever sailed, all the parliaments that ever sat, and all the kings that ever reigned put together have not affected the life of man on this earth as much as that one solitary life. . . . He didn't have anything. He just went around serving, and doing good.[21]

Even though "he didn't have anything" much in terms of material means, he had a lot of love to share with the world. It is this love of Christ that the body of Christ is also called to share in unconditional, disinterested ways.[22]

Church on a Mission

As the body of Christ on earth, the church does not exist for itself but for others. Thurman's concept of "the Spirit of God Without-Within" indicates that the Spirit mingles one's personal needs with the needs of others.[23] The fellowship of the Spirit within a congregation is connected with fellowship outside of the local church because the Spirit cannot be divided. James Evans notes that "while the church is centered in the communal memory and ritual presence of Jesus of Nazareth, it is moved by the Pentecostal imperative to seek its epicenter in the world. . . . It is always seeking to establish peace and justice where they do not yet exist."[24] The Pentecostal Spirit empowers the church to be witnesses (Acts 1:8) and grants the church the necessary gifts to fulfill the divine mission in the world, leading some scholars to speak of a "charismatic ecclesiology."[25]

Through the Spirit, the Church is socially active and preachers can declare, "We are on the move now. . . . We must keep going."[26] The church moves in the presence and power of the Spirit, for without the Spirit of fellowship, it would implode. The *charismata*, as signs of the Spirit, are full of new life in the midst of death in the world. These powers of new life encompass the entire scope of one's existence because "the Spirit makes the whole biological, cultural, and religious life history of a person charismatically alive."[27] Accordingly, these gifts are socially oriented and not only individually or ecclesially focused. They serve not the interests of an existing church or human cravings but the kingdom of God on earth. Essential to a gifted, welcoming church is the idea of *diakonia* and a particular way of life in the social world.[28] The Spirit of fellowship unifies a church for a common purpose of life-giving service to others. There may be diverse gifts, but they support the same common goal of serving the kingdom of God in the world, with the ultimate goal of a future new creation.

As the church reaches out into the world through the Spirit of fellowship, it confirms the impulse of Christianity, which "is the human *will to share* with others what one has found meaningful to oneself elevated to the height of a moral imperative."[29] The Spirit guides the church beyond fear to recognize the worth and dignity of every human being. King reveals his "will to share" in the face of opposition to his ideas on war. He says this about the ministry of Jesus Christ:

> To me the relationship of this ministry to the making of peace is so obvious that I sometimes marvel at those who ask me why I am speaking against the war. Could it be that they do not know that the good news was meant for all men— for Communist and capitalist, for their children and ours, for black and for white, for revolutionary and conservative? Have they forgotten that my ministry is in obedience to the one who loved his enemies so fully that he died for them? What then can I say to the "Vietcong" or Castro or to Mao as a faithful minister of this one? Can I threaten them with death or must I not share with them my life?[30]

Christians are called to reach out to others with life because of the dignity of every human being—enemy, stranger, or friend. In the Spirit, a welcoming and missional Church can say "Git on board . . . dere's room for many a mo'" because there is "no second class aboard dis train, no difference in de fare."[31] All have need; thus all need to be served. "Facilitating the well-being of others" unconditionally should be the aim of the Church's mission.[32] Through the power of the Spirit, any Church can serve. As King preached:

> You don't have to have a college degree to serve. You don't have to make your subject and verb agree to serve. You don't have to know about Plato and Aristotle to serve. You don't have to know Einstein's theory of relativity to serve. You don't have to know the second theory of thermodynamics in physics to serve. You only need a heart full of grace. A soul generated by love. And you can be that servant.[33]

A church in the fellowship of the Spirit will embody a "messianic way of life," which gives a "stamp to life in the Spirit."[34] This messianic way is the way of Christ in his life of service to the world in the power of the Spirit before God. The external activities of a church (that is, social mission) authenticate its internal communal spirituality. "If I say I love God and don't love you—I lie. If I say I love you and don't love God—I lie."[35] The church lives a lie and will die if either of the variables, God or humanity, are missing in their love life. The two directions of the church as a local congregation led by the Spirit are inward and outward, the gathering of the congregation and its sending by way of its vocations in society. The sending into every day is just as important as the festal worship of the church.[36] In its sending out, the church is motivated in mission by the Christian hope created through the eschatological orientation toward the future. This eschatological horizon informs the church to change the present world in the direction of the future kingdom, making believers a "constant disturbance in human society."[37]

Christians will disturb society and fight for justice because they realize that the "universe is on the side of justice."[38] In fact, God is a God of justice (Amos 5:21-24; cf. Isa.58:1-9) and through the Spirit, the Church works for justice. African American Christians can "have church" outside of the traditional church setting because the Spirit creates an atmosphere for hospitality through service opportunities. The status quo of society is not the pulse of the church; thus, the mission of the church calls for more than evangelization, because a "missionary church cannot be apolitical."[39] Particularly in the black church, *diakonia* relates to "participation in God's liberating work on behalf of the oppressed."[40] Social outreach emphasizes care for the widows and orphans (James 1:27), the poor (Luke 4:18), and the "least of these" (Matthew 25:40, 45). "We are called to speak for the weak, for the voiceless, for victims of our nation and for those it calls enemy, for no document from human hands can make these humans any less our brothers."[41] This stress on social fellowship, service to others, especially the needy in society, does not negate a vibrant personal or ecclesial spirituality, but it does suggest that in the Spirit one cannot separate spiritual and social hospitality, the individual, communal, and social realms. Historically, African American Christians have aimed for matching creeds and deeds. Riggins Earl captures this core trait of many black churches when he writes of spiritual and social hospitality and says, "the former, without the latter, makes church worship a ritualistic exercise in spiritual escapism; the latter without the former, makes it a ritualistic exercise in comraderie. Whenever either is sacrificed for the other, the church becomes an impotent witness for Christ."[42]

When one is born again to a living hope, this rebirth does not isolate one but sets one in the movement of the Spirit that is poured out on all flesh. The creative tensions of this life are threefold: prayer and earthiness, contemplation and political struggle, and transcendental religion and religion of solidarity.[43] All three categories attempt to maintain a healthy dialogue between meditation and action because Christian spirituality necessarily includes political action in the world and not personal prayer only. For instance, transcendence is not transcendence of the risen Christ if it is not linked to solidarity with those he came to free and save. Solidarity is not solidarity with the crucified Jesus if it does not lead to transcendence of the future for which he was raised. Social fellowship embraces the real presence of Christ and the reality of human pain, and what is most crucial as a welcoming church on a mission is the "sign of the lived life."[44] Indeed, a congregation's missional work will speak louder than any word from the pulpit. In the fellowship of the Spirit, a church cannot resist to engage with the Spirit's larger ministry in the world. If it does, it is not a part of the social fellowship of the Spirit. The Spirit broadens the mission of the church because the Spirit leads the church and not vice versa. Moltmann makes this absolutely clear when he writes:

> It is not the church that administers the Spirit as the Spirit of preaching, the Spirit of the sacraments, the Spirit of the ministry or the Spirit of tradition. The Spirit "administers" the church with the events of word and faith, sacrament and grace, offices and traditions. . . . It then has no need to look sideways in suspicion or jealousy at the saving efficacies of the Spirit outside the church; instead it can recognize them thankfully as signs that the Spirit is greater than the church and that God's purpose of salvation reaches beyond the church.[45]

Because the Spirit of fellowship is a "spirit abroad in life,"[46] the entire creation is included in the social fellowship of the Spirit. Ecological crises cry out for the ministries of the church, calling the church to be a "church of the cosmos" if it is truly to be the salt of the earth it is called to be.[47] The fellowship of the Spirit, service to others, includes loving God's creation.

Loving Creation, Loving Life

Preachers, and all Christians, are "kinsman of all living things."[48] The Spirit brings reverence for the life of every living thing into adoration of God, which leads to expanding our understanding of worship and service to God to include service to God's creation. The Spirit is the "source of life,"[49] whether transient life (ends in death) or the eternal life of the new creation (continuity of creation and salvation). The Spirit of God is the Spirit of the resurrection of the dead, the quickening power of the new creation of all things, and the empowering rebirth of everything that lives; thus an affirmation and love of life are key traits of a life in the Spirit of fellowship. "The Spirit is life" (Rom. 8:10); thus anyone or anything in the Spirit will also love life, the life of God in the world, and will work toward this life through the "Spirit of Life." In his important pneumatological work with the same title, *The Spirit of Life*, Moltmann writes, "The operations of God's life-giving and life-affirming Spirit are universal and can be recognized in everything which ministers to life and resists its destruction. This efficacy of the Spirit does not replace Christ's efficacy, but makes it universally relevant."[50]

In the power of the Spirit, the church's ministry is one of life, not death. The only relationship to deathly powers is resisting them, because the Spirit in whom our "life wakes up"[51] is the life-giver for all of creation. The Spirit is a Mother who "purposes life."[52] The church or person in the wind of the Spirit will stress the love of life, saying "yes" to life and loving everything living. The Spirit is the *fons vitae*, the well of life, because

> Life in God's Spirit is *life against death*. It is not life against the body. It is life that brings the body's liberation and transfiguration. To say "yes" to life means saying "no" to war and its devastations. To say "yes" to life means saying "no" to poverty and its humiliations. There is no genuine affirmation of life in this world without the struggle against life's negations. [53]

Anything that dehumanizes or destroys is not of the Spirit and must be resisted. King resists dehumanizing societal structures for the love of creation and life when he declares,

> True compassion is more than flinging a coin to a beggar; it is not haphazard and superficial. It comes to see that an edifice which produces beggars needs restructuring. . . . A nation that continues year after year to spend more money on military defense than on programs of social uplift is approaching spiritual death.[54]

King yearned that all would experience spiritual life because he knew that the Spirit is life. The Spirit resists death and destruction because "everything in God's history with men and women and earthly creation draws towards the fellowship of the Holy Spirit."[55] God the Spirit aims for a fellowship of life that is rooted in the Trinity, who draws everything into a *perichoresis*, revealing that life in the Spirit is not solitary confinement but community involvement in the world, loving creation for the pure love of life and God. In the Spirit, "there is no such thing as solitary life.... All living things—each in its own specific way—live in one another and with one another, from one another and for one another."[56] Any entity that resists fellowship resists its own life potential. Without the Spirit of fellowship, the ministry of the Church will be ailing and suffer from disequilibrium. But we can only know this if the Spirit of fellowship, the Spirit of life, teaches us. If Christians possess this love of life for the love of God, they will also engage in battles to fight for the life of all of creation, because divine social fellowship sometimes calls for a nonviolent, loving struggle against death.

Preaching and Fellowship

Engaging Society Hospitably

The Spirit of fellowship challenges preaching to transform more than just the local congregation. Through preaching, the Spirit shapes and spurs social ethics in the world. The Spirit's work is holistic through preaching and cannot be limited to individual grace or ecclesial unity because God is concerned with the whole of life. Preaching empowered by the Spirit aims to minister to the world, not just the church. "The world [is] the arena where God's Spirit is even now working making the impossible, creating faith where there is nothing else to believe in, creating love where there is nothing lovable, creating hope where there is nothing to hope for."[57] Preaching in the Spirit reaches far beyond the confines of the local church in matters of social ethics because sermons "travel on in the lives of those who listen."[58] Listeners live in the world and ideally act on the Word they hear, but even their response to the proclaimed Word is only possible by the Spirit.[59] "No sermon or homily is over when it is delivered. It is completed in the life of the people throughout the week as they carry God's good news to the world."[60] The work of the Spirit through preaching continues in the public realm.

Anointed preaching is not primarily for personal edification but "it is to enable us to be an embodiment of divine intent," which includes acts of mercy and justice in the world.[61] The Spirit causes preaching to transform individuals and communities and to confront injustices.[62] Arthur Van Seters concurs when he states, "The work of the Spirit in preacher, congregation, and the Word is the dynamic force empowering the sermon for transformation."[63] The Spirit empowers the church through preaching to live out its ethical obligations in a hospitable manner. Engaging society hospitably is vital because "hospitality is the practice by which the church stands or falls."[64] Preaching that ignores hospitality to others will fail to be what it ought to be in the Spirit. However, preaching that taps into the holy hospitality of God the Spirit will "enable and sustain persons to *be* good news in the larger world," a world that sorely needs the welcome of God.[65]

Living the Sermon

If a preacher teaches love of creation and life, then he or she is expected to also demonstrate that love with how he or she lives. There is a desire on the part of observers to see the equation of the spoken and enacted word. In the light of this notion of fellowship, preachers cannot emphasize speaking the Word over living the Word, because the Spirit manifests through his or her entire life. In the Spirit, words *and* deeds matter; therefore, how well preachers conduct their lives is just as important as how well they proclaim the Word.

The Spirit works within preachers to shape the word preached into a word lived in the Spirit. One cannot urge social engagement and service in the world and not demonstrate that kind of fellowship with their own life of Christian discipleship. This would be disingenuous and hypocritical, since Jesus "preached not only with words, but his life was the 'amen' to the proclamation of his lips."[66] The preacher's life should be the "amen" to what has been preached in the pulpit. The Spirit of fellowship would have it no other way, for the Spirit longs for a life of homiletical integrity that does not focus so much on how well one whoops but on how well one helps others. African American preaching traditions and other communities will not be sustained or strengthened by fancy rhetoric without concrete Christ-like living in the world, "a demonstration of the Spirit and of power" (1 Cor. 2:4) in society. The preacher's lip service should match his or her life service because as Martin Luther King, Jr. prophetically pronounces, "It's possible to affirm the existence of God with your lips and deny his existence with your life."[67] The importance of the preacher's life in the Spirit of fellowship should not be downplayed, because one's life can serve as a "death threat" to all the powers of death at work in the world.[68]

Resisting Deathly Powers

Preaching that wishes to be in the Spirit must be ready to engage the world by resisting death, which in fact is a way of serving others. Preaching as resistance is not only an announcement but also an action by the preacher that is necessary to overcome evil.[69] The Spirit resists oppressive powers in the world and this is a sign of God's love for the world, and preaching that loves the world must also engage in resistance. By flowing with the Spirit in this work, one reveals a concrete love of neighbor, revealing how the Spirit cannot be detached from the ethically demanding commands of Christ in the Spirit, including this concrete love that resists powers of death. As William Willimon notes, "To be a preacher is to be willing to assert that the powers are not in power."[70]

Preachers declare that another Power is actually in power. Through the power of the Spirit of fellowship, God's new social order can begin to emerge with the help of preaching. God's social order is one of charity instead of profit, peace instead of war, and mercy instead of dominant power. The world's social order of power is a power of death and self-destructiveness, whereas God's power creates life through the power of the resurrection. Preaching as resistance will "unmask the pretensions of the powers that be."[71] Anointed preachers expose death; reveal its structure of oppression; speak truth plainly, which leads to transformation of life for the oppressor and oppressed; overthrow the power of death in all its forms; and cast out demons of institutions whether ecclesial, political, or social.[72] The ethical context of preaching is the principalities and powers. Preaching is another power fueled by God, because it is the "sword of the Spirit, which is the Word of God."[73] The Word (that is, preaching) is the tool that the Spirit uses to resist the deathly powers. The Word, the sword of the Spirit, is the only weapon wielded by Jesus in his nonviolent action against the powers of death. Through the Spirit, preaching becomes active resistance, as opposed to a passive, irrelevant act that puts people to sleep.

Summary

Fellowship is a manifestation of the Spirit that should also be evident in preaching. The fellowship of the Holy Spirit is seen in the collaborative relationship between the Persons of the Trinity, their *perichoresis*; but this fellowship reaches out to all of creation because of God's hospitable initiative of love toward us. Most poignantly, one sees the fellowship of the Spirit in the life history of Christ, whose pattern was one of loving service to all. This inspires a charismatic church, the body of Christ, to welcome all through its mission, especially the needy and oppressed of society, and to love creation, and thus love life. Preachers must engage society hospitably, not only through their sermons, but through their lives, while resisting any power that propagates death. The Spirit is life and fellowship that require one to bestow life wherever one goes. Preaching will aim to be a lifeline to the world, making all things new, turning injustice into justice and death into life. The "Spirit of fellowship" will help one read sermons pneumatologically, and the following chapter will integrate the five manifestations of the Spirit—lament, celebration, grace, unity, and fellowship—and use them as a lens to discern the presence of the Spirit in sermons.

Chapter Six

The Rhetoric of the Spirit through Lament and Celebration

God made manifest his power among the people.
Some wept, while others shouted for joy.
—Jarena Lee, *The Life and Religious Experience of Jarena Lee*

If the Spirit is vital to and present in the *entire* process of preaching, as many scholars declare, then the Spirit must also be evident in the actual sermon—its language, content, and structure.[1] Studies have inadequately described on what the manifestations of the Spirit looks like in the sermon, perhaps, because of homileticians, like David Buttrick, who say, "We cannot identify the Spirit with particular rhetoric or particular moments in preaching."[2] However, preaching is an expression of the gracious gift of the Spirit, and as such, it must show and use "rhetoric of the Spirit."[3]

For our purposes, the rhetoric of the Spirit consists of the five manifestations of the Spirit already presented in the previous chapters—lament, celebration, grace, unity, and fellowship. These manifestations provide the theological-hermeneutical lens for discerning and describing the presence of the Spirit in preaching, implying that we can claim more about the Spirit in preaching than what has been said. It is true that "the wind blows where it chooses...you do not know where it comes from or where it goes"; however, "you hear the sound of it" (John 3:8). The Spirit of God is mystery but not *all* mystery. There is a sound associated with the divine wind. This rhetoric of the Spirit gives us a sense of the sound of the Spirit in preaching and may help us become more concrete with our Spirit talk in homiletics. By overcoming the generalizations about the Spirit's role in preaching and by emphasizing specific manifestations of the Spirit—signs of lament, celebration, grace, unity, and fellowship in sermon language, content, and structure—teachers of preaching may be able to point students in more concrete directions that are congruent with the work of the Spirit in the church and the world.

This chapter will first integrate the five manifestations of the Spirit for a homiletical discussion that fosters the theory and practice of preaching. Then these five manifestations of the Spirit will be treated as a lens for interpreting two African American sermons pneumatologically, revealing that one can discern the presence of the Spirit in preaching.

Homiletical Implications of the Manifestations of the Spirit

Lament

The Spirit can be discerned in sermons because the Spirit manifests outwardly. In the case of preaching, sermon language, content, and structure manifest the Spirit in various ways that are culturally dependent. Sermonic lament follows the pattern of psalmic lament, the songs of the Spirit, in that its topics are multilayered, covering various human predicaments and it basically asserts that life is not right and God must and will change things. In psalmic lament, "Israel insists that Yahweh has a precise responsibility to right wrong, to restore order, and to establish justice."[4] Preaching that laments will operate in the same manner in that the onus for justice is placed on God. Sermonic lament of the Spirit also takes its cues from the insights of biblical lament in that it too not only directly and concretely names life's harsh realities (plea) but also anticipates God's intervention in faith and hope (praise) because of the belief in the reign of God. Direct speech in preaching lament is necessary as a means to exposing life's harsh realities, as the psalms illustrate. This idea parallels Charles Campbell's advocacy for direct speech in exposing the deathly powers present in the world.[5] Explicit and direct speech about hope in God is vital, for as Emilie Townes notes, lament appeals are "always to God for deliverance."[6] Homiletical lament is no different; it is a sermon form that begins with the truthful declaration of human pain but moves toward hope because of a strong belief in the presence and power of God. At times, the anticipation of hope is evident through the interjection of statements of good news while painting the picture of bad news, as is the case with the sermons that will be studied later in this chapter. Lament is faith speech, implying that all preaching assumes a measure of faith in God; thus, one should not preach against God in a sermon. One may be angry with God, but even this implies a relationship with God that does not seek the demise of God. If one preaches against God, then one can necessarily presume that what occurs is not in fact Christian preaching nor the lament of the Spirit that one finds in the suffering Christ's cry of dereliction, "My God, my God, why have you forsaken me?" (Mark 15:34; cf. Ps. 22).

Lament is important for all homiletical cultures because of the travail of the world in which we live. War, genocide, famine, and child-trafficking are just a few of the serious problems pervading the global society. African American communities in particular are burdened with issues such as the high rate of imprisonment for black males, a high percentage of people with AIDS, and the ongoing struggle against racism. The language of lament is vital for African American preaching communities because it links to the particular reality of pain and suffering experienced by African Americans in the past and present. A denial of lament is a denial of African American history, the Holy Spirit, and the history of Christ; the embrace of lament is an embrace of the Spirit of Christ and historical memory. Also, lament allows a preacher to "descend into hell," giving depth to sermons.

In many ways, the concept of "trouble," articulated poignantly in the work of Paul Scott Wilson, is a homiletical precursor to homiletical lament. Trouble is sin or brokenness experienced by humanity, which places a burden on people. According to Wilson, this trouble serves as part of the deep grammar of sermons. Trouble is the existential context for the response of lament.[7] However, trouble does not necessarily link to the work of the Spirit explicitly nor does it point to human expressions of the Spirit (for example, lament) in preaching. Lament implies human activity, not passivity, before God in the Spirit during the preaching event. Moreover, it anticipates the eventual overcoming of vast trouble. Lament also echoes Samuel Proctor's "antithesis" in his sermon method. Antithesis is the "woe is me" sermon section that is not the final answer of hope, though it anticipates it. Proctor describes antithesis as the following:

> It could be an error that must be corrected, a condition that must be altered, a mood that must be dispelled, a sin that cries out for confession and forgiveness, some ignorance that needs to be illumined, a direction that has to be reversed, an idolatry of worshiping things that are corruptible that should cease in favor of praising an incorruptible God, some pain and hurt that await the balm of Gilead, or some lethargy that needs to be replaced.[8]

Antithesis raises the need, as does lament, but lament also actively longs for God's answer to the particular struggles. Lament has a Godward direction and is important for preaching because it keeps God in focus, but not to the neglect of humanity. Lament coincides with the "hermeneutic of God" discussed by Cleo LaRue, who says that the

> hermeneutic of God, the mighty sovereign who acts mightily on behalf of the powerless and oppressed, is the longstanding template blacks place on the

scriptures as they begin the interpretive process. . . . Blacks historically and to this present day believe God is proactively at work on their behalf. This is what they bring to scripture, see in scripture, and preach from scripture.[9]

Furthermore, lament, in its naming of reality, nurtures truthfulness and anger, two key virtues of any preacher, according to some homileticians.[10]

Lament is embedded in black cultures and has been a part of the experience of oppressed people across the world. In particular, studies on the spirituals stress the struggle and lament of African Americans.[11] However, lament in sermons has not been discussed in depth. Barbara Holmes, in her work, *Joy Unspeakable*, shares a concern that people in general, but African Americans in particular, "have forgotten how to lament," though she realizes that some churches engage in this practice, even if they do not recognize it. Even the moans on the slave ships of the Middle Passage were generative and "the precursor to joy yet unknown." Holmes poetically writes "on the deck after evening rations, lament danced and swayed under the watchful eyes of the crew."[12] African Americans have not forgotten how to lament in most settings but just have not named the phenomenon in preaching as lament or realized its vital and necessary partnership with homiletical celebration.

Albert Raboteau notes that African American spirituality intones a "sad joyfulness,"[13] and it is this mixed texture that represents the relationship of lament and celebration in preaching. This mixture of sorrow and joy is already emphasized in the singing of African Americans. William McClain writes:

> In our melancholy, our songs are not always mournful songs. Most often, they are joyous, lifting the spirit above despair. Yet, our sad songs sometimes come in the midst of our joy, in moments of jubilation and celebration. Without warning caution emerges to remind us that songs of joy must be tempered by the stark realities of the plight of our people. In the midst of our joyful singing the soul has not forgotten depression, pain, and expressions of hopelessness on the faces of our young. Laughter turns to tears and our glad songs into laments. But we refuse to give up or give in. There is a God sense that has become a part of the fabric of the race. We refuse to let God alone, and we know God has never let us alone! At the moment of our deepest despair we sing, "sometimes I feel like a motherless child a long way from home." Then, in the midst of our sadness, we sing with assurance, "I'm so glad that trouble don't last always!"[14]

This same pattern is present in African American preaching. Preaching in the Spirit is bi-focal, lamenting and celebrating. Though it has not been emphasized in homiletics, it has been recognized. James Cone says the Word "arises out of the totality of the people's existence—their pain and joy, trouble and ecstasy."[15] Homiletician James Earl Massey recognizes there is a "trouble-glory" mixture in black praise, even though he emphasizes the festive nature of black preaching. He says black preaching "majors in the celebrative aspects of faith even as it sings of the troubles nobody knows."[16] James Harris notes that "Black preaching is indeed exciting and jubilant, but it is also sad and reflective. It represents the ebb and flow of the Holy Spirit that correlates with the ups and downs of life."[17] Evans Crawford in his book, *The Hum,* says the sermon pitch and voice of the preacher "can sound life's laments and its laughter, its grief, and its glory."[18]

Other African American homileticians, such as Teresa Fry Brown, also capture this relationship between lament and celebration in the experience of black preaching with her notions of "weary throats" and "new songs." In her most recent work, *Weary Throats and New Songs: Black Women Proclaiming God's Word,* Fry Brown hints at the dialectic of lament and celebration undergirding the preaching of African American women in particular. She refers to the resistance to the call of women to pulpit ministry as the "weary throats," indicating the weariness of women due to their struggle for full access to the pulpit; the weary throat is reason for lament. The "new song" is the support given to black women preachers, even if the support is only from God; the new song is reason for celebration. She says of her own homiletical history:

> My throat was sometimes parched due to human machinations, but I was able to sing a new song when God's word coursed through my marrow. There was life on the other side of the church restrictions. There was a light in the tunnel of discrimination. There was energy in the midst of fatigue. There was an "any-how" in the gift of preaching. There was a dialectic balancing of the weary throat and the new song.[19]

Brown's work is significant not only because of her recognition of the close relationship between lament and celebration, but also because she reclaims black women's voices as potential conduits of the Spirit in the pulpit and not only in testimony on the main floor.

In one sense, lament and celebration may be viewed as a grammar of the Spirit underlying the preaching of African Americans. Harold Dean Trulear argues that the preacher "fashions that trouble into a litany in which every sentence of sorrow is punctuated with an exclamation point of God's care," sorrow balanced with joy. He notes that the "drama" of black preaching moves from crucifixion (sorrow, lament) to resurrection (joy, celebration), rehearsing the crucifixion-resurrection motif rooted in Jesus Christ.[20] Trulear's perspective on African American sermon movement coincides with

Paul Wilson's understanding that the sermon should move *"from* trouble *to* grace...*from* the exodus *to* the promised land, *from* the crucifixion *to* the resurrection and glory."[21] One does not have to agree with the idea that *all* African American sermons move from the Crucifixion to the Resurrection in order to embrace the observation that both lament (crucifixion), and of course celebration (resurrection), are present within the homiletical discourse of many African Americans.

If sermons move from lament to celebration, this homiletical movement of the Spirit echoes the lament psalms. As indicated earlier, lament psalms *generally* move from plea or cry to praise or celebration because of hope in God for present and future intervention. Some laments, such as Psalms 39 and 88, seemingly do not resolve in praise. Likewise, there may be situations when cries of lament alone are the only appropriate response in a sermon, thus a lament-celebration paradigm does not predetermine every individual sermon.[22] Despite this fact, the very turning to God in lament glorifies God, because even in lament humanity does what it was created to do—turn to God (that is, conversion in its literal sense).[23] The linking of lament to celebration and viewing it as a sermon movement, parallels law/gospel, trouble/grace, antithesis/thesis, exposing/envisioning sermon patterns propagated by others.[24] Also, uniting lament and celebration is similar to the stereoscopic apocalyptic homiletic espoused by James Kay, who suggests that from the vantage point of the cross, preachers should proclaim the gospel through a "bifocal" lens of Paul's "old creation" (reason for lament) and Paul's "new creation" (reason for celebration).[25]

Furthermore, the juxtaposition and unity of lament and celebration in preaching may be called doxology because as a unified tensive pairing these manifestations of the Spirit in preaching represent the full glorification of God during times of joy and sorrow. When expressing lament and celebration, preachers are at "full stretch" as *homo adorans* before God, capturing the breadth of worship stances before God. "Full stretch" is an idea liturgical theologian Don Saliers propagates when speaking about humanity coming before God in times of joy and sorrow, in the entire scope of human pathos: "Christian liturgy without the full range of the Psalms becomes anorexic—starving for honest emotional range."[26] Liturgical theologian Gordon Lathrop believes that the juxtaposition of lament and celebration, or what he calls beseeching and praise, along with other biblical juxtapositions, compose the heart of the liturgical *ordo*, grammar or pattern, of Christian liturgy. Thus, what is presented here about preaching is also present in liturgies.[27] This is to say that doxology implies neither the negation of lament nor celebration but the unified balanced linking of the two.

Neither lament nor celebration should be omitted from the homiletical toolbox. Otherwise, a sermon performance loses its christological grounding by neglecting either the Crucifixion (lament) or the Resurrection (celebration). As Amy Plantinga Pauw has said, "The resurrection does not erase from Christ's hands and feet the wounds of the crucifixion."[28] The challenge is to maintain a balanced relationship between these two expressions of the Spirit because the "'yes' of the gospel does not instantly make the 'no' of human doubt and struggle disappear."[29] Without lament or celebration in a sermon, the sermon loses its doxological nature, because doxology, as defined here, is the juxtaposition and unity of lament and celebration. The two exist in tension, and doxology is a third identity that is produced because of their union; it is what they are together, an act of fulsome praise, that puts life into perspective before God. Doxology entails both manifestations of the Spirit. The juxtaposition and unity of lament and celebration as doxology function as a sermonic metaphor in that "the tension or energy generated between the poles" of lament and celebration "produces a third identity (or spark)," which in this case is doxology.[30] This is a tensive relationship that does not diminish or erase any one of the variables or poles but maintains the integrity and identity of each. Doxology through the Spirit upholds the truthfulness about the grace and power of God and the truthfulness about human reality.

Moreover, lament and celebration as doxology reclaim preaching as an act of worship be(for)e God and not only an act within worship. Lament and celebration are languages of worship and can help homiletics regain its doxological thrust through an exploration of African American preaching specifically. In my estimation, preaching has been divorced from its true doxological nature in the academy and the church. Particularly, in church contexts that emphasize contemporary worship, the musical portion of a service is spoken of as "worship" to the neglect of preaching. Lament and celebration is what preachers do before God through the Spirit to glorify God in view of all creation. Elizabeth Achtemeier says, "It is for God's glorification alone that the Christian preacher labors."[31] Thinking of doxology (lament and celebration) in relation to preaching can blaze the trail for a homiletic theology that burns with the fire of worship for God. Philosophical, rhetorical, or performance-oriented discussions about preaching may then take a backseat to the doxological, thus theological, identity of preaching, leading all who engage in this act to celebrate, and even lament, before God in the Spirit. Preaching in the Spirit means that one "descends into hell" but also "ascends into heaven," which is celebration.

Celebration

African American homileticians, in particular, highlight celebration as a manifestation of the Holy Spirit in preaching and as a specific sermon form.

As a sermon form, celebration is the peak, or climax, of a sermon that ecstatically reinforces the good news about God's action in the world through Jesus Christ. It represents the height of preaching. Poetic license, heightened rhetoric, hyperbole, joyous emotion, personal testimony, with appropriate facial expression and tonal qualities, are all part of celebratory sermonic performances in the Spirit. This study has not attempted to negate what has been taught about celebration, but it does try to expand on the church's understanding of celebration by linking it to lament. The relationship of celebration to lament keeps celebration rooted in pain and sorrow and the groans of the Spirit, allowing preaching to remain honest and genuine. Paule Marshall artfully demonstrates sorrowful lament as the foundation for any expression of joyful celebration, particularly within the context of the African diaspora, when she writes about the mixture of festivity with solemnity in a cultural celebration known as the Big Drum. When the drum is beaten, she writes:

> And the single, dark, plangent note this produced, like that from the deep bowing of a cello, sounded like the distillation of a thousand sorrow songs. For an instant the power of it brought the singing and dancing to a halt—or so it appeared. The theme of separation and loss the note embodied, the unacknowledged longing it conveyed summed up feelings that were beyond words, feelings and a host of subliminal memories that over the years had proven more durable and trustworthy than the history with its trauma and pain out of which they had come. After centuries of forgetfulness and even denial, they refused to go away. The note was a lamentation that could hardly have come from the rum keg of a drum. Its source had to be the heart, the bruised still-bleeding innermost chamber of the collective heart.
>
> For a fraction of a second the note hung in the yard, knifing through the revelry to speak to everyone there. To remind them of the true and solemn business of the fete. [32]

Lamentation is the thread through this cultural fête because of the reality of historical suffering. Through this literary depiction Marshall confirms what Brueggemann notes, "Praise always happens midst the irreducible reality of pain," and if praise does not include pain, it is a false world.[33] The "true business" of praise includes suffering. In fact, pain is the "matrix of praise."[34] "The grounds of our thanksgiving are found in a crucified man," in brokenness and suffering.[35] Without the practice of lament, there can be no true celebration, which is an acknowledgment of God's intervention in the midst of pain. Preachers will not be able to reach the height of preaching unless they first plumb the depth of preaching. In human experience, epitomized in the life of the Christ, lament (the Crucifixion) precedes celebration (the Resurrection), and this movement of the Spirit may shape sermon movements as well. What one laments in preaching turns to celebration because of God's imminent intervention. What God does in the world through grace leads to homiletical celebration. What Paul Wilson calls "grace" in his *Four Pages of a Sermon* is the context for the response of the Spirit through celebration.[36] Grace is God's action that leads to celebration of the good news of the presence of God's activity.

Homiletical celebration is the "celebration of God's presence and participation in human affairs"[37] in the present and anticipated in the future. Though homiletical literature typically presents celebration as unique to African American preaching traditions, it is not. The performance of celebration may take a particular shape in African American settings and African American homiletics may serve as a teacher about the importance and nature of celebration and even as a model for what can be done, but celebration is not limited to a specific cultural milieu. African American homiletical celebration, in particular, traditionally entails hooping, the musical intonation of the Word, which is highly emotive and involves the entire community in the Word through a call-response homiletic performance. Black preaching expressions tend to be embodied through passionate delivery of the voice and body of the preacher that then ignites the embodied celebration of the congregation. In this sermonic performance of the Spirit, there is a surplus (*glossa*) expressed in music that accompanies a rational content (*logos*) expressed in words. During the glossal, musical portion, the preacher becomes a "flute through which divine air is blown, a harp upon which eternal strings vibrate," causing the preacher to become a divine oracle.[38] Related to this musical performance of the Spirit through celebration is "tonal semantics," a black mode of discourse, according to Geneva Smitherman. Voice rhythm and voice inflection convey meaning; thus, "the sound of what is being said is just as important as 'sense'" because in this cultural homiletical tradition sound and sense deliver the Word. Included in this semantic family are talk-singing, repetition and alliterative wordplay, intonational contouring, and rhyme.[39] All of this suggests that sermonic celebration as a manifestation of the Spirit is accompanied by a particular, embodied performance that also reveals the presence of the Spirit.

African American performance of sermonic celebration is distinct, but celebration as a theological response to God spans various Christian homiletical contexts, indicating that there are many ways to perform celebration. Others may emulate African American homiletical celebration, but there should not be any attempt to duplicate it in tone or bodily expression, because this would lead to inauthentic preaching. Furthermore, the manner of celebration in African American preaching will even manifest differently within different African American churches. Celebration is not monolithic, but rather, at its theological core it is a response to the good news about God's grace that is essential for any kind of Christian proclamation. All preaching should celebrate in some manner because of God's present and future intervention in the human realm. This call to celebrate is what is vital for all homiletics, and its connection to the Spirit is significant for any homiletical tradition that yearns to be deeply rooted in the Spirit. Celebration is what the Spirit invites us to do and is what the Spirit does through us.

Celebration's union with lament is vital for the doxological life of preaching, yet celebration is significant in and of itself. In African American history, celebration has been a form of resistance in the face of oppression. In the midst of harsh realities, black people found reason to celebrate, signifying hope for the future. Likewise, in an age filled with bad news of war, disease, and famine, homiletical celebration acts as the resistance of the Spirit to fatalism or nihilism. Celebration as a form of resistance to deathly circumstances parallels the notion of preaching as resistance in the homiletical thought of Christine Smith and Charles Campbell. Smith argues that preaching must resist radical evil in the world, while Campbell contends that preaching is a practice of nonviolent resistance to the work of principalities and powers.[40] Celebration is rooted in lament, yet signals that there is hope because of God; therefore, there is life in the midst of death because of the presence of the Spirit. Spirit-instilled celebration of God produces hope because "to celebrate the presence of God in the face of suffering is to say that pain and evil shall not have the final victory."[41] Hope is a valued virtue of any preacher who by God's Spirit can envision God's future for the world.[42] Celebration acknowledges that there is good news found in Jesus Christ that is relevant for living in a broken world. Celebration assures that sermons will have good news, but by itself it may lead to a false optimism, while lament alone can lead to fatalism. Sermons that only lament the world and provide social critique do not provide the necessary hope grounded in the Spirit of the Resurrection; and sermons that only celebrate do not present a realistic picture of human life grounded in the Spirit of the Crucifixion. This is why preaching in the Spirit necessarily includes doxology, the unified relationship of lament and celebration. Yet a pneumatological study of preaching entails more than homiletical lament and celebration.

Grace, Unity, and Fellowship

Lament and celebration as manifestations of the Spirit in preaching are incomplete without taking into account a holistic theology of the Spirit. Rooted in the African American Christian conviction that the Spirit manifests holistically, this study turned to biblical and theological resources for further insight into the manifestations of the Spirit. What was discovered were three further variables representing the holistic work of the Spirit— grace, unity, and fellowship, which correspond to the individual, communal (church), and social realms, respectively. Grace refers to the embrace of existential grace for one's personal spiritual life and growth. Unity refers to the movement of the Spirit in fostering ecclesial harmony in particular. Fellowship is the work of the Spirit to encourage social fellowship, which is service and social outreach to others. Grace, unity, and fellowship are not sermon forms like lament and celebration that possess a certain theological homiletical movement, but they are theological themes with particular theological content that function as manifestations of the Spirit anywhere in a sermon regardless of the sermon forms within which they are present. They are not exclusive to sermonic lament and celebration but find their fullest expression in lament and celebration taken together as doxology. Doxology is Christocentric and Christ is our grace, unity, and fellowship. Lament and celebration provide depth and height in preaching, while grace, unity, and fellowship provide breadth, leading to cruciform preaching. Cruciformity as an image is helpful in keeping Christian preaching in the Spirit "Christian."

The Relationship between Grace, Unity, and Fellowship

Grace, unity, and fellowship together reveal the holistic manifestation of the Spirit. To speak about one without mention of the other does an injustice to the holistic understanding of the work of the Spirit. Homiletical theory and practice that wishes to be engulfed in the Spirit should engage the person, church, and society, because the Spirit manifests and moves in all realms. Usually, homiletical literature limits dialogue about preaching to one of these realms, focusing on the individual, the communal, or the social,[43] but legitimate conversation about the Spirit in preaching necessarily encompasses a wider scope and vision; thus, preaching should touch on all three arenas of the Spirit's domain if it wants to bathe in the life of the Spirit.

The African American church has made a valiant effort to bridge the emphases of personal piety and social concerns with an interest in issues related to the church community. Cleo LaRue notes that African American Christians have a communal interpretive strategy and a biblical hermeneutic for preaching that incorporates varied "domains of experience" such as personal piety, care of the soul, social justice, corporate concerns, and maintenance of the institutional church, revealing how black preachers have attempted to preserve the breadth of the human experience for the spiritual health of the community.[44] This is not to say that all African American preachers are perfect in their preaching. In fact, a current trend among certain "Spirit-filled" black congregations is the proliferation of the so-called prosperity gospel that emphasizes the personal realm, especially to the neglect of the social realm.[45] However, I would argue that African American preachers, in general, though not always successful in proclaiming a holistic gospel, see the importance of maintaining a broad vision for the power and work of God in the world. Yet, even if espousing LaRue's "domains of experience" implicitly or explicitly, African American preachers have not linked the Spirit to these sermonic expressions of experience.

Grace, unity, and fellowship belong together as manifestations of the Spirit. Individual, personal grace sparks unity, which is itself a sign of grace and spiritual growth within a congregation. If one does not acknowledge the grace experienced within, there will be no desire to share this grace without, in social fellowship. Without the personal experience of grace, one may assume the that work of unity and fellowship are human ventures when in fact they are the work of the Spirit through grace. With grace, one may think of unity and fellowship as other expressions of grace through the Spirit and collaborate with the Spirit in fostering unity and encouraging social fellowship. In addition, grace points to the personal nature of preaching, as well as indicating the divine source of preaching. Ecclesial unity points to the necessary ideal of community for effective preaching to occur, for without unity, both the individual spiritual growth (grace) and the social outreach dimensions (fellowship) of a church will diminish, leaving preaching ailing and a community broken. A church that is divided and broken will not be concerned with *the other*; thus, it will become insular, losing sight of the vastness of God's grace and the holistic mission of the Spirit. With unity, a person's experience of grace through spiritual growth is fostered and a clearer vision of social outreach is possible. With fellowship, an individual and congregation may maintain the mission of the church, realizing that the domain of the Spirit's work is the entire world. Social outreach is a result of grace and unity operating in the life of a community. A unified community reaches out to the world in love as a continued expression of proclamation in and of the Spirit. Without fellowship, Christian spirituality and preaching become incestuous, leading one to question whether the proclaimed Word was truly propelled by the Spirit.

One of these variables may be emphasized more than the others at some point in preaching, yet none of the themes related to the Spirit's holistic manifestation should be ignored or forgotten. Some African American preaching moments even suggest how these themes relate to each other through the embodied sermon performance. For instance, sermonic celebration has been noted to be highly personal, involving the preacher's emotions and own testimonies of experiential *grace*.[46] As a preacher, one appropriates the good news for oneself and celebrates accordingly; yet this celebration is not only for the self but is contagious and leads other people to rejoice. In the context of a worshiping community, genuine sermonic celebration enables the congregation to join in the celebration too, thereby reflecting a certain *unity* expressed through mutual celebration. This unity of the community sparked by the grace experienced by the preacher and at work in the lives of the hearers, leads this celebrating community to engage in social *fellowship* manifesting in loving service to others in the world. Authentic celebration leads to mission. The Spirit who is manifest in the corporate worship experience continues to be manifest through Christians at work in the world. The Spirit gathers the community for worship and sends them into the world, demonstrating a continuum among the manifestations of the Spirit.

In conjunction with homiletical celebration, African Americans propagate a participatory pneumatology. Robert Hood notes, "In black religion, the model of the Spirit imbues a spirituality that is not the classic *imitati Christi* but rather *participati Christi*, through performance, drama, emotion, and ritual."[47] Thus, the sermonic performance of celebration as an expression of grace, unity, and fellowship is participation in the life of Christ through the Spirit. This performance of the Spirit through the congregation and preacher ideally continues with the participation of African Americans in acts of justice in the world, continuing the participation in the life of Christ. The movement of the Spirit of grace, unity, and fellowship in this cultural context as *participati Christi* is not coincidental with its Christocentrism, because Jesus Christ serves as a unifying force for the variables of grace, unity, and fellowship.

These themes of the Spirit sustain a relationship because each focuses on Christ. The individual and personal experience of God's grace happens through justification by faith in Christ and the work of sanctification. The unity of a church community happens with a focus on Christ, particularly on the way of the cross, which suggests humility in human relationships. Social fellowship that serves others is the messianic way of life, guided by the Messiah, Jesus Christ. The love one receives from God in justification is the same love that unifies a congregation and must be shared with a suffering world. With this understanding, one can see how the Spirit is a source of life on all levels. The Spirit manifests holistically as grace, unity, and fellowship. These manifestations help form a pneumatology *of* preaching, a theological context for preaching that laments and celebrates. They also imply a pneumatology *in* preaching, theological components within sermons that lament and celebrate. In the following, how grace, unity, and fellowship interact with homiletical lament and celebration will become evident.

Relationship with Lament and Celebration

Homiletical lament basically states that life is not right, indicating a dissatisfaction with the way things are in the present; yet it possesses a tone of hope in anticipation of future change through divine intervention. Therefore, lament reveals where there is *not* an embrace and reception of grace individually, *not* church unity, and *not* an encouragement to engage in social fellowship or outreach. Lament, as the voice of the Spirit, expresses where the Spirit is not present, but it always does this in faith and hope that one day the Spirit will manifest through grace, unity, and fellowship. Homiletical celebration, on the other hand, articulates through the Spirit the hope and joy in knowing that God does intervene in present human situations and will continue to do so in the future. Thus, celebration names where the Spirit is present and manifest in the life of an individual, church, and society.

Expressing Grace through Lament and Celebration

Celebration is an expression of grace that focuses on the generosity and saving care of a loving God. Grace manifests itself in embracing existential grace personally through the sermon. Homiletical lament links to this experience of grace in one's life because it names the "dis-grace"[48] present among and within humanity. Lament, in terms of grace, deals with personal, spiritual suffering. It names the spiritual reality of sin, rebellion, and disobedience to God, which is a rejection of Jesus Christ as the divine source of salvation. Lament notes moments or episodes where resistance to grace is noticed such that doubt and a lack of faith pervade a human life. Instead of an embrace of God's grace, there is resistance to it; thus, a testimony of faith is absent and perhaps not even desirable. There is no sense of God's presence and definitely not an awakening of faith. Lament can paint a portrait of life sans grace, which would not reveal any fruit of the Spirit or actions of love that are associated with a sanctified life in the Spirit. What can be presented is basically a person without any evidence of God in Christ being at work in their life through the Spirit. There is no sign of spiritual growth and the "dis-grace" is a deep personal despair. Because of this mood, it is essential that the performance of homiletical lament be appropriate to this intense disappointment and sadness with the way things are (for example, lack of grace) in one's personal life; thus, the vocal and facial gesture should exemplify this mood of the Spirit. Though lament states "dis-grace" emphatically, the very articulation of lament, the raising of one's cries to God, implies that life does not have to remain as it is; as with the Psalmist, through truthful naming of personal spiritual reality, lament includes, though subtly, a desire for the embrace of existential grace by a subtextual yearning for it. Lament implies the necessity of grace for Christian living.

During celebration, the embrace of personal existential grace as a manifestation of the Spirit is most evident. As some African American homileticians note, God speaks the divine promise of the gospel by "possessing the preacher."[49] Through the vocal and physical musical performance of African American preachers, grace is received and embraced, especially by the preacher. The passionate performance of the preacher is a sign of the embrace of God's grace in one's life through the Spirit. What the preacher proclaims about God's goodness is real and personally meaningful to the proclaimer. As mentioned, celebration is personal and the "testimony of real experiences such as one's own conversion is a powerful catalyst for celebration."[50] Personal testimony represents an assurance of faith in Christ, part of forgiving grace, for why would any preacher celebrate what he or she did not know or believe? Celebration requires a firm personal faith in God without which celebration would be pure emotionalism and inauthentic Christian proclamation. Genuine homiletical celebration stems from the personal experience of grace found in Jesus Christ, and celebration magnifies the salvific work of Christ on the cross and through his resurrection. Celebration rejoices in divine justification but also celebrates existential evidence of divine sanctification. Human lives that bear the fruit of the Spirit and manifest actions of love are celebrated because of God's concrete work in the human realm. Celebration is a focused homiletical rejoicing about the grace of God, especially in a person's life.

Furthermore, the importance of the personal testimony of grace as content and context for homiletical celebration connects with Tom Long's core idea of the preacher as witness. Long, borrowing from Paul Ricoeur, notes that "testimony is not merely one of words but rather demands a total engagement of speech and action. The whole life of the witness is bound up in the testimony."[51] Celebration through the personal testimony of grace sustains the continuum of celebration in a lived testimony in the world. The witness of African American preaching does not cease with the end of the sermon but lives on in the lives of all the hearers of the Word when the divine grace received is offered to others through a life of Christian witness. Not only in the African American performance of homiletical celebration does one see the engagement of speech and *actio* but also this testifying mode of preaching should lead to and encourage a certain kind of vocal and embodied performance of the Spirit in the community of faith (for example, unity).

Expressing Unity through Lament and Celebration

Unity is an expression of the love of the Persons of the Trinity, one for another. Unity may be discerned where the Spirit fosters ecclesial harmony in Christ's name.[52] By noting the disunity in a dissatisfied tone through lament, the preacher implies an earnest desire for ecclesial unity; this can be one method for fostering unity among the members of the community. The performative tone or content of lament can be so sharp that it may create a feeling and belief within the congregation that God must have something better for the church. Lament can spur unity when the content presented resonates with the congregation. In some African American churches, the call-and-response nature of the proclamation event indicates that the Word spoken is congruent with all; this may happen throughout the sermon, whether in lament or celebration, which is a sign of the Spirit's work of forming a unified community through the preaching performance. Call and response "embodies communality rather than individuality. Emphasis is on group cohesiveness, cooperation, and the collective common good," says Geneva Smitherman.[53] She adds, "call-response seeks to synthesize speakers and listeners in a unified movement."[54]

Through celebration in preaching, call and response as the unity of the Spirit is most poignant. Celebration is personal, but it also enables others to celebrate, contributing to the fostering of ecclesial unity. When the unity of the Spirit is present, all participate in the celebration of God's gracious deeds. Many times in sermonic celebration, Christ is magnified in his whole history, including the Crucifixion and the Resurrection; this Christocentrism unifies the Christian community around a common confession and purpose. Through the Spirit of *anamnesis* and *prolepsis*, the preacher remembers the past work of Christ and anticipates his future work, which instigates a homiletical celebration about the present work of Christ that incorporates the lives of all Christian believers. If the selfless love of Christ for the world is accentuated during celebration, this has the capacity of sparking praise within the entire community because of the truth of Christ's love for the hearers. In addition, celebration may reinforce the desired work of the Spirit in the community.

Expressing Fellowship through Lament and Celebration

Fellowship as a manifestation of the Spirit in preaching may be discerned where there is a sense that one is encouraging social fellowship, that is, social outreach and service to the other, through the sermon. Homiletical lament can highlight happenings of "mis-fellowship," where fellowship has seemingly missed the mark and goal of the Spirit to serve others in the world. "Mis-fellowship" could speak to the ecological crisis and the apparent lack of care for God's creation. Lament would highlight signs of ruin in the world as in the ongoing divisions and conflicts in the global society, demonstrating the lack of fellowship among humanity rather than lives offered in loving service and outreach to others. In crying out in sermonic lament, preachers detail signs of death in opposition to the Source of life, the Holy Spirit; but naming the "mis-fellowship" in the world and its devastating effects can be a method of actually encouraging social fellowship.

In celebration, the messianic way of life, preeminently expressed in the life of Jesus Christ, is emphasized and amplified. There is a natural excitement and passion for the social outreach ministry of the church because of the impetus of the Spirit of mission. Celebration highlights what God is doing in the world through human beings and uses these manifestations of the Spirit as a reason for present and future hope. Signs of life are accentuated and social death is presented as defeated by the Giver of life. Contagious celebration would instill and spark a desire for fellowship to such an extent that the listening community, those in the pulpit and the pew, would engage in life-giving social outreach in the world.

This suggests an underlying assumption about how homiletical lament and celebration function in the life of the Christian community. Long argues that preachers should have an idea of how they want their sermons to function in the lives of the hearers as a "hoped-for change."[55] In this case of African American homiletical lament and celebration, the hope is that lament and celebration would function in such a way to enable lives of doxology that are permeated with the Spirit of grace, unity, and fellowship. Thus, a sermon is not only for the hearing in a community but also for the doing in the world. *Actio* in sermon performance through the Spirit leads to *action* in the world. Zora Neale Hurston notes that an African American worship service is "drama with music. And since music without motion is unnatural among Negroes there is always something that approaches dancing—in fact IS dancing—in such a ceremony."[56] Dancing and bodily movement in a service continues in the world through just actions toward others. This is vitally important, especially if Elsie McKee is correct when she says, "In some instances, love of neighbor may be better evidence for the actual faithful worship of God than are liturgical or devotional practices."[57] This idea of just action in the world coincides with Wilson's call to mission on "Page Four" of *Four Pages of a Sermon,* his book on his sermon method; mission is transformed into invitation and empowerment by the nature of the gospel proclaimed. As Wilson writes, "In identifying one mission, we affirm that a sermon should result in faith and action."[58] Lament and celebration through the Spirit of grace, unity, and fellowship may serve as stimuli for loving Christian service in the world through the Spirit.

In the following segment, two sermons by African American preachers will be studied through this theological-hermeneutical lens in order to demonstrate how lament, celebration, grace, unity, and fellowship may manifest in sermons.

Manifestations of the Spirit in African American Sermons

The two sermons analyzed are by J. Alfred Smith, who is the senior pastor emeritus of Allen Temple Baptist Church in Oakland, California, and professor of Christian ministry and preaching at the American Baptist Seminary of the West in Berkeley, California, and Deborah K. Blanks, who is the associate dean of religious life and of the chapel at Princeton University in Princeton, New Jersey.[59] The choice to analyze sermons preached by a man and a woman is intended as a way of indicating that the Spirit, who is poured out on all flesh (Acts 2), calls women to preach and not only men, which is contrary to some patriarchal opinions in the black church. Through a pneumatological approach to these sermons, it should become clear that it is possible to discern the presence of the Spirit in sermons.

Sermon: Foundations of Our Faith
(1 Corinthians 15:12-18)

The overall movement in J. Alfred Smith's sermon begins with homiletical lament and journeys through lament to homiletical celebration, or as he says of his general "personal approach," "I move from a tear, which is bad news, to a smile, which is good news."[60] In his sermon introduction, the lament of the Spirit is evident, not only because of the naming of life's harsh realities, but because there is an anticipation in hope of what God has done and will do in the human sphere to cause change. There is not just pure lament but the presence of hope and anticipation of celebration in the midst of lament. Though there are "earthquakes," an image he uses to demonstrate human suffering, Smith states forthrightly that "retrofitting" is imminent. He preaches:

> We live in earthquake country. At any given moment our foundations can be shaken. Our possessions can be shattered. Without warning you and I can lose every precious presence or any potential ever promised. Foundations that we thought to be secure can crumble into dust beneath our feet. When the recent Loma Prieta earthquake surprised us on the eve of an opening World Series baseball game between the San Francisco Giants and the Oakland Athletics (As), freeways fell, cars were crushed, buildings burned, lives were lost, and the foundations for the future of many persons were flung far away in the land of nowhere. After some two decades, buildings and bridges that were damaged by the Loma Prieta earthquake are being retrofitted....
> Our spiritual lives are lived under the constant threat of earthshaking reali-

ties. Our foundations are in danger of being destroyed by disease, death, disappointment, divorce, and destruction. Today is God's time to retrofit the feeble and fragile faith of persons whose foundations have been or may be fractured by the earthquakes of life. In 1 Corinthians 15:12, spiritual engineer Paul sets out to retrofit the faith of all Christian believers. He asks, "Now, since our message is that Christ has been raised from death, how can some of you say that the dead will not be raised to life?" Paul calls attention to the "if" of doubt.[61]

At the outset, Smith laments the literal and figurative "earthquakes" in human life. When he speaks of losing "every precious presence or any potential ever promised" or of foundations crumbling under human feet, he alludes to the lack of grace or "dis-grace" one is experiencing personally. The remarks about the damage caused by the Loma Prieta earthquake points to uncontrollable circumstances, yet it is implicitly a cry to encourage social fellowship, social outreach and service to those who were deeply affected by the earthquake, because all creation is interconnected. His pathetic voicing through the Spirit of the "many persons" "flung far away" is a call to seek fellowship with those "in the land of nowhere." However, this lament echoes a hope by revealing that the buildings and bridges damaged "are being retrofitted." This is a homiletical hint that there is good news somewhere and in fact it will arrive through celebration.

Lament continues in the remarks about the demolition of foundations by disease, death, disappointment, divorce, and destruction; these references evoke all the realms of life in a general manner; thus, lament links to grace, unity, and fellowship. Disappointment may touch on the lack of grace being experienced by a person. Disease or divorce may be destroying the unity of a church, while death and destruction annihilate any opportunity for real fellowship. Moreover, disunity is obvious in the Corinthian tension over whether the dead will be raised to life, showing how the lens of unity may be appropriated for reading scripture. To say "Paul sets out to retrofit the faith of all Christian believers" indicates that there is a need for unity in the Christian community because of its theological discord and lack of love towards one another. Nonetheless, through this lament of the Spirit, Smith says, "Today is God's time to retrofit the feeble," another explicit sermonic anticipation of the celebration to come.

As his sermon continues, the Corinthian situation of disunity and dis-grace is lamented even more. Smith says, "They doubted the testimony of their peers and predecessors, who preached the resurrection of Jesus Christ."[62] This doubting not only stirred disunity but represented the lack of grace embraced by so-called Christian believers. Their spiritual growth was stumped because of the disbelief in the resurrection. Even with the numerous testimonies, "some of the Corinthians gave a negative response to many positive testimonies that Jesus Christ has been raised from death. They raised the word of denial, defeat, and despair. Their cry was, 'If Christ be not risen.' "[63] Here Smith laments the lack of faith exhibited by some Corinthians. In this biblical situation, there is no sure testimony of faith at all, and therefore, no spiritual sense of God, but only despair. Smith repeats this refrain "If Christ be not risen" with an antiphon of its result (for example, "then gospel preachers are masquerading clowns of foolishness") in the subsequent paragraph, not only as a way of pointing to the disunity and dis-grace in the sermon text, but as a rhetorical method of asserting that "Christ is risen," which is in fact how he ends forthrightly in the paragraph by stating, "On the other hand, since our message is true, then those who are guilty of the 'if' of doubt logically must embrace the death of hope."[64] Smith assures the listener of an anticipated hope because "our message is true," but he takes the listener deeper into the Spirit of lament with the utter despair of hope's death, which leads to lives without any sense of existential grace, or of social fellowship in particular. He says,

> We are miserable without hope. When hope dies there is no sense of right or wrong, good or evil because everything goes. Nothing is off limits. When hope dies, the grace is a dead-end street....Without hope there is no heavenly city, no new world a-coming, nothing eternal to look forward to experiencing. A hopeless world is a heartless world without compassion, a hellish world, where goodness is wasted work, and a helpless world where there is no amazing grace to save sinners like you and me.[65]

In his lament, Smith focuses on "no heavenly city," "no amazing grace," and a "world without compassion," indicating a lack of grace and fellowship. However, as is characteristic of this sermon, his lamenting is an encouragement to practice social fellowship and to embrace grace. He names popular music and talk shows as social signs of the death of hope but when he says "Your heart will feel a heavy burden for a generation starved for hope,"[66] this is a call to a fellowship in the Spirit that would bring hope. Even a more explicit episode of the anticipation of hope, especially in terms of grace and fellowship, is seen in the following excerpt:

> But thanks be to God who has given us the victory over the "if" of doubt and the "death of hope," with the reality of the Resurrection Christ, who retrofits our faith's foundations.
> In a century when AIDS seeks to destroy Africa and African Americans, hope is a tiny sprout growing in cracked concrete. In a world where our youth live by the secular gospel of rappers, who profane the holy with cursed speech, hope

lives. In a sensate culture where pleasure-intoxicated persons live from their waist down, rather than from their shoulders up, hope in Christ is present for the preservation of the moral fiber of society. In an era of racism, ageism, classism, and homophobism, hope survives in the name of the Living Christ, who has torn down and continues to tear down the devilish dividing walls of Lucifer, the evil one. In an era when the privilege, power, and purses of countries defy environmental health, because they value capitalistic greed far more than the ecological harmony bequeathed to us by God, our originating, sustaining, and continuing Creator.[67]

The energy and emotion of this sermon begins to enliven even more as Smith turns his sermonic attention to the reason for celebration—"the reality of the Resurrection Christ, who retrofits our faith's foundations." In the midst of lament is the anticipated hope and future celebration rooted in Christ. This is a call to embrace existential grace found in Christ, who is the reason for celebration as the later portion of the sermon will indicate. As Smith transitions to homiletical celebration, he holds the "mis-fellowship" in the world (for example, AIDS, racism, environmental crisis) and the "disgrace" in people's lives (for example, "profane the holy," "live . . . waist-down") together with a profound sense of hope, which is a part of lament, as noted. He indicates that "hope is a tiny sprout growing in cracked concrete," "hope lives," "hope in Christ is present," and "hope survives in the name of the Living Christ." Eventually, Smith moves into homiletical celebration by using hope as a metaphor for Christ by saying, "Hope, crucified and buried, rose again in the bosom of elders whose salty tears and moaning voices were cleared away with the reality of the resurrected Christ in their midst."[68]

At this juncture, Smith moves into a strong Christocentric theological development that with some preachers could be heavy and dull, but here it is fast-paced and energetic, and functions as a manifestation of the Spirit. Through his focus on Christ and celebration of the work of Christ through the end of the sermon, Smith links grace, unity, and fellowship. His celebration has already started, but it picks up throttle as he continues:

This mystical Christ continues to retrofit the faith of faithful followers in every generation. Retrofitted faith is God's way of empowering each generation with stability during times of volcanic upheaval and vicious earthquakes in our social order. Let the earth shake. Let foundations tremble. There is the activity of God, who has a glorious record in the retrofitting business.

God continuously retrofits the foundations of our faith conversion . . . God continuously retrofits the foundations of resurrected faith with a commission. God commissions cowardly disciples with a history of denying Jesus into becoming courageous witnesses of the power of Christ's resurrection and the richness of the fellowship of Christ's suffering. Christ becomes the companion of those who have been retrofitted with foundations of resurrected faith. Like the apostle Paul, those who are companions of the Christ are able to say, "I can do all things through Christ who comforts me, who consoles me, who counsels me. Christ is the one who gives me the courage to stand with the minority against injustice and oppression in society. Christ is living in my convictions, Christ is living in my conversations, Christ is living in my commitments, and because Christ lives in me, I will courageously face my future, because all fear is gone. All fear is gone, because Christ holds the future. Christ is Alpha! Christ is Omega! Christ lives!"[69]

As the celebration of God's activity grows, Smith celebrates God's retrofitting foundations of conversion and the action of Christ to comfort, console, and counsel, which addresses personal grace accepted and received. He celebrates God's retrofitting foundations with a commission and the courage to oppose injustice and oppression, which relates to social fellowship in the world. Then as he magnifies Christ, who lives in convictions, conversations, commitments, and within individuals, Smith demonstrates how Christ's living in a person impacts all realms, including the communal venue of unity and the social scene of fellowship. The exclamation of Christ living is the voice of the Spirit shouting out through this sermon. This celebration rolls over into hymnic jubilation, alluding to hope for the future, not just the present, because Christ is the one who is the Living One at the beginning (Alpha) and the ending (Omega) of all time. During African American homiletical celebrations, hymn excerpts are often used. These are part of the heightened poetics of celebrations. In this case, the phrases "because Christ lives in me," "all fear is gone," and "because Christ holds the future," reflects the hymn, "Because He Lives."[70]

In the climactic ending, Smith rehearses the history of Christ in his death, resurrection, and imminent return, gathering all listeners in a unity centered on the common story of the Christian faith. During this sermonic climax, the unity of the Spirit would be clear in the sermon performance within the congregation because most of the listeners would also be celebrating. Smith celebrates the work of Christ in relation to grace (for example, conversion, cleansing from guilt, courage, comfort) and fellowship (for example, commissions to serve), while unity is implicit through his Christocentricism, which unifies a Christian community. The last portion of the sermon resounds with the emphasis on life, not death, which resonates with the Spirit of life. In the end, the "earthquakes" are not lamented, as in the beginning, but celebrated because "Christ who lives today offers you earthquake security."[71] He proclaims in the celebratory closing,

You can accept his offer of protection today; death did not destroy the Lord Jesus Christ. The grave could not hold him. Doubters, unable to blot out the name of Jesus from the blackboard of history, come and go. Their names are forgotten in the graveyard of generations past and present. But there is a person who is the same, yesterday, today, and tomorrow. He is your resurrection and your life. He converts you from corruption. He cleanses you from guilt and self-condemnation.... He commissions you to serve him in a compassionate ministry to those who need help and healing. He retrofits your faith for times of trouble, trial, and testing. Through the Holy Spirit, he gives you courage for every challenge, comfort for every crushing earthquake, and in the end when death has brought your early life to a conclusion, Jesus Christ offers your commencement in a place he has prepared for prepared people.[72]

Smith's proclamation represents preaching that manifests the Spirit through homiletical lament and celebration, while embracing existential grace, fostering ecclesial unity, and encouraging social fellowship that is outreach to others. The movement from lament to celebration is important. Though some variables of the pneumatological lens were less present and less explicit, one can discern all of the manifestations of the Spirit discussed in this study.

Sermon: Telling God Where It Hurts (Mark 5:25-35)

Though Blanks' sermon is based on a Gospel text, rather than an epistle text as Smith's sermon is, her sermon also moves from homiletical lament to homiletical celebration while revealing the holistic manifestation of the Spirit through her dealing with grace, unity, and fellowship. Blanks begins her lament through the biblical text, noting how the unnamed woman's situation represents "dis-grace" personally and "mis-fellowship" socially. She sets the scene:

She has no identity. She has no renown. She has no name. We do not have any background information on her. We do not know anything about her family tree. We do not know whether at one time she was the Martha Stewart of the region or the Jerusalem Idol competing for national fame and acclaim. We do not know if she was ever the center of attention or someone who was never noticed. The facts are straightforward: she had suffered for twelve years; she was bleeding to be exact; she had exhausted her HMO plan and could not obtain another referral; some of the physicians she had seen had taken advantage of her; her prognosis was not good, because the Scripture says that, "she was not better but rather grew worse."[73]

Blanks highlights the lack of apparent personal grace in this situation evidenced by the woman's suffering, bleeding, no referrals, a bad prognosis, and the fact that her state was growing worse. Yet this dis-grace was connected to how others treated her, revealing the mis-fellowship in this story, for "some of the physicians she had seen had taken advantage of her," a clear sign that the Spirit was not present in those doctors.

As the lament of the Spirit continues, it is noted how the woman "seeks out the help that she needs" and "tells God where it hurts," which in fact is a sign of one willing to embrace the grace of the Spirit and serves as an encouragement to the listener to do the same.[74] This is why Blanks turns to her listeners and asks a litany of questions, "What about us? How many of us feel safe enough to tell God where it hurts?...Can we share the upsetting, the seemingly unforgivable, the things that hurt us so deeply that it causes an unrelenting ache in our souls? How many of us feel safe enough to tell God where it hurts, even though God already knows everything about us?"[75] Blanks alludes to the lack of faith and evidence of grace due to human pain through homiletical lament by suggesting our spiritual lives are not what they might be. On the other hand, this questioning lament is a call to assurance of faith and the embrace of grace in one's life. This is why she ends her questioning with a word of hope, anticipating the experience of personal grace.

> The ancient prophet Jeremiah posed the question, "Is there anything too hard for God?" In other words, "Are there hurts beyond healing? Is there brokenness beyond repair? Is there misery beyond a miracle?" The answer to these questions and others is a resounding "no"! For the text suggests that faith that presses its way will find the miracle in an unexpected place.[76]

Like Smith's, Blanks's lament anticipates the future with hope in God's imminent "miracle," which in itself is an embrace of grace. But, this hope is not fully celebrated at this point. Instead, she returns to the unnamed woman and laments her life in terms of the mis-fellowship, disunity, and dis-grace caused by her bleeding.

> Her situation had stigmatized her social standing in the community. The Levitical laws rendered her ritually unclean, which meant that she could not associate with family or friends. She was bleeding! She could not join other women around Jacob's well.... She was bleeding! She could not sit in the congregation and hear the Shammah from the Torah read, "Hear O Israel, the Lord is one!" She was bleeding! She was cut off from her community, excommunicated from her ethnic heritage, and separated from her spiritual birthright. She was bleeding![77]

The repetition of "bleeding" accentuates the lament and actually represents being distanced from grace, unity, and fellowship. Her uncleanliness represents the lack of grace experienced. Not being able to sit in her congregation demonstrates the disunity present. The lack of association with others in the society presents the absence of social fellowship.

In the next major section of the sermon, Blanks magnifies and expands the lamentable situation of bleeding to the plight of African Americans and to other trouble in the world. She says,

> People of color do not have to dig too deep to understand what the unnamed sister might have been experiencing. We know what it is like to be treated differently just because we have more melanin in our skin—that is to say, that our tan is naturally browner.... There is bleeding in our society.... 840 million people in the world are hungry.... 1400 women a year die as a result of domestic violence.[78]

This homiletical lament emphasizes the lack of social fellowship and the presence of death, but it is also a form of encouraging or crying out for social fellowship through the Spirit by highlighting the need in the world. As the sermon moves, "bleeding!" still resounds with examples of dis-grace or mis-fellowship by stating "bleeding because of...," yet there is still an anticipation of future hope when she says that the unnamed woman is a "living example of survival."[79] This indicates that her bleeding does not kill her. Rather, something happens when she touches Jesus. This gives Blanks reason to encourage the listener to tell God where it hurts and embrace divine grace. She says, "I wonder whether you have heard any reports about Jesus. Have you heard about what he has done? Have you heard about what he will do? Have you heard about what he can do?"[80] These questions begin to transition this sermon into celebration, with its focus now on what Jesus can do for bleeding people.

Even though Blanks focuses on what the woman hears about Jesus, she is actually magnifying the work of Christ throughout scripture to build faith in Christ.

> This woman must have heard where Jesus had just been. She must have heard that he had just delivered the demoniac. She must have heard that he had just spoken the words "Peace be still" and caused a cosmic *chill out* of the contrary wind and misbehaving sea. She must have heard that he had just touched the mother-in-law of Peter and her fever had left. She must have heard that he only spoke the word and the servant of the centurion was healed.
>
> The Scriptures do not tell us what, but we do know that something within her reached out in faith to receive the cure for her condition, the deliverance of her disease, the panacea for her pain, and the healing for her hurt....
>
> When she touched Jesus a transfusion of power, of healing, and deliverance went out of him to her.[81]

This homiletical celebration rejoices in the work of the Christ to bring grace and salvation, in their full meaning, to this woman—"cure for her condition." The sermon continues to exhort the listeners to "tell God where it hurts!" during this celebration; this implies hope based on this particular biblical narrative. By stating "tell God where it hurts," Blanks is suggesting "God heals," just as in the situation of the bleeding woman. The celebration does not cease there but surges forward climactically to encompass grace, unity, and fellowship:

> God has a miracle for the somebody and the nobody.
> God has a miracle for the learned and the unlearned.
> God has a miracle for the pulpit and pew.
> God has a miracle for the single one and the married couple.
> God has a miracle for the man and the woman.
> God has a miracle for the corporate executive and the cleaning lady.
> God has a miracle for the African and the European.
>
> Jesus looked and saw this no-name woman, and called her "daughter." That designation signifies kinship, relationship, and lineage. Her touch of the hem of his garment healed her bleeding. His words healed her soul. If we want the bleeding to stop, we must tell God where it hurts.
>
> And if you tell God where it hurts, heaven and earth will exchange a holy kiss. If you tell God where it hurts, divinity will perform a dance on the stage of eternity. If you tell God where it hurts, grace and mercy will give thunderous applause.[82]

The litany "God has a miracle" asserts the good news of God's intervention on all levels of life. There is the embrace of grace for "somebody and nobody," indicating that grace is available for all people and Blanks celebrates this. There is the fostering of ecclesial unity when there is the celebration of God's miracle for "the pulpit and pew." Even the breadth of the examples indicating for whom God has a miracle fosters a unity within a community because it implies no one is ignored. This celebration also entails God's miracles in the world through the encouraging of social fellowship, particularly in the announcing of "the corporate executive and the cleaning lady" and the "African and European." By this sermonic inclusion, Blanks, through homiletical celebration, is calling for a wider vision of social fellowship and outreach through the Spirit. Jesus even calls the unnamed woman "daughter," bringing her into relationship and kinship with him, signs of grace and fellowship. In the end, the celebration blasts forth in such a manner that heightened poetics is required to express the movement of the Spirit through grace, unity, and fellowship (for example, "divinity will perform a dance on the stage of eternity"). Just as Blanks says, "grace and mercy will give thunderous applause," one can assume, based on prior experience of African American homiletical celebration, that the applause is probably also literal throughout the congregation.

Teaching the Manifestations of the Spirit

These five manifestations of the Spirit are not only important for homiletical theory and practice but for homiletical pedagogy in the classroom. As noted, the "trouble" and "grace" grammar of the *Four Pages of a Sermon* are linked to lament and celebration in that lament is a response to trouble and celebration is a response to grace. The "four pages" as a sermon method and movement means: trouble in the text, trouble in the world, grace in the text, and grace in the world. As mentioned, trouble and grace may also be viewed as a grammar underlying any gospel sermon.[83] Lament and celebration extend beyond trouble and grace in being actions of worship in and through the Spirit; however, if one were to use *The Four Pages of a Sermon* as a main textbook for the teaching of preaching, then one could easily speak of lament and celebration in conjunction with trouble and grace as grammar and sermon method and movement. This would open a dialogue between African American homiletics and Euro-American homiletics in the same intellectual space, which is not always common.

In addition, the other manifestations of the Spirit (grace, unity, fellowship) may provide a necessary theology of preaching that is sensitive to the Spirit; thus forming a theological context for proclaiming trouble and grace, or lament and celebration. These manifestations of the Spirit are also theological content within preaching; thus, they may suggest avenues for expressing the issues of life in relation to God as they relate to individuals, churches, and the larger society. Preachers are called to declare "the whole counsel of God."[84] Preaching does not only deal with God and scripture, but also with real individual, communal, and social contexts. Grace, unity, and fellowship present thematic categories that should be present in any sermon; thus, they may help students of preaching obtain a holistic vision for the work and power of God through trouble and grace or lament and celebration. Furthermore, the concept of doxology as the juxtaposition and unification of lament and celebration may not only link further with the tensive relationship of trouble and grace but could provide an opportunity for a class segment on preaching as worship, viewing what speakers and listeners of preaching events do as worship before God.

Moreover, rather than teaching the manifestations of the Spirit as described in *The Four Pages of a Sermon,* another option would be to teach an entire course on "Preaching in the Spirit," whose content would be the five manifestations of the Spirit as they relate to the theology, theory, and practice of preaching. These brief pedagogical musings should indicate some of the possibilities for teaching the manifestations of the Spirit in the classroom. Teaching on the manifestations of the Spirit in preaching is viable because the presence of the Spirit can be discerned; but ultimately, the Spirit is a free wind that blows where she wills; thus, the first step in any sermon preparation is not the turning of the pages of the Bible but the crying of the human heart to God—Come, Holy Spirit.

Summary

This chapter attempted to demonstrate the homiletical importance and implications of each manifestation of the Spirit presented in this study—lament, celebration, grace, unity, and fellowship. Their interaction is significant for homiletical theory and practice. The juxtaposed unified relationship between lament and celebration in African American preaching creates a new homiletical identity, doxology. Doxology is necessary to maintain in preaching truthfulness about the scope of human experience and God's nature. In this way, preaching represents the history of Christ in the Crucifixion (lament) and Resurrection (celebration), echoing the descent and ascent of Christ, giving depth and height to preaching. When grace, unity, and fellowship (breadth of preaching) interface with lament and celebration (depth and height of preaching), there is a holistic manifestation of the Holy Spirit in preaching because no aspect of life is left untouched homiletically; through the Spirit, the individual, church, and society are considered and engaged, enveloped in the cruciform proclamation (depth, height, breadth) created by the Spirit of Christ.

Through analyzing the sermons, it is possible to describe concretely the presence of the Spirit in preaching and to confirm the thesis of this book that the presence of the Spirit can be discerned in sermon language, content, and structure, even if the Spirit is not explicitly mentioned. This homiletic of *Spirit speech* is an implicit, embedded pneumatology, undergirding and guiding preaching, and does not rest on repeated references to the Spirit. The discernment of this "rhetoric of the Spirit" also reveals that the rhetorical form and theological content of sermons will look different if preachers take lament and celebration seriously. In the next, and final, chapter, I will tease out the practical implications of lament and celebration as sermon forms.

Chapter Seven

Practicing Lament and Celebration

Because this book is a work in practical theology, this chapter will emphasize the practical implications of lament and celebration for preaching, by demonstrating how the practice of preaching looks different when a preacher utilizes the forms of lament and celebration in his or her preaching. The marks of lament will be presented first, followed by a discussion of the marks of celebration. This discussion of the content and form of lament and celebration will not be exhaustive, but suggestive, and it is offered with the hope of improving the practice of preaching in the Spirit.

Marks of Sermonic Lament

Lament is the foundation for celebration. One cannot truly reach the height of celebration in preaching until one plunges to the depth of lament. Foremost in sermonic lament is the (1) *naming of the human reality of pain concretely,* whether it be individual (grace), communal (unity), or social (fellowship). The preacher asserts that in some area of life, things are not right. For instance, in his sermon "Are We For Real?" Zan Holmes names the struggles within African American communities, declaring:

> Racism is still alive and well. African Americans have the fastest growing AIDS rate, the highest teenage pregnancy rate, the second highest school dropout rate, and the highest rate of drug-driven violence in the nation. There are still more young black men in prison than in college. We are still the last hired and the first to be fired. We still have less access to medical care and many social services than others.[1]

Holmes paints the picture of pain with concrete examples, foregoing abstract language. Carolyn Ann Knight insinuates human pain directly in the title of her sermon "When All Hell Breaks Loose." This human "hell" is not solely metaphorical in her usage but becomes literal as she names the reality of hurt we endure in various aspects of life:

The events of September 11, 2001, and beyond can be described as nothing short of all hell breaking loose. . . . When the Twin Towers of the World Trade Center in Manhattan went down, when the Pentagon in Washington was seriously damaged, and when a fourth plan crashed into a field in Pennsylvania, it set off a chain of events that altered forever the way we live our lives. . . . All hell breaks loose. It happens to individuals, it happens to nations, and it happens to churches. Love dies and divorce follows. Cancer strikes and the primary source of income is taken away. An only child turns to drugs. . . . All hell breaks loose![2]

In the naming of human reality, the (2) *mode of lament language is not usually indicative but imperative and direct,* which is another mark of lament in preaching. Prathia Hall preaches about the woman with the "issue of blood" in Mark 5:

In the church we often sow seeds that become a harvest of pain because we fail to speak plainly about life, about the facts of life, and certainly about the facts of women's lives. We relegate to backroom whispers, mythology, and mystery subjects that are so much better understood if only allowed the light of day. Having made that preliminary comment or disclaimer, I want to discuss plainly the suffering of the sister in our text.[3]

In preaching lament, one does not back away from dealing with tough issues in the "light of day" but names them directly and firmly within the listening community. One instance of this, along with the other previous examples, is when Teresa Fry Brown says, "Children are still dying. Adults are still abusing one another. Diseases are still killing thousands of our brothers and sisters daily. Nations are still fighting over land."[4] Through the direct mode of speech, there is an honest approach to revealing the nature of human life.

The one who preaches lament does not distance him or herself from the situation being lamented. Thus, sermonic lament (3) *entails self-inclusion.* This is noticeable in the use of first person speech, either in singular ("I") or plural ("We") form. Howard Thurman questions, "What, as a human being, can I do about all the pain that I have when armies run over my land, destroy my family, desecrate what is precious to me? What shall I do with that? How can I handle it?"[5] Like Thurman, Gardner Taylor includes himself within the lamenting community in first person plural. "Look Up!" Taylor preaches, "So many of our churches are little more than social clubs or places for purposeless emotional orgy. Too many of us who preach seem to have little else in mind except how much we can get, how much money we can filch and scheme out of people for our own comfort and luxury."[6] Taylor includes himself within the lamentable situation.

Not only does sermonic lament include the reality of pain for an individual

("I") or a community ("We"), but lament (4) *explicitly notes faith in God/Christ in the midst of naming the pain.* Faith in God is implied in the act of preaching, but before lament moves to blatant celebration, it anticipates the future praise by interjections that make explicit reference to faith and hope in God/Christ. Carolyn Ann Knight, when speaking about the "hell" of Job, captures the tension of the Christian life between the reality of suffering and the embrace of faith in saying, "Our faith in God is not immunization from the storms of this life."[7] Those who lament in preaching about the "storms" of life make known their faith in the God of life despite the named struggles. Sermonic lament reveals how faith is an aspect of lament. Zan Holmes notes the struggles of African Americans and declares, "Yes, in the face of these and all other challenges, the love of Jesus saves and liberates us to get real by hanging together in acts of love."[8]

An excerpt from J. Alfred Smith's "Foundations of Our Faith," which was discussed in the previous chapter, reveals the interjection of statements of faith during the naming of human pain. He says,

> In a sensate culture where pleasure-intoxicated persons live from their waist down, rather than from their shoulders up, hope in Christ is present for the preservation of the moral fiber of society. In an era of racism, ageism, classism, and homophobism, hope survives in the name of the Living Christ, who has torn down and continues to tear down the devilish dividing walls of Lucifer, the evil one.[9]

Ideally, these explicit statements of faith in God/Christ during lament anticipate a future sermonic celebration; thus, the lament form eventually (5) *moves toward celebration and praise of God.* J. Alfred Smith finishes his lament, and soon moves into a fuller celebration of God's presence,

> Hope, crucified and buried, rose again in the bosom of elders whose salty tears and moaning voices were cleared away with the reality of the resurrected Christ in their midst: This mystical Christ continues to retrofit the faith of faithful followers in every generation. Retrofitted faith is God's way of empowering each generation with stability during times of volcanic upheaval and vicious earthquakes in our social order. Let the earth shake. Let foundations tremble. There is the activity of God, who has a glorious record in the retrofitting business.[10]

James Earl Massey makes this sermon more explicit even in his sermon title, "Looking Beyond Our Laments." As he begins to shift out of lament into celebration, Massey declares, "There is a way out of the lament mood." He then speaks of his slave ancestors, showing how they looked beyond their laments. He says:

They caught a glimpse of God that helped them to look beyond their laments. Yes, they did sing "Nobody knows the trouble I see, nobody knows my sorrow," but having looked beyond themselves to catch a vision of the justice and mercy of God, they went on to sing, "Glory, Hallelujah!" Our slave ancestors made it through the dark valley of slavery because they learned to look beyond their laments to see the bright mountain peak of a coming freedom.[11]

Lament is only one aspect of an understanding of doxology and the Spirit in preaching. The Spirit begins in lament but moves the speakers and hearers of the gospel to the celebration of the gospel.

One final mark of lament as a form is noticeable on the page—(6) *heightened, passionate rhetoric*. While rhetoric is a strategy for persuasion or identification and arguably is not a form, it nonetheless may have visible traits, such as short balanced phrases and parallelism, which aid the musicality of African American preaching. "Heightened rhetoric" is named by Henry Mitchell as an aspect of the "material of celebration," contributing to its form; but heightened rhetoric is also a part of lament as a sermon form.[12] This kind of rhetoric does not necessarily "signal closure" or only belong at the end of a sermon and not in the body, as Mitchell claims, because heightened, passionate rhetoric is also present in lament, as will soon be evident. Mitchell, however, is right in saying, "Embellished language is more suitable for the expression of deep feeling," though he is only speaking of celebration.[13] The "deep feeling" of lament is expressed in creative rhetorical ways because pure logical prose is not sufficient to capture the depths of human pain expressed in lament. Expressions of lament go beyond mere description of the trouble to an attempt to move all hearers to experience the immensity of trouble and lament such that the voice of lament becomes their own. This idea is rooted in the tradition of African American preaching, whose basic structure is "prone to generate experiential encounter."[14]

Experiencing lament through preaching is generated by some of the rhetorical devices that will now be discussed. It is clear that some features evident on the page of the passionate rhetoric which shapes lament include, but are not limited to, balanced phrases, alliteration, anaphora, epistrophe, asyndeton, concrete pictures/images, and the use of repetition, all contributing to the homiletical rhythm of lament. Lament may be a sentence in a sermon, but usually it appears as a paragraph or two, which gives ample time for one to proclaim and experience the overwhelming sense of lament.

Teresa Fry Brown says:

Our lives are permeated with talk of social injustice, infectious diseases, familial decimation, racial profiling, political machinations, global poverty, ethnic cleansing, terrorism, unmanageable addictions, interpersonal alienation, and spiritual bankruptcy.

The Bible says there is nothing new under the sun.... God has an answer for any situation careening down the information superhighway. God knows, in times like these,

> Too many dreams are dying at dawn
> Too many aspirations are asphyxiated in apathy
> Too many visions are eviscerated in valleys
> Too many blessings are buried in boredom
> Too many joys are jilted by jealousy...

God is still the author and finisher of the "good news," the "saving word," the "empowered message," and the "naked truth" that frees us from debilitating rumors and unsubstantiated predictions of the demise of God's world.[15]

Lists can be a signal of lament as a form. Fry Brown begins by listing some social, communal, and individual situations of human pain and she does so without using any conjunctions until her last example in the first paragraph; this is the rhetorical scheme of asyndeton, which is a way of beginning to stir up the immensity of trouble by moving along without pauses. She also incorporates balanced phrases here as well, as when she proclaims her list of "too many." The lack of pause in this initial listing suggests the persistent nature of trouble that gives us no pause in human life. As she moves along, she interjects faith statements about God. When she moves back into naming the pain, the pathos increases, indicated by her use of alliteration, anaphora, and the use of repetition of the words "too many." Her sermonic lament "paints a picture" of trouble through the pulsing, rhythmic quality of her words. Listing various kinds of problems creates a pulsating litany that amplifies the pain. If one were to lament in only one sentence, this amplifying litany would be impossible and in fact not capture the heavy burden of suffering. The litany of "too many" resounds in the ears of hearers, suggesting that it is not necessarily always the kind of trouble that is named that creates identification with the hearers in lament, but it is the "size" of lament that stirs the laments of others. Her lament is finished once the litany ceases and she begins to speak of hope in God as the finisher of "good news."

Later in this same sermon, she engages in lament again, this time adding rhyme and concrete images or pictures to her rhetorical repertoire. Fry Brown declares:

Folk running around looking for salvation in all the wrong places.
Church-hopping and Holy Ghost-shopping.
Denominational damnation.
Advertisements of "We preach and teach the whole world," as if the gospel can

be segmented. Throwing away one's religious heritage for a cup of instant popularity.

Perpetuating the prosperity of a few, while millions exist in poverty.

Competitions for same market share while millions remain unchurched.

Big churches with little spirituality.

Loud music with no theology.

Hand-clapping with no mention of Christ.

Choreographed praise, as if humans command the Spirit.

Sermons about serving the pastor, but no realization that God is still on the throne.

Preachers, leaders hiding behind artificial barriers of

    Powder-filled vials

    Weak theology

    Cloned delivery styles

    Unlimited credit lines

    Competitive market shares

    Private jets

    Faddish clichés

    Designer labels

    Back scratching-officers

    Made-up titles

    Colorful, oversized, flowing robes

    Calvary-sized crosses

    Multiple rings

    Ill-fitting collars

    "Big chair syndrome"

    Perspiration, anticipation, handkerchiefs

    Cowering committees

    And powerless positions.

Is it a wonder that the people are in darkness? Look at their models of Christian love.[16]

She begins with rhyming "hopping" and "shopping," continues to utilize alliteration, incorporates antithesis (big churches with little spirituality), but her lament intensifies when she begins her amplifying litany of the barriers behind which preachers hide, beginning with "powder-filled vials." The length of this litany, along with the balanced phrases, creates the feeling of the "size" of trouble. In this litany, she also utilizes concrete images or pictures of life as in "back-scratching officers" and "colorful, oversized, flowing robes." All of her heightened rhetoric contributes to the sense of lament she wants to create for the hearers to see and experience. Once again, her lament ends when she finishes the litany.

Another sermon that is a fine example of the form of lament is Vashti McKenzie's "Same No More." She says:

The same mistakes roll over you, followed by the same poor decision-making process. The wheels of life roll over you and grind you into the ground.

Every day people are going up to the temple . . . and you are still in the same place.

Every day they go into the temple to pray . . . and you are still in the same place.

Every day they are passing you by . . . and you are still in the same place.

Every day their prayers are being answered . . . and you are still praying your same prayer.

You can see them go up and you can see them come down . . . but you are still in the same place.

People going in one way and coming out another . . . but you are still in the same place.

They are walking in and out, but you are sitting in the same place. You are close enough to see them go into the presence of God. You are close enough to look at them being blessed and being a blessing in worship. It is just an arm's length away, but you can't get in. You are still in the same place. Change never crossed your mind.

The man asked for alms, and Peter simply replied, "We do not have what you want. We don't have what you are asking for; but we do have what you need." Sometimes, beloved, we need to remember that there is a difference between our wants and our needs. We want a lot of things, but we need only some things. We want a Mercedes, but need only a Chevrolet. We want a black diamond, but need only a fabulous fake. We want caviar, but fried chicken is what we need. Wants tend to satisfy a desire and needs tend to satisfy a necessity. Peter said, "We do have what you need; it is the name of Jesus." "In the name of Jesus Christ of Nazareth rise up and walk." (Acts 3:6)[17]

After some basic description of human problems, McKenzie enters lament by using epistrophe, the repetition of the same phrase at the end of each sentence (you are still in the same place). She heightens the sense of lament in this case with her use of hyperbole, a feature also found in celebration.[18] In this sermon, "every day" is both anaphora and hyperbole and is used to accentuate the static situation of sameness of those who remain in the "same place," creating a greater feeling of lament. She then utilizes antithesis (you can see them go up . . . come down) to stress this point. All of this is said through an amplifying litany to create size for lament, as was done in Fry Brown's sermon. McKenzie continues to repeat, "You are still in the same place," seemingly ending the lament by shifting to the words "change never crossed your mind," coming out of the litany, which is a usual indication of the end of lament. However, she makes a transition into more lament through the biblical text, this time heightening the lament by lifting up the antithesis of "wants" and "needs." After this brief lament, she begins her move into celebrating the name of Jesus.

One more example will present another variation of sermonic lament that may not be as embellished as Fry Brown or McKenzie's sermons. This sermon still represents lament in preaching because what is prevalent in its passionate rhetoric is repetition through the motif of a "dream shattered" paired with concrete images and pictures from life, formed into an amplifying litany that emphasizes the magnitude of lament. In this sermon, "The American Dream," Martin Luther King, Jr. states:

> About two years ago now, I stood with many of you who stood there in person and all of you who were there in spirit before the Lincoln Monument in Washington. As I came to the end of my speech there, I tried to tell the nation about a dream I had. I must confess to you this morning that since that sweltering August afternoon in 1963, my dream has often turned into a nightmare. I've seen it shattered. I saw it shattered one night on Highway 80 in Alabama when Mrs. Viola Liuzzo was shot down. I had a nightmare and saw my dream shattered one night in Marion, Alabama, when Jimmie Lee Jackson was shot down. I saw my dream shattered one night in Selma when Reverend Reeb was clubbed to the ground by a vicious racist and later died. And oh, I continue to see it shattered as I walk through the Harlems of our nation and see sometimes ten and fifteen Negroes trying to live in one or two rooms. I've been down to the Delta of Mississippi since then, and I've seen my dream shattered as I met hundreds of people who didn't earn more than six or seven dollars a week. I've seen my dream shattered as I've walked the streets of Chicago and seen Negroes, young men and women, with a sense of utter hopelessness because they can't find any jobs. And they see life as a long and desolate corridor with no exit signs. And not only Negroes at this point. I've seen my dream shattered because I've been through Appalachia, and I've seen my white brothers along with Negroes living in poverty. And I'm concerned about white poverty as much as I'm concerned about Negro poverty.
>
> So yes, the dream has been shattered, and I have had my nightmarish experiences, but I tell you this morning once more that I haven't lost the faith. I still have a dream....[19]

Here, as in many sermonic laments, King expands the notion of shattered dreams by the sheer number of examples he presents consecutively in conjunction with his repetitive motif (dream shattered), and by doing this, he is able to stir the listeners to lament also. He does not just name troubles in society but organizes the presentation of them in such a way that is rhetorically sophisticated and creative, drawing the listener into the experience of pain. By rhetorically stacking the different examples of the dream shattered, King burdens the hearers with the extent of the shattering problems, or rather "stacks" on them human pain, such that there is no other response than to lament. Even here, however, the lament of shattered dreams does not have the final word, because King does say that he has not lost the faith and still has a dream, an idea which he expands in a celebratory fashion from the last sentence of the sermon excerpt quoted above.

Marks of Sermonic Celebration

As for celebration, it is important to remember Frank Thomas' insight into the theological core of celebration—that is, Jesus Christ is the good news and he is the reason for sermonic celebration.[20] It should be no surprise then that the primary mark of celebration in preaching is the (1) *amplification of God's action in the world through Jesus Christ*. In his sermon "Nevertheless," Henry Mitchell climaxes his preaching with a rehearsal of the history of Christ, his life, death, resurrection, ascension, and imminent return. He declares:

> At the name of him who went from crying and complaining "if it be possible let this cup pass from me," but ended up declaring, "Nevertheless not as I will but as thou wilt." Because of his nevertheless. His name is above every name.
> Because of his nevertheless, his name is the only name given under the heavens by which men, women, boys, and girls must be saved. Because of his nevertheless, he suffered the humiliation of the Cross. Nevertheless, he got up from the grave on Easter Sunday morning. Nevertheless. He ascended into heaven and sitteth at the right hand of the Father. Nevertheless he's coming back again. Nevertheless, eyes have not seen, ears have not heard, nor hath it entered into the hearts of men what the Lord has in store for those that love his appearing. Amen.[21]

Mitchell's sermon pattern represents Frank Thomas's definition of celebration as "the culmination of the sermonic design, where a moment is created in which the remembrance of a redemptive past and/or conviction of a liberated future transforms the events immediately experienced."[22] Mitchell remembers the past work of Christ and declares the future of Christ; thus, by Thomas' standards this would create a moment of transformation for the congregation. Highlighting what God has done in Christ is seen in Deborah Blanks's sermon when she presents a litany of biblical examples of the actions of Christ. She says:

> This woman must have heard where Jesus had just been. She must have heard that he had just delivered the demoniac. She must have heard that he had just spoken the words "Peace be still" and caused a cosmic *chill out* of the contrary wind and misbehaving sea. She must have heard that he had just touched the mother-in-law of Peter and her fever had left. She must have heard that he only spoke the word and the servant of the centurion was healed.[23]

Furthermore, J. Alfred Smith offers another possibility by describing God and Christ as subjects who act. He preaches:

> God continuously retrofits the foundations of our faith conversion.... God continuously retrofits the foundations of resurrected faith with a commission. God commissions cowardly disciples with a history of denying Jesus into becoming courageous witnesses of the power of Christ's resurrection and the richness of the fellowship of Christ's suffering. Christ becomes the companion of those who have been retrofitted with foundations of resurrected faith.... Christ is the one who gives me the courage to stand with the minority against injustice and oppression in society. Christ is living in my convictions, Christ is living in my conversations, Christ is living in my commitments, and because Christ lives in me, I will courageously face my future, because all fear is gone. All fear is gone, because Christ holds the future. Christ is Alpha! Christ is Omega! Christ lives![24]

Another mark of sermonic celebration is the (2) *accentuation of the nature and identity of God/Christ*. This accentuation can be done by asserting the various names for Christ or God. Martin Luther King, Jr. does this in "Drum Major Instinct" when he declares:

> His name may be a familiar one. (*Jesus*) But today I can hear them talking about him. Every now and then somebody says, "He's King of Kings." (*Yes*) And again I can hear somebody saying, "He's Lord of Lords." Somewhere else I can hear somebody saying, "In Christ there is no East nor West." (*Yes*) And then they go on and talk about, "In Him there's no North and South, but one great Fellowship of Love throughout the whole wide world." He didn't have anything. (*Amen*) He just went around serving and doing good."[25]

Charles Booth follows suit by saying, "We know who God is and what he can do. He is El Shaddai—the Lord God Almighty! He is Jehovah—the Lord! He is Jehovah Elyon!—the Lord Most High! He is Jehovah Shammai—the Lord Ever Present! He is Jehovah Shalom—the Lord my Peace! He is Jehovah Jireh—the Lord who will provide!"[26] The two above-mentioned marks of celebration are two key reasons for a third mark of sermonic celebration—(3) *hope for the future*. As Teresa Fry Brown affirms, "God says Hope is not dead."[27] Because of the nature and activity of God/Christ, Christians can have hope not only in the present but for the future. Some preachers take the traditional route and preach about the future hope found in going to heaven. One who does so is Ella Mitchell. She declares:

> When my time down here is ended, and I get on the train bound for glory, I want to hear the Great Conductor say, "Well done! Well done, good and faithful servant. You have healed broken hearts. Well done! You have ministered to

troubled minds. Well done! You have brought peace and joy to those without homes. Well done! You have let my Spirit work in you. Well done! Now get on board little sister, get on board! You may enter...enter...enter...into the joy of your healing Lord and Savior."[28]

J. Alfred Smith also focuses in on the promise of a prepared home for God's children. He preaches, "Through the Holy Spirit, he gives you courage for every challenge, comfort for every crushing earthquake, and in the end when death has brought your early life to a conclusion, Jesus Christ offers your commencement in a place he has prepared for prepared people."[29] In cele-bration, the future is embraced because "Christ holds the future," leading some to say, "I will courageously face my future, because all fear is gone. All fear is gone."[30] The hope for the future is also expressed in terms of hope for what is to come on the earth due to Christ. Charles Adams asserts:

> Good religion is shaped like a cross, the vertical beam reaching up to God for power, and the horizontal beam, reaching out and sharing love.... Is you got good religion?
>
> When we get good religion...whenever you go, wherever you preach, wher-ever you pray, wherever you work, problems will be solved, prayers will be answered, doors will be opened, barriers will be shattered, nations will be freed, races will be reconciled, churches will be saved, burdens will be lifted, yokes will be broken, people will be liberated, children will be educated, churches will be empowered, and religion will be responsible.[31]

Adams emphasizes what will happen in the world if faith is propelled by Christ, who is alluded to when he says "shaped like a cross." "Will be" indi-cates a hope for the future of earthly existence.

The hope embedded in celebration functions as (4) *empowerment for mis-sion*; this is a fourth mark of sermonic celebration that is discernable in many sermons. Intertwined with the good news of the power of Jesus Christ is the call to serve in the world empowered by Christ. There are indications that service cannot happen without the presence of Christ. Prathia Hall preaches, "Keep your eyes on Jesus. Turn things around in his name, by his word, and with his power. Turn our community right side up and make sure you never take your eyes off Jesus. Watch him. Watch him. Keep your eyes on Jesus."[32] Her admonition to keep one's eyes on Jesus suggests that proper action in the world can only happen in relation to Christ; this is why she speaks of action "in his name, by his word, and with his power." During celebration, there are calls to mission but this is deeply linked with God's empowerment to act in the world. Charles Adams makes this point explicit:

Empowered ministry is not so much getting something from God as having an enlivening, energizing, and transformative encounter with God because you have made yourself available to God. It is to accept the invitation of God to be in partnership with God where God is at work in the world. It is hearing the voice and call of God and answering... "If you send me to liberate the oppressed in China, I'll go." "If you send me to stand and bleed with dying students in Tiananmen Square in Beijing, I'll go."[33]

A person can say, "I'll go," and serve because God empowers individuals to act in the world. Zan Holmes asserts that Christian action is possible "by the liberating love of Jesus." His sermonic climax establishes a litany that includes the following: "If there is a race, by the liberating love of Jesus that enables us to hang together in acts of love, we can run it together. If there is a fence, by the liberating love of Jesus that enables us to hang together in acts of love, we can climb over it together."[34] It is clear here that it is the love of Jesus "that enables"; thus, mission in the world does not happen without Christ, an assertion present in many homiletical celebrations.

Furthermore, celebration does not only serve the larger social mission of the Church, but celebration is deeply personal, as indicated earlier, in that preachers have a sure knowledge of God's goodness and power in their lives. This suggests that another mark of sermonic celebration is the (5) *use of personal testimony*. Frequently, first person speech in the singular, "I," is used to indicate testimony. A fine example of testimony in celebration is the ending of Carolyn Ann Knight's "When All Hell Breaks Loose." She concludes her sermon by saying, "Even though all hell has broken loose in this world, I know that God is able to deliver me from hell or he will deliver me in hell. God is keeping me even while I go through hell. God is providing for me in the midst of my hell."[35] Henry Mitchell boasts of God's pedigree as an "investment counselor" and testifies to God's provision in his and his family's life. He says, "All I can say is that God is the best investment counselor I know—anywhere, anyplace, anytime—because all these things have been added. All that our children needed to get through school came from somewhere. The fact that it didn't come from our pockets doesn't matter. They got through school, and we don't owe anybody a dime.... Jesus is the world's greatest investment counselor."[36] Mitchell testifies about the past. Knight focuses on the present with a mention of the future; but J. Alfred Smith testifies wholeheartedly about the future when he declares, "because Christ lives in me, I will courageously face my future, because all fear is gone."[37]

Lastly, another trademark of celebration hinted at in Smith's testimonial use of hymnic material is a (6) *heightened sense of rhetoric and poetics*.[38] Various rhetorical devices are utilized throughout the body of sermons, but during the celebration there appears to be a more intense and emotive use of rhetoric as the sermonic climax approaches. For instance, in Deborah Blanks's sermon "Telling God Where It Hurts," she utilizes the rhetorical devices of anaphora and antithesis, where the former refers to starting a sequence of clauses with the same word or phrase, and the latter means the pairing of contrasting words or ideas. She preaches:

> God has a miracle for the somebody and the nobody.
> God has a miracle for the learned and the unlearned.
> God has a miracle for the pulpit and pew.
> God has a miracle for the single one and the married couple.
> God has a miracle for the man and the woman.
> God has a miracle for the corporate executive and the cleaning lady.
> God has a miracle for the African and the European.[39]

Her rhetoric stirs further celebration about the breadth of God's work in the world. Henry Mitchell uses anaphora also in "Nevertheless" as he concludes, "Nevertheless, he got up from the grave on Easter Sunday morning. Nevertheless, he ascended into heaven and sitteth at the right hand of the Father. Nevertheless, he's coming back again. Nevertheless..."[40] Another common rhetorical device is repetition of a short motif, such as when Ella Mitchell interjects "Well done" and Gardner Taylor interjects "Look up" between their other sentences, as they approach the end of the sermon. Mitchell says, "Well done! You have ministered to troubled minds. Well done! You have brought peace and joy to those without homes. Well done!" Taylor declares, "Look up and, by faith, face skyward....Up above the clouds of gossip and meanness there is a fellowship, a joy divine. Look up. God lives and by faith...you may see the blessed sunshine and move in the calm, pure atmosphere of the Holy Spirit. Look up!"[41] Creative and heightened rhetoric is a part of celebration, but even more distinct in celebrations is the turn to poetics, particularly hymnody.

Many African American preachers enter into the poetry of hymns as they celebrate the gospel of God. Teresa Fry Brown completes her hope theme and proclaims, "Hold on to your hope. How do you know, Preacher? Psalmist writes: 'My hope is built on nothing less than Jesus' blood and righteousness. I dare not trust the sweetest frame but wholly lean on Jesus' name. On Christ the solid rock I stand. All other ground is sinking sand. All other ground is sinking sand.' Hold on to your hope."[42] Prathia Hall declares:

> Then we can join both the wonderful unnamed woman and Jairus. They came to Jesus with a story about death and left with a brand-new story of life—a first-century version of a brand-new song. Blessed assurance, Jesus is mine, Oh what

a foretaste of glory divine. Heir of salvation, purchase of God, Born of his spirit, washed in his blood. This is my story, this is my song, Praising my savior, all the day long.[43]

This discussion about the marks of lament and celebration as sermon forms and manifestations of the Spirit establishes their presence in African American preaching and reveals again that these manifestations of the Spirit in preaching can be discerned.

Summary

This chapter has attempted to demonstrate the theological and rhetorical practical difference lament and celebration would make to a sermon if these forms were utilized. Marks of sermonic lament and celebration were presented as a way of revealing what it might mean to practice preaching in this manner. African American sermons were used as examples, but lament and celebration may be practiced in any culture because the Spirit is not captive to anyone or anything, including culture. Just because practical implications for preaching were offered does not imply that if one practices these guidelines exactly as written one will necessarily be preaching in the Spirit with transformative power. The Spirit cannot be controlled or coerced. The right sermon content and form do not guarantee that the Right Spirit will be present. Practicing lament and celebration in preaching is a move in the right direction because it follows the movement of the Spirit of Christ, rooted in suffering and hope, "descending into hell" and "ascending into heaven." Nonetheless, uttering these words of lament and celebration is only a humble prayer for the Spirit to come and bless these human efforts to make preaching "a demonstration of the Spirit and of power" (1 Cor. 2:4).

CONCLUSION

This book has argued that the presence of the Spirit can be discerned in sermon language, content, and structure. It has shown that lament, celebration, grace, unity, and fellowship are five key manifestations of the Spirit that one can discern in sermons. Though some may assert this is an unattainable task because the Spirit of God is total mystery, I have attempted to demonstrate that this aim is attainable in some way because even the sound of the wind can be heard (John 3). The movement of the Spirit is mystery, but not *only* mystery, because even the wind leaves traces of its presence. There is a homiletical tongue of the Spirit that one can hear in the air and see on the page; thus in light of the homiletical aims of this study, one can say that there is a *Spirit speech* available to preachers.

To make this case, I explored the work of the Spirit through the lenses of African American Christianity, homiletics, the Bible, and theology; thus what is presented is actually an ecumenical pneumatology for preaching. This was done because the presence of the Spirit is not confined to one source or culture or discipline. However, I used African American culture and preaching traditions as a case study for this book because the black church has traditionally emphasized the Holy Spirit and the ministry of preaching such that it helps to provide a language to talk about the role of the Spirit in churches, particularly in preaching. This does not mean that all churches are to imitate African American ones, that is, attempt to duplicate the experience of the Spirit found in many black churches; but it does suggest that other ethnic ecclesial communities should search for ways to authentically experience this *same* Spirit in their contexts. The Spirit is the same; how she expresses herself through others may be different.

This study began with a close look at the understanding of the Spirit within African American Christianities with the stress on outward manifestations of a holistic working Spirit. The Spirit's presence in human language was confirmed as lament, celebration, grace (individual), unity (ecclesial), and fellowship (social). Lament and celebration are manifestations of the Spirit in preaching that mirror the descent (lament) and ascent (celebration) of Christ, giving depth and height to preaching, even if much more work needs to be done on lament. Together, grace, unity, and fellowship give breadth to Christian preaching, enlarging the scope of sermons that aim to be rooted in the Spirit, and bring a further degree of concreteness to this pneumatological discussion for homiletics. Grace may be discerned to be a sign of the Spirit in sermons when the preacher embraces existential grace.

Unity relates to the ecclesial realm, focusing on the work and experience of the Spirit to unify the community of faith through preaching. Fellowship is how the Spirit encourages service to others in the world through preaching.

These five manifestations of the Spirit—lament, celebration, grace, unity, and fellowship—emerge as a theological-hermeneutical lens for discerning, or reading, the presence of the Spirit in sermons. They are a lens and language for discerning and describing the presence of the Spirit in actual sermons that reveal a "rhetoric of the Spirit." The final chapter argued that if one laments and celebrates, preaching will look and feel different, not only on the surface, rhetorically or theologically, but also deep within the heart of the preacher. Preaching in the Spirit entails a robust theology and a renewed practice for the life of the church and world.

Because the Spirit can be discerned in preaching, it is possible to answer the homiletical question that this book presented in the introduction— "Where Is the Spirit in Sermons?" The Spirit is in the sermon speech of lament, celebration, grace, unity, and fellowship. The possibility of discerning a speech of the Spirit in sermons does not imply that just because one uses this language, the Spirit will be present. The Spirit cannot be controlled, coerced, or tricked into blessing our sermons. These manifestations do not suggest a mechanical approach to preaching that guarantees the Spirit's presence nor does naming the Spirit explicitly do so because the Spirit is a free wind who blows where she wills, blessing whatever she chooses, even our imperfect, fallible, limited, spiritless words. The truth is that every sermon is only an *epiclesis*, a yearning for the triune God to be present in a transformative way. Nonetheless, this book has attempted to help preachers find more fruitful ways of connecting with the movement of the Spirit in their preaching. By doing so, the depth (lament), height (celebration), and breadth (grace, unity, and fellowship) of preaching can be restored. In their interaction, cruciform preaching in the Spirit emerges. At least, this is the hope.

One other hope is that Christian preachers who practice lament will embrace these groans of the Spirit as crucial to the development of a mature homiletic. Lament is vital for homiletical studies because it provides a theological language that embraces God and human suffering *simultaneously*, therefore maintaining the truthfulness and "Christic center" of our preaching. "Christic center" means that the person of Jesus Christ "is central and foundational for all of Christian faith and Christian action, and therefore also for Christian theology."[1] Moreover, as lament partners with celebration in African American homiletics, it offers more opportunities for African Americans to serve as teachers to other cultural traditions at the homiletical table in the future. Lament may be on life support in some circles of Christianity, but this study is an invocation of the Spirit to breathe new life into us so that we may live fully in the Spirit, not only celebrating, but also lamenting, individually (grace), communally (unity), and socially (fellowship).

Normally, discussions about preaching are limited to conversations about sermon preparation, construction, and delivery. Yet a conversation about the holistic Spirit and preaching cannot be limited to those sermonic domains but must include all of our living, for the Spirit is life.[2] Thus, just as the community helps Baby Suggs finish her heartfelt sermon in Toni Morrison's *Beloved* when she can say no more and can only dance with her twisted hip, I can say no more at this point but can only allow the Spirit to finish this literary "sermon" in your life. These words were not just for a change in our way of preaching but for a transformation in the manner of our living. In the end, preaching is not about our eloquent rhetorical words of wisdom, but about "a demonstration of the Spirit and of power" (1 Cor. 2:4). Without power, preaching will be pitiful; but with God's power, anything is possible. Come, Holy Spirit!

NOTES

Introduction

1. Nicholas Wolterstorff, *Lament for a Son* (Grand Rapids, MI: Eerdmans, 1987), 6.

2. See R. C. D. Jasper and G. J. Cuming, *Prayers of the Eucharist: Early and Reformed* (Collegeville, MN: Liturgical Press, 1990).

3. See his work, *On the Holy Spirit* (ca. 329–79; reprint, New York: St. Vladimir's Seminary Press, 1980), 97.

4. Yves Congar, *I Believe in the Holy Spirit*, vol. 3, trans. David Smith (London: Geoffrey Chapman, 1983), 271. Jürgen Moltmann concurs by saying, "The church's first relation to the Holy Spirit is the *epiclesis*." See Moltmann, *The Spirit of Life: A Universal Affirmation*, trans. Margaret Kohl (Minneapolis: Fortress, 1992), 230.

5. James Forbes, *The Holy Spirit and Preaching* (Nashville: Abingdon Press, 1989), 19.

6. For a classic study of homiletical celebration, see Henry Mitchell, *Celebration and Experience in Preaching* (Nashville: Abingdon Press, 1990).

7. See Yves Congar's *I Believe in the Holy Spirit*, vol. 2, in which he beautifully discusses how the Spirit combines everything, including the church's life of praise, in doxology. See pp. 113, 221–28. Congar takes his cue from the biblical tradition in which it is noted that the Spirit is the one who causes believers to cry, "Abba, Father!" (Rom. 8:15ff; Gal. 4:5-7).

8. Olin Moyd, *The Sacred Art: Preaching and Theology in the African American Tradition* (Valley Forge, PA: Judson, 1995), 101.

9. Peter Paris, "When Feeling Like a Motherless Child," in *Lament: Reclaiming Practices in Pulpit, Pew, and Public Square*, eds. Sally Brown and Patrick D. Miller (Louisville: Westminster John Knox, 2005), 111.

10. See Mary Catherine Hilkert, *Naming Grace: Preaching and the Sacramental Imagination* (New York: Continuum, 2003), particularly chapter 7, "Grace at the Edges: Preaching and Lament," 108–27. For Sally Brown's essay, see "When Lament Shapes the Sermon," in *Lament*, eds. Brown and Miller, 27–37.

11. Hughes Oliphant Old declares that worship is not "spoiled by tears" because "when the godly weep, they weep unto God, and weeping before God is worship just as much as rejoicing before God." See his *Themes and Variations for a Christian Doxology: Some Thoughts on the Theology of Worship* (Grand Rapids, MI.: Eerdmans Press, 1992), 17–21.

12. For a homiletical discussion about the tensive language of metaphor, law, and gospel, see Paul Scott Wilson, *Imagination of the Heart: New Understandings in Preaching* (Nashville: Abingdon Press, 1988). For a brief discussion of the idea, see Wilson's *Preaching and Homiletical Theory* (St. Louis: Chalice, 2004), 91–94.

13. For her succinct introduction to some of the issues involved in naming blacks and insight into the discourse of black identity politics, see Smitherman, *Black Talk:*

Words and Phrases from the Hood to the Amen Corner (Boston: Houghton Mifflin, 2000), 5–11. For a fuller examination of this racial discourse in relation to African American cultural philosophy and theology, see Victor Anderson, *Beyond Ontological Blackness: An Essay on African American Religious and Cultural Criticism* (New York: Continuum, 1995).

14. See C. Eric Lincoln and Lawrence Mamiya, *The Black Church in African American Experience* (Durham, NC: Duke University Press, 1990), 1.

15. For Delores Williams's statement, see Barbara Holmes, *Joy Unspeakable: Contemplative Practices of the Black Church* (Minneapolis: Fortress, 2004), 5.

16. Ibid.

17. Ibid.

18. Ibid., 6.

19. Karen Baker-Fletcher, *Sisters of Dust, Sisters of Spirit: Womanist Wordings on God and Creation* (Minneapolis: Fortress, 1998), 112; cf. Mark Sturge and Melva Costen, "Black Churches' Worship," in *The New Westminster Dictionary of Liturgy and Worship*, ed. Paul Bradshaw (Louisville: Westminster John Knox, 2002), 61–64; cf. Robert E. Hood, *Must God Remain Greek? Afro Cultures and God-Talk* (Minneapolis: Fortress, 1990), 193, 204–9.

20. See Saint Augustine, *On Christian Doctrine*, Book 4, XXIV (ca. 396–427 CE); reprint, trans. D. W. Robertson Jr. (New Brunswick, NJ: Prentice Hall, 1958), 160–61.

1. Toward a Pneumatology for Preaching

1. W. E. B. Dubois, *The Souls of Black Folk* (1903; reprint, New York: Penguin, 1969), 275.

2. See her "Voice, Vision, and Spirit: Black Preaching Women in Nineteenth Century America," *Sisters Struggling in the Spirit: A Women of Color Theological Anthropology*, eds. Nantawan Boonprasat Lewis, Lydia Hernandez, Helen Locklear, Robina Marie Winbush (Louisville: Women's Ministries Program Area and National Ministries Division, Presbyterian Church [U.S.A.], 1994), 38.

3. For Mitchell's perspective, see his "The Holy Spirit: A Folk Perspective," *The Living Pulpit* 5:1 (January–March 1996): 40–41.

4. Geneva Smitherman, *Talkin and Testifyin: The Language of Black America* (Boston: Houghton Mifflin, 1977), 93.

5. James H. Cone, *God of the Oppressed* (San Francisco: HarperSanFrancisco, 1975), 17–18.

6. Cecil W. Cone, "The Black Religious Experience," *Theology and Body*, ed. John Y. Fenton (Philadelphia: Westminster, 1974), 83.

7. Howard Thurman, *Disciplines of the Spirit* (Richmond, IN: Friends United, 1963), 64. He also says that "suffering is universal for mankind. There is no one who escapes." See pp. 64–65.

8. Cleophus LaRue, *Heart of Black Preaching* (Louisville: Westminster John Knox, 2000), 1, 14; Warren H. Stewart, Sr., *Interpreting God's Word in Black Preaching* (Valley Forge, PA: Judson, 1984), 18, 27.

9. Anthony B. Pinn, *Terror and Triumph: The Nature of Black Religion* (Minneapolis: Fortress, 2003), 12, 15, 21, 31, 52.

10. See her *Joy Unspeakable: Contemplative Practices of the Black Church* (Minneapolis: Fortress, 2004), 75.

11. Carol E. Henderson, *Scarring the Black Body: Race and Representation in African American Literature* (Columbia: University of Missouri Press, 2002), 4, 7, 20–21. Henderson notes that a white Georgian physician in the antebellum period says of blacks, "So notoriously filthy are Negroes that many persons will doubtless smile at the very mention of cleanliness when used in connection with a people closely allied to hogs in their nature and habits." This statement confirms the overall feeling towards black people during slavery times; see p. 29.

12. Richard Burton, *Afro-Creole: Power, Opposition, and Play in the Caribbean* (Ithaca, NY: Cornell University Press, 1997), 32.

13. See the chapter entitled "Of the Sorrow Songs" in Dubois, *The Souls of Black Folk.*

14. See "Many Thousand Gone," *Songs of Zion* (Nashville: Abingdon Press, 1981), 137.

15. For the complete lyrics of this spiritual, see "Oh, Freedom," *Songs of Zion*, 102.

16. This is a reference to the spiritual "Sometimes I Feel Like a Motherless Child." The words and music may be found in *Songs of Zion*, 83.

17. For a musical arrangement of this spiritual for voice and piano, see "Death, Oh Me Lawd!" in Edric Connor, ed., *The Edric Connor Collection of West Indian Spirituals and Folk Tunes Arranged for Voice and Piano by Max Saunders and Hal Evans* (London: Boosey & Hawkes, 1945), 22–25.

18. Pinn, *Terror and Triumph*, 143.

19. Diane J. Austin-Broos, *Jamaica Genesis* (Chicago: University of Chicago Press, 1997), 42.

20. David Walker, *Appeal to the Coloured Citizens of the World, but in Particular, and Very Expressly, to Those of the United States of America* (New York: Hill and Wang, 1965; orig. 1829), 7.

21. Riggins Earl Jr., *Dark Symbols, Obscure Signs: God, Self, and Community in the Slave Mind* (Maryknoll, NY: Orbis, 1993), 15–16.

22. Clarence E. Hardy, *James Baldwin's God: Sex, Hope, and Crisis in Black Holiness Culture* (Knoxville: University of Tennessee Press, 2003), 27.

23. For the complete lyrics of this hymn, "Whiter than Snow," see www.cyberhymnal.org (accessed June 23, 2009).

24. Hardy, *James Baldwin's God*, 6.

25. Ibid., 26, 28.

26. Cheryl Townsend Gilkes, "The 'Loves' and 'Troubles' of African-American Women's Bodies," in *A Troubling in My Soul: Womanist Perspectives on Evil and Suffering*, ed. Emilie M. Townes (Maryknoll, NY: Orbis, 1993), 232–34.

27. Ibid., 234.

28. Emilie M. Townes, *Breaking the Fine Rain of Death: African American Health Issues and a Womanist Ethic of Care* (New York: Continuum, 1998), 122–23.

29. N. Lynne Westfield, *Dear Sisters: Womanist Practice of Hospitality* (Cleveland: Pilgrim, 2001), 98.

30. See the spiritual, "I've Been 'Buked," *Songs of Zion*, 143.

31. Cheryl J. Sanders, *Saints in Exile: The Holiness-Pentecostal Experience in African American Religion and Culture* (New York: Oxford University Press, 1996), 123–25. In these pages, Sanders claims that her exilic dialectic goes beyond the idea of African American identity as a dichotomized "double consciousness" as presented in the work of W. E. B. Dubois, *The Souls of Black Folk*.

32. See the spiritual "I've Been 'Buked" in *Songs of Zion*, 143.

33. Joseph Murphy, *Working the Spirit: Ceremonies of the African Diaspora* (Boston: Beacon, 1995), 3.

34. George C. L. Cummings, "The Slave Narratives as a Source of Black Theological Discourse: The Spirit and Eschatology," in *Cut Loose Your Stammering Tongue: Black Theology in the Slave Narratives*, ed. Dwight N. Hopkins and George C. L. Cummings (Louisville: Westminster John Knox, 2003), 38.

35. James Cone, *The Spirituals and the Blues: An Interpretation* (Maryknoll, NY: Orbis, 1991), 32.

36. These phrases are references to the spirituals "Nobody Knows the Troubles I See" and "Balm in Gilead," respectively. A fuller version of these songs can be found in *Songs of Zion*, p. 170 and p. 123.

37. Paule Marshall, *Praisesong for the Widow* (New York: Putnam, 1983), 39.

38. Melva Costen, *African American Christian Worship* (Nashville: Abingdon Press, 1993), 13–15. Further expressions of this same sentiment can be seen in the work of Dwight Hopkins, specifically in *Being Human: Race, Culture, and Religion* (Minneapolis: Fortress, 2005), in which he teaches that spirit inherently dwells in culture; thus, culture contains the sacred. A similar trajectory can be found in *Noise and Spirit: The Religious and Spiritual Sensibilities of Rap Music* (New York: New York University Press, 2003), edited by Anthony Pinn, who believes rap emphasizes the spiritual found in culture.

39. See "Over My Head," *Songs of Zion*, 167.

40. See "I Want Jesus to Walk with Me," *Songs of Zion*, 95.

41. John S. Mbiti, *African Religions and Philosophy* (New York: Doubleday, 1970), 2–3. For more on the African view of sacredness, see Mbiti, *Concepts of God in Africa* (New York: Praeger, 1970), chapters 8–13.

42. Marshall, *Praisesong*, 94, 159, 194.

43. Ibid., 194.

44. Diana Hayes, "Slain in the Spirit: Black Americans and the Holy Spirit," *Journal of the Interdenominational Theological Center* 20, no. 1–2 (Fall–Spring 1992–1993): 98.

45. See Nalo Hopkinson, *Brown Girl in the Ring* (New York: Warner Books, 1998); and Karen McCarthy Brown, *Mama Lola: A Vodou Priestess in Brooklyn* (Berkeley: University of California Press, 1991). For more about the African worldview of spirits, see Henry M. Mitchell, *Black Belief: Folk Beliefs of Blacks in America and West Africa* (New York: Harper & Row, 1975), 65. Mitchell says that the spiritual

worldview in West Africa consists of the following: Supreme or High God, hierarchy of lesser divinities and spirits, ancestral spirits, and evil spirits.

46. Howard Thurman, *The Inward Journey* (New York: Harper and Bros., 1961), 7; cf. Thurman, *Deep Is the Hunger* (New York: Harper and Bros., 1951), 146–47.

47. Ibid., 126.

48. Ibid., 136, 128. He says, "There is a spirit within and about us that broods over every tiding, encircling all our needs. It breathes through the Waiting Moment, cradling all that is." The "quiet ministry of the Spirit" includes healings, a word, silence, a smile, images, old musical refrains that can bring unexpected healing to hurts. The Spirit may even soften the hard heart of a person. For the softening influence of the Spirit, see Thurman, *Meditations of the Heart* (New York: Harper and Bros., 1953), 183.

49. Ibid., 133. Thurman stresses that it is important to remember that "God has not left himself without a witness in our spirits" and in our lives.

50. In his article, "The Holy Spirit: A Folk Perspective," Henry Mitchell testifies that the Spirit is a "living reality" and a presence with whom he is familiar. See *The Living Pulpit* 5, no. 1 (January–March 1996): 40.

51. Costen, *African American Christian Worship*, 18.

52. Walter F. Pitts Jr., *Old Ship of Zion: The Afro-Baptist Ritual in the African Diaspora* (Oxford: Oxford University Press, 1993), 130. Italics mine. Melva Costen insightfully points out that "Unlike the Western-oriented Christian, whose theology is rooted in Greco-Roman concepts and culture, African peoples tend to seek to *know* God personally rather than to *know about* God from doctrines and creeds." See Costen, *African American Christian Worship*, 20.

53. Gilkes, 242.

54. Westfield, *Dear Sisters*, 81, 85–86. Westfield grounds her view in the incarnation. She writes, "The incarnation of Jesus is proof of the importance of the body as a means of grace."

55. Cheryl J. Sanders, "African-American Worship in the Pentecostal and Holiness Movements," *Wesleyan Theological Journal* 32, no. 2 (Fall 1997): 120. Cf. Murphy, *Working the Spirit*, 169–70, 173–74. Murphy writes, "The spirit of the Black Church is the ceremonial experience of God's ultimate freedom in the body of the congregation. In word, song, music, and movement, the spirit is brought down to become incarnated in the very bodies of the devotees, showing them its power to sustain, heal, and liberate the community."

56. Robert E. Hood, *Must God Remain Greek? Afro Cultures and God-Talk* (Minneapolis: Fortress, 1990), 204, 193. An explicit literary expression of the Spirit taking human shape in black religion is found in *Praisesong for the Widow*. The main protagonist, Avey Johnson, is also known as "Avatara," a Sanskrit name meaning "incarnation" or "spirit-in-the-flesh." Avatara is the Spirit incarnated in black flesh.

57. Sanders, *Saints in Exile*, 63.

58. James H. Evans Jr., *We Have Been Believers: An African-American Systematic Theology* (Minneapolis: Fortress, 1992), 125.

59. Albert Raboteau, *Slave Religion: The "Invisible Institution" in the Antebellum*

South (Oxford: Oxford University Press, 1978), 61–62. For more about spirit possession in black religion, see pp. 62–73.

60. Will Coleman, *Tribal Talk: Black Theology, Hermeneutics, and African American Ways of "Telling the Story"* (University Park: Pennsylvania State University Press,
2000), 51.

61. Costen, *African-American Christian Worship*, 48–49.

62. See Marshall, 34. Cf. Melva Costen's *African American Christian Worship*,
52–54; and Raboteau, *Slave Religion*, 70–71.

63. Clifton H. Johnson, ed., *God Struck Me Dead: Voices of Ex-Slaves* (Cleveland:
Pilgrim, 1993), 10–12.

64. To W. E. B. Dubois, the three salient elements of slave religion were the
preacher, the music, and the frenzy. See *The Souls of Black Folk*, 211–12.

65. Zora Neale Hurston, *Sanctified Church* (Berkeley: Turtle Island, 1983), 91.

66. Wallace Best, "Lucy Smith and Pentecostal Worship in Chicago," *Religions of
the United States in Practice*, vol. 2, ed. Colleen McDannell (Princeton, NJ: Princeton
University Press, 2001), 14–15.

67. C. Eric Lincoln and Lawrence H. Mamiya, *The Black Church in the African-
American Experience* (Durham, NC: Duke University Press, 1990), 6. The "theater"
quality of African American worship in the Spirit is also portrayed through the ethno-
graphic work of Glenn Hinson and the sociological analysis of Timothy Nelson. See
Hinson, *Fire in My Bones: Transcendence and the Holy Spirit in African American
Gospel* (Philadelphia: University of Pennsylvania Press, 2000); and Nelson, *Every
Time I Feel the Spirit: Religious Experience and Ritual in an African American
Church* (New York: New York University Press, 2005).

68. Ibid., 6.

69. Anthony B. Pinn, "Black Theology, Black Bodies, and Pedagogy," *Cross Currents* 50, no. 1/2 (2000): 200.

70. For Geertz's approach, see "Deep Play: Notes on the Balinese Cockfight,"
Readings in Ritual Studies, ed. Ronald L. Grimes (New Brunswick, NJ: Prentice Hall,
1996), 217–29.

71. This is a quote by communication theorist, James Carey in Richard F. Ward,
Speaking of the Holy: The Art of Communication in Preaching (St. Louis: Chalice,
2001), 18.

72. Murphy, *Working the Spirit*, 175.

73. Hurston, *Sanctified Church*, 91. In black religion, when the Spirit "enveloped"
individuals through crying and jerking movements, this was believed to show that
they had experienced something that gave deeper meaning to their lives. See Baker-
Fletcher, "Voice, Vision, and Spirit: Black Preaching Women in Nineteenth Century
America," 37.

74. Pinn, *Terror and Triumph*, 99–100.

75. Ibid., 100.

76. Coleman, *Tribal Talk*, 51.

77. For this idea and more, see Hood, *Must God Remain Greek?* 193, 204–9.

78. Baker-Fletcher, "Voice, Vision, Spirit," 37; Pipes as quoted in James Harris,
Preaching Liberation (Minneapolis: Fortress, 1995), 34.

79. Johnson, *God Struck Me Dead*, 5, 8.

80. Henry Mitchell, *Black Preaching: The Recovery of a Powerful Art* (Nashville: Abingdon Press, 1990), 123.

81. Harris, *Preaching Liberation*, 35.

82. Cone, *God of the Oppressed*, 19.

83. Lincoln and Mamiya, 6. Cf. Evans Crawford, *The Hum: Call and Response in African American Preaching* (Nashville: Abingdon Press, 1995).

84. Sanders, "African-American Worship," 105. When Melva Costen speaks of singing, she says that it is a "divine channel through which God speaks and believers respond." See Costen, *African American Christian Worship*, 44.

85. See his article, "The Heavenly Anthem: Holy Ghost Singing in the Primal Pentecostal Church (1906–1909)," *Journal of Black Sacred Music* 1, no. 1 (Spring 1987): 1–33.

86. Cited in Lincoln and Mamiya, *Black Church*, 81.

87. See Riggins Earl, *Dark Salutations: Ritual, God, and Greetings in the African-American Community* (Harrisburg, PA: Trinity, 2001), pp. 151–69, 171–200.

88. For further terms and concepts that come out of the traditional black church, see pp. 57–58 in Smitherman, *Talkin and Testifyin*.

89. Cummings, "Slave Narratives," 46.

90. Howard Thurman, *The Centering Moment* (New York: Harper and Bros., 1969), 21.

91. Thurman, *Inward Journey*, 138. Throughout his writings, he asserts the importance of righting relations with others. For example, see *The Centering Moment*, 35.

92. Ibid., 48. "Miracles in the Spirit" are also

the resolving of inner conflict upon which all the lances of the mind have splintered and fallen helplessly from the hand; the daring of the spirit that puts to rout the evil deed and the decadent unfaith; the experiencing of new purposes which give courage to the weak, hope to the despairing, life to those burdened by sin and failure; the quality of reverence that glows within the mind, illumining it with incentive to bring under the control of Spirit all the boundless fruits of knowledge; the necessity for inner and outer peace as the meaning of all men's striving.

93. Westfield, *Dear Sisters*, 82. Westfield says, "The revealing of God in concealed gatherings is a hallowing of kitchens, an immersion in Holy Communion." Her perspective is tied to her sacramental perspective that "there is a sacramentality inherent in living life." For more on this, see pp. 80–82.

94. Ibid., 89.

95. Smitherman, *Talkin and Testifyin*, 87.

96. Westfield, *Dear Sisters*, 89.

97. Ibid., 70.

98. Ibid., 49.

99. Westfield draws on the thinking of Henri Nouwen for her understanding of hospitality. Nouwen asserts freedom as crucial for an encounter to be hospitable—to create a "free space where the stranger can enter and become a friend instead of an

enemy"; to "offer freedom not disturbed by dividing lines"; to inspire "the liberation of fearful hearts"; to allow strangers "to discover themselves as created free; free to sing their own dances; free also to leave and follow their own vocations." For West-field's use of Nouwen, see pp. 46–47.

100. I note specifically that working for liberation is hospitality for the *oppressed* because fighting for the liberation of the oppressed will probably be viewed through the eyes of the oppressor as inhospitality toward the oppressor. This implies that one's celebration could be another's lament.

101. J. Deotis Roberts, "The Holy Spirit and Liberation: A Black Perspective," *Mid-Stream* 24 , no. 4 (October 1985): 409–10. In a similar tone, Thurman asserts, "There is no alternative to the insistence that we cannot escape from personal respon-sibility for the social order in which we live." See *Meditations of the Heart*, 135. Both Roberts and Thurman demonstrated that "no man is an island," and people have a responsibility to be involved with other human beings in service to the liberation of oppressed people.

102. Albert B. Cleage, "Let's Not Waste the Holy Spirit," in *Black Theology: A Documentary History, 1966–1979*, eds. Gayraud Wilmore and James Cone (Mary-knoll, NY: Orbis, 1979), 338.

103. Ibid., 332–33.

104. Thurman, *Meditations of the Heart*, 174.

105. For this article, see *Quarterly Review* 8:2 (Summer 1988): 19–35.

106. Thurman, *Deep Is the Hunger*, 144.

2. The Spirit of Lament and Celebration

1. Michael Welker, *God the Spirit*, trans. John F. Hoffmeyer (Minneapolis: Fortress, 1994), ix.

2. Walter Brueggemann, *Israel's Praise: Doxology against Idolatry and Ideology* (Philadelphia: Fortress, 1988), 141.

3. Stephen Breck Reid, *Listening In: A Multicultural Reading of the Psalms* (Nashville: Abingdon Press, 1991), 35.

4. Ibid., 34.

5. Ibid., 13.

6. Walter Brueggemann, *The Psalms and the Life of Faith*, ed. Patrick D. Miller (Minneapolis: Fortress, 1995), 69.

7. Brueggemann, *Israel's Praise*, 140.

8. The use of "I"/first person speech may (1) reflect vulnerability, innocence, trust; or (2) statements of loyalty; or (3) performative liturgical language (for example, I will give thanks) (Ps. 6:6–7).

9. Brueggemann, The *Psalms and the Life of Faith*, 34.

10. Claus Westermann, *Praise and Lament in the Psalms* (Atlanta: John Knox, 1981), 267; cf. Reid, *Listening In*, 9.

11. Reid, *Listening In*, 9.

12. Brueggemann asserts that the movement of human experience is from orienta-tion to disorientation to reorientation. He names the psalms of lament "psalms of dis-

orientation." See his *Psalms and the Life of Faith*, 24, 30, and his *Message of the Psalms: A Theological Commentary* (Minneapolis: Augsburg Publishing House, 1984), 51–77.

13. Reid, *Listening In*, 7, 10–11.

14. Claus Westermann, *The Praise of God in the Psalms*, trans. Keith R. Crim (Richmond, IN: John Knox, 1965), 66–69, n. 4. For further description of these traits, see Brueggemann, *Psalms and the Life of Faith*, 70–72; and Brueggemann, *The Message of the Psalms*, 54–57.

15. Reid, *Listening In*, 9.

16. Westermann, *Praise of God in the Psalms*, 75, 80; cf. Westermann, *Praise and Lament in the Psalms*, 11–12, 33, 75.

17. Brueggemann, *Psalms and the Life of Faith*, 115, 99.

18. Ibid., 56.

19. Brueggemann, *Message of the Psalms*, 54.

20. Brueggemann, *Psalms and the Life of Faith*, 72.

21. Patrick Miller, "Heaven's Prisoners: The Lament as Christian Prayer," in *Lament: Reclaiming Practices in Pulpit, Pew, and Public Square*, eds. Sally Brown and Patrick D. Miller (Louisville: Westminster/John Knox, 2005), 19.

22. Brueggemann, *Psalms and the Life of Faith*, 54.

23. Brueggemann, *Message of the Psalms*, 56–57.

24. Westermann, *Praise and Lament in the Psalms*, 270–71.

25. James L. Mays, *Psalms: Interpretation: A Bible Commentary for Teaching and Preaching* (Louisville: Westminster/John Knox, 1994), 30.

26. "God Is a God," *Songs of Zion* (Nashville: Abingdon Press, 1981), 140.

27. Hughes Oliphant Old, *Worship That Is Reformed According to Scripture* (Atlanta: John Knox, 1984), 43. Old also says, "When they sang the Psalms the Holy Spirit was praising the Father within their hearts." See p. 44.

28. Thomas L. Hoyt Jr., "Romans," *True to Our Native Land: An African American New Testament Commentary*, eds. Brian K. Blount, Cain Hope Felder, Clarice J. Martin, and Emerson B. Powery (Minneapolis: Fortress, 2007), 262.

29. Gordon D. Fee, *God's Empowering Presence: The Holy Spirit in the Letters of Paul* (Peabody, MA: Hendrickson, 1994), 574–75.

30. Ibid., 582–83.

31. Hoyt, "Romans," 263.

32. Emerson B. Powery, "The Groans of 'Brother Saul': An Exploratory Reading of Romans 8 for 'Survival,'" *Word and World* 24: 3 (Summer 2004), 321.

33. Martin Luther King, Jr., "Eulogy for the Martyred Children," *A Testament of Hope: The Essential Writings and Speeches of Martin Luther King, Jr.*, ed. James Melvin Washington (San Francisco: Harper & Row, 1986), 221.

34. Ibid., 222.

35. Apostle Paul speaks to this same idea, using different terms, in 2 Corinthians 1:22 and 5:5, where he talks about the Spirit as a "first installment" and "guarantee."

36. Fee, *God's Empowering Presence*, 571.

37. Ibid., 572.

38. "Soon-a Will Be Done," *Songs of Zion*, 158.

39. See the spiritual "Nobody Know the Troubles I Seen" in *Songs of Zion*, 170.

40. Jürgen Moltmann, *The Way of Jesus Christ: Christology in Messianic Dimensions*, trans. Margaret Kohl (Minneapolis: Fortress, 1993), 78, 94.

41. Jürgen Moltmann, *The Spirit of Life: A Universal Affirmation*, trans. Margaret Kohl (Minneapolis: Fortress, 1994), 60.

42. Ibid., 81.

43. Ibid., 93; cf. Moltmann, *Spirit of Life*, 62.

44. JoAnne Marie Terrell, *Power in the Blood? The Cross in the African American Experience* (Maryknoll, NY: Orbis, 1998), 34.

45. James Cone, "Strange Fruit: The Cross and the Lynching Tree," *The African American Pulpit* 11/2 (Spring 2008): 24.

46. Ibid.

47. See "Were You There?" in *Songs of Zion*, 126.

48. "He Nevuh Said a Mumbalin' Word," *Songs of Zion*, 101.

49. Carla A. Jones, "Forgiven," *This Is My Story: Testimonies and Sermons of Black Women in Ministry*, ed. Cleophus J. LaRue (Louisville: Westminster/John Knox, 2005), 170.

50. Moltmann, *The Crucified God: The Cross of Christ as the Foundation and Criticism of Christian Theology*, trans. R. A. Wilson and John Bowden (Minneapolis: Fortress, 1993), 50–51.

51. James Weldon Johnson, "The Crucifixion," *God's Trombones: Seven Negro Sermons in Verse* (New York: Penguin, 1927), 42.

52. King, "Eulogy for the Martyred Children," 222.

53. Moltmann, *Spirit of Life*, 192.

54. See "He Arose," *Songs of Zion*, 168.

55. Moltmann, *Theology of Hope: On the Ground and the Implications of a Christian Eschatology*, trans. James W. Leitch (Minneapolis: Fortress, 1993), 161–62, 211–12, 216.

56. King, "Eulogy for the Martyred Children," 222.

57. Mary Catherine Hilkert, *Naming Grace: Preaching and the Sacramental Imagination* (New York: Continuum, 1997), 53.

58. Moltmann, *Theology of Hope*, 22, 34–35, 288–90.

59. Henry Mitchell, "Nevertheless," *Fire in the Well: Sermons by Ella and Henry Mitchell*, ed. Jacqueline B. Glass (Valley Forge, PA: Judson, 2003), 77–78.

60. Theo Witvliet, "In Search of a Black Christology," *Cross Currents* 37/1 (1987): 21–22.

61. The Apostle's Creed states, "He descended into hell. The third day, he rose again from the dead. He ascended into heaven."

62. Melva Costen, *African American Christian Worship* (Nashville: Abingdon Press, 1993), 127.

63. For an overview of perspectives on the Spirit in the history of homiletics in the twentieth century, see chapter 2 in Luke Powery, *The Holy Spirit and African American Preaching*. Dissertation. University of Toronto, 2007.

64. Olin Moyd, *The Sacred Art: Preaching and Theology in the African American Tradition* (Valley Forge, PA: Judson, 1995), 101.

65. Evans Crawford and Thomas H. Troeger, *The Hum: Call and Response in African American Preaching* (Nashville: Abingdon Press, 1995), 23.

66. Moyd, *The Sacred Art*, 101.

67. Frank Thomas, *They Like to Never Quit Praisin' God: The Role of Celebration in Preaching* (Cleveland: Pilgrim, 1997), 2–3. Thomas also argues that Jesus Christ is the good news that makes the church a "celebrative community" because "celebration is not an optional emotion that we attach to the preaching of the gospel, but part of the natural experience of emotions that is at the heart of the gospel." See Thomas, 23, 26–27. For a more recent exploration of celebration as a form of proclamation, see Paul Scott Wilson, *Setting Words on Fire: Putting God at the Center of the Sermon* (Nashville: Abingdon Press, 2008).

68. Mitchell, *Celebration and Experience in Preaching* (Nashville: Abingdon Press, 1990), 34.

69. Ibid., 66.

70. Mitchell asserts that celebration is relevant empowerment and is necessary because it empowers people. He believes that "people do what they celebrate." See *Celebration and Experience*, 62, 131.

71. Thomas, *They Like to Never Quit Praisin' God*, 32ff.

72. Ibid., 31.

73. Moyd, *The Sacred Art*, 109.

74. Mitchell, *Celebration and Experience*, 71.

75. Mitchell, *Black Preaching: The Recovery of a Powerful Art* (Nashville: Abingdon Press, 1990), 132. Mitchell boldly declares, "The sermon that celebrates without giving help is an opiate. The sermon that tries to help without celebration is, at least in the Black church, ineffective. The celebration is a necessity."

76. Mitchell, *Celebration and Experience,* 146–47.

77. Thomas, *They Like to Never Quit Praisin' God*, 30.

78. Thomas asserts that much of the transformative work of celebration is contingent upon the Spirit. "The Holy Spirit causes and allows transformation to occur through celebration, and we preachers are junior partners and facilitators in celebrative emotional process. We assist the Spirit, but the work is that of the Holy Spirit." See Thomas, *They Like to Never Quit Praisin' God*, 26–27, 34–35. Also, Olin Moyd says, "God is the author of celebration. God ordained celebration. God expects celebration among his people, and God honors celebration," implying that genuine celebration is not constructed by human beings. See Moyd, *The Sacred Art*, 104.

79. See William Turner, "The Musicality of Black Preaching: A Phenomenology," *Performance in Preaching: Bringing the Sermon to Life*, eds. Jana Childers and Clayton Schmit (Grand Rapids, MI: Baker Academic, 2008). Teresa Fry Brown notes that this hooping is "spirit-endowed" and a "form of singing the songs of Zion in a strange land." The content is varied—listing heroes of faith, history of God's action in the world, talk about Christian grandma or mother, Jesus to cross-resurrection-second coming, sing a song, tell a story—one that is fixed in black oral tradition, share

testimony. In terms of performance, it is intensified, poetic, alliterative, verbal or nonverbal, and usually at the end of a sermon. The voice does gymnastics like gasping for air, panting, long pauses, or rapid speech; voice quality becomes harsh the voice runs the tonic scale; articulation is with elongated vowels; there is repetition of phrases or initial consonants; word endings are omitted. It is physical activity and sometimes preachers are drenched in perspiration. See Brown, *Weary Throats and New Songs: Black Women Proclaiming God's Word* (Nashville: Abingdon Press, 2003), 171–72.

80. Mitchell, *Black Preaching,* 130.

81. Thomas, *They Like to Never Quit Praisin' God,* 26–27. Indeed, as Moyd says, "Authentic African American celebration embodies spiritual transcendence," but it is also "spiritual and social empowerment." See Moyd, *The Sacred Art,* 105.

82. See Suchocki's final chapter about the sermon as worship in *The Whispered Word: A Theology of Preaching* (St. Louis: Chalice, 1999).

83. Walter Brueggemann says that the preacher's task is to bring to speech the yearning for the lost communion with God and includes the "voice of the worshiper in pain, protest, and need," speaking rage and resentment to God, yet with hope in God. He further writes, the "sermon is an invitation, a modeling, and a permit. Such speech is courageous faith which addresses God about the pain in the world." See Brueggemann, *Finally Comes the Poet: Daring Speech for Proclamation* (Minneapolis: Fortress, 1989), 51, 53, 57.

84. James Harris, *Preaching Liberation* (Minneapolis: Fortress, 1995), 52–53.

85. For his perspective on these matters, see his *Preaching and Homiletical Theory* (St. Louis: Chalice, 2004), pp. 87–115. In chapter 10 of his book, *Setting Words on Fire: Putting God at the Center of the Sermon*, Paul Scott Wilson actually presents lament as a form of proclamation.

86. "Rudolf Bohren: The Spirit as Giver and Gift of the Word," *Theories of Preaching: Selected Readings in the Homiletical Tradition,* ed. Richard Lischer (Durham, NC: Labyrinth Press, 1987), 330.

87. Justo L. González and Catherine G. González, *The Liberating Pulpit* (Nashville: Abingdon Press, 1994), 65.

88. Hilkert says, "Preaching remains always a profound act of worship. Whether in the mode of thanks and praise or of lament, preaching is a calling on the mystery of the transcendent God who alone can save us." See Hilkert, *Naming Grace,* 193–94.

89. Ibid., 111.

90. Ibid., 117.

91. Ibid., 119.

92. Sally A. Brown, "When Lament Shapes the Sermon," in *Lament: Reclaiming Practices in Pulpit, Pew, and Public Square*, eds. Sally A. Brown and Patrick D. Miller (Louisville: Westminster John Knox, 2005), 28–29.

93. Brown calls lament "nonoptional dialogue with God." See Brown, "When Lament Shapes the Sermon," 30.

94. Ibid., 35.

95. Ibid., 31.

3. The Spirit of Grace

1. Howard Thurman, *Creative Encounter: An Interpretation of Religion and Social Witness* (New York: Harper and Bros., 1954), 20–21.

2. W. E. B. Dubois, *The Souls of Black Folk* (1903; reprint, New York: Penguin, 1969), 275. Italics mine.

3. Howard Thurman, *Meditations of the Heart* (New York: Harper and Bros., 1953), 48.

4. Howard Thurman, *Inward Journey* (New York: Harper and Bros., 1961), 133. Thurman stresses that it is important to remember that "God has not left himself without a witness in our spirits" and in our lives.

5. Howard Thurman, *Mysticism and the Experience of Love* (Wallingford, PA: Pendle Hill, 1961), 4.

6. *A Farther Appeal to Men of Reason and Religion,* Part I, vol. 28, *The Works of John Wesley,* ed. Albert C. Outler (Grand Rapids, MI: Baker, 1996), 8:106.

7. Martin Luther King, Jr., "The Strength to Love," *A Testament of Hope: The Essential Writings and Speeches of Martin Luther King, Jr.,* ed. James M. Washington (San Francisco: Harper & Row, 1986), 509.

8. Theodore Runyon, *The New Creation: John Wesley's Theology Today* (Nashville: Abingdon Press, 1998), 146–48. In Wesley's theology, it is not only orthodoxy or orthopraxy that are important to the Christian faith but also orthopathy, which Runyon defines broadly as right experience. Runyon also defines orthopathy as right feelings or affections. It should be noted that Wesley's embrace of experience as a valid epistemological source was influenced by the work of John Locke and his emphasis on the empirical sciences. For this discussion of Locke's influence, see Runyon, *New Creation,* 72–74.

9. Howard Thurman, "The Grace of God," *The Growing Edge* (Richmond, IN: Friends United Press, 1956), 74.

10. Sermon 12, "The Witness of Our Own Spirit," *Works of John Wesley,* 5:141.

11. This is from Wesley's *Instructions for Children* as presented in Randy Maddox's *Responsible Grace: John Wesley's Practical Theology* (Nashville: Abingdon Press, 1994), 120; also, for commenary on grace as the power of the Holy Ghost reigning in hearts, see Sermon 9, "The Spirit of Bondage and Adoption," III.1, *Works of John Wesley* 5:106.

12. "Give Me Jesus," *Songs of Zion* (Nashville: Abingdon Press, 1981), 165.

13. *Sisters of the Spirit: Three Black Women's Autobiographies of the Nineteenth Century,* ed. William L. Andrews (Bloomington: Indiana University Press, 1986), 15.

14. With this fourfold understanding of the forms of grace, I am influenced by Wesley, who primarily discusses preventing, justifying, and sanctifying grace as keys for understanding the process of salvation. Albert Outler confirms this in his introduction to *John Wesley* but also keenly identifies sacramental grace or what Wesley calls "means of grace," as another aspect of the powerful work and experience of the Spirit. For two places where Wesley distinguishes the types of grace, see *Journal, November 1, 1739–September 3, 1741, John Wesley,* 365, and Sermon 16, "The Means of Grace," II.1, *Works of John Wesley* 5:187; cf. *John Wesley,* 33.

15. Howard Thurman, *Disciplines of the Spirit* (Richmond, IN: Friends United Press, 1963), 87.

16. According to Wesley, this type of grace is called "preventing grace" or prevenient grace. In Wesley's metaphorical image of salvation as a house, prevenient grace is the porch, the first step of salvation through the action of the Holy Spirit. See Runyon, *New Creation*, 27.

17. In a discussion about dispensations of grace in his eighteenth-century sermon, "On Faith," Wesley asserts that there is a "small degree of light" given to "heathens." Sermon 106, "On Faith," 2–3, I.4, *Works of John Wesley* 7:195–97.

18. Thurman, *Inward Journey*, 129; on God's gracious initiative, see Wesley's Sermon 85, "On Working Out Our Own Salvation," III.3, *Works of John Wesley* 6:511–12. Cf. Runyon, *New Creation*, 28.

19. James Weldon Johnson, "The Creation," *God's Trombones: Seven Negro Sermons in Verse* (New York: Penguin, 1927), 20.

20. King, "A Christmas Sermon on Peace," *A Testament of Hope: The Essential Writings and Speeches of Martin Luther King, Jr.*, ed. James M. Washington (San Francisco: Harper & Row, 1986), 255.

21. Wesley's Sermon 85, "On Working Out Our Own Salvation," III. 4, *Works of John Wesley* 6:511–12.

22. The human conscience is a "supernatural endowment" from God in Wesleyan thought, further accenting the point that no one is unaffected by divine grace. Sermon 105, "On Conscience," I.5, *Works of John Wesley* 7:187–88; cf. Runyon, *New Creation*, 32. For more on preventing grace, see "Scripture Way of Salvation," I.1–2, *John Wesley*, 273.

23. Johnson, *God's Trombones*, 43.

24. Thurman, "The Grace of God," *The Growing Edge*, 76.

25. Sermon 16, "The Means of Grace," *Works of John Wesley* 5:189.

26. Runyon, *New Creation*, 81. If one is "born again" or regenerated, one is "being inwardly changed by the almighty operation of the Spirit of God." This is from Wesley's *Doctrine of Original Sin* as quoted in Maddox, *Responsible Grace*, 159.

27. I am influenced by John Wesley, who speaks of faith in terms of senses. That faith "is with regard to the spiritual world what sense is with regard to the natural. It is the spiritual sensation of every soul that is born of God." Faith is "the eye of the new-born soul" to see God. It is the "ear of the soul" to hear God. It is the "palate of the soul" to taste God and even the world to come. It is the "feeling of the soul" through which one feels the existence, presence, and love of God in his or her heart. See his *An Earnest Appeal to Men of Reason and Religion*, *John Wesley*, 386–87. For another discussion of how Wesley connects the Christian life with the senses, see his Sermon 19, "The Great Privilege of Those That Are Born of God," I.3–10, *Works of John Wesley* 5:224–227. Wesley also spoke of faith as "medicine" that heals human sickness; thus the Spirit can be viewed as a Physician through the work of divine grace. For this perspective, see Sermon 17, "Circumcision of the Heart," I.5, *Works* 5:205.

28. Wesley, "Scripture Way of Salvation," *John Wesley*, 276.

29. Thurman, *Inward Journey*, 133.

30. For the account of this story about Mother Pollard, see "The Strength to Love," *A Testament of Hope*, 517.

31. Historically, the tradition of testimony has played a significant role in the black church. For further insight into African Americans and testimony, see Thomas Hoyt, "Testimony," *Practicing Our Faith*, ed. Dorothy Bass (San Francisco: Jossey-Bass Publishers, 1997), 91–103. For testimony in relation to the struggle of black women, preaching, and ordination, see *This Is My Story: Testimonies and Sermons of Black Women in Ministry*, ed. Cleophus J. LaRue (Louisville: Westminster John Knox, 2005); and Teresa Fry Brown, *Weary Throats and New Songs: Black Women Proclaiming God's Word* (Nashville: Abingdon, 2003). For more on testimony in general, see Tom Long's *Testimony: Talking Ourselves into Being Christian* (San Francisco: Jossey-Bass, 2004), and for more about testimony in relation to preaching, see Anna Carter Florence, *Preaching as Testimony* (Louisville: Westminster John Knox, 2007).

32. Thomas Hoyt Jr., "Testimony," *Practicing Our Faith*, ed. Dorothy Bass (San Francisco: Jossey-Bass Publishers, 1997), 91.

33. Sermon 18, "The Marks of the New Birth," I.1–3, *Works of John Wesley* 5:213; cf. Maddox, *Responsible Grace*, 127.

34. *Doctrines and Discipline in the Minutes of the Conferences, 1744–47, John Wesley*, 137. For Wesley, this sure confidence, or assurance, through the witness of the Spirit is one of the traits that differentiate between an "altogether Christian" and "an almost Christian." See Sermon 2, "An Almost Christian," *Works of John Wesley* 5:17–25.

35. "Aldersgate Experience," *John Wesley*, 66.

36. Andrews, *Sisters of the Spirit*, 180.

37. Hoyt, "Testimony," 95.

38. Sermon 10, "Witness of the Spirit, Discourse I," I.8, *Works of John Wesley* 5:115.

39. Ibid., I.7.

40. A person is so sure of the testimony that "while it is present to the soul he can no more doubt the reality of his sonship than he can doubt of the shining of the sun while he stands in the full blaze of his beams." See ibid., I.11–12.

41. Ibid., I.11–12.

42. In a letter to one of his theological opponents, Wesley writes: "We affirm that inspiration of God's Holy Spirit whereby he fills you with righteousness, peace, and joy, with love to him and to all people. And we believe it cannot be, in the nature of things, that a person should be filled with this peace and joy and love . . . without perceiving it. . . . This is . . . the main doctrine of the Methodists." Letter to "John Smith" (30 Dec. 1745) as quoted in Maddox, *Responsible Grace*, 128.

43. Sermon 11, "Witness of the Spirit, Discourse II," *John Wesley*, 209–20. Galatians 5:22–23 notes the fruit of the Spirit to be love, joy, peace, patience, kindness, generosity, faithfulness, gentleness, and self-control.

44. Runyon, *New Creation*, 82.

45. This is what Wesley preaches in Sermon 12, "The Witness of Our Own Spirit," *Works of John Wesley* 5:141. Because of the influence of Eastern thought, Wesley

viewed salvation as therapeutic in that it was the healing of a sin-diseased nature, and thus it entailed a process of moving closer to God, including the sanctification process of recovery of the image of God in one's life. For this discussion, see Maddox, *Responsible Grace*, 22, 67, 145.

46. *Letter to a Roman Catholic, John Wesley,* 495. Cf. Sermon 138, "On Grieving the Holy Spirit," *Works of John Wesley,* 7:486.

47. Thurman, "The Grace of God," *The Growing Edge,* 76.

48. Randy Maddox, *Responsible Grace: John Wesley's Practical Theology* (Nashville: Abingdon, 1994), 179.

49. Andrews, *Sisters of the Spirit,* 30.

50. Sermon 10, "Witness of the Spirit, Discourse I," II.12, *Works of John Wesley* 5:122.

51. Thurman, *Mysticism and the Experience of Love,* 5.

52. Thurman, "Grace of God," *The Growing Edge,* 73. In this same sermon, he also says, "Every kind act, every tender movement of the heart, every gracious deed, becomes a sacrament of the living God." See p. 76.

53. King, "The Drum Major Instinct," *A Testament of Hope,* 265.

54. *John Wesley,* ed. Albert Outler (New York: Oxford University Press, 1964), 28. Wesley's theological mantra was the Galatians verse "faith worketh by love."

55. "Of Salvation of Mankind," *John Wesley,* 128; "The Law Established by Faith; Discourse II," II.1, *John Wesley,* 226. In Wesley's theology, good works representative of sanctification are classified as "works of piety" (that is, prayer, Lord's Supper, scripture reading, fasting) and "works of mercy" (feeding the hungry, clothing the naked, visiting prisoners and the sick). See "Scripture Way of Salvation," III.9–10, *John Wesley,* 280.

56. See "Wesleyan Spirituality and Faith Development: Working Group Paper," in *The Future of Methodist Theological Traditions,* ed. M. Douglas Meeks (Nashville: Abingdon Press, 1985), 195–96.

57. King, "I See the Promised Land," *A Testament of Hope,* 279.

58. Theodore Runyon, "Introduction: Wesley and the Theologies of Liberation," in *Sanctification and Liberation: Liberation Theologies in Light of the Wesleyan Tradition,* ed. Runyon (Nashville: Abingdon Press, 1981), 34. For more about the connections between Wesley's idea of sanctification and social liberation, see the entirety of this book.

59. Katie Geneva Cannon, "Transformative Grace," *Feminist and Womanist Essays in Reformed Dogmatics,* eds. Amy Plantinga Pauw and Serene Jones (Louisville: Westminster John Knox, 2006), 139.

60. "Law Established by Faith, Discourse II," II.1, *John Wesley,* 227. In fact, love is the primal affection or temper for Wesley. See Maddox, 69.

61. James H. Evans Jr., *We Have Been Believers: An African-American Systematic Theology* (Minneapolis: Fortress, 1992), 125.

62. Sermon 138, "On Grieving the Holy Spirit," *Works of John Wesley,* 7:487.

63. Wesley called for a "catholic or universal love" of humankind, regardless of divergent belief systems, in "Catholic Spirit," *John Wesley,* 93; cf. *A Plain Account of Genuine Christianity, John Wesley,* 184–85.

64. See Sermon 16, "The Means of Grace," *Works of John Wesley* 5:185–201.

65. Wesley defined means of grace as "outward signs, words, or actions, ordained of God, and appointed for this end, to be the ordinary channels whereby he might convey to men, preventing, justifying, or sanctifying grace." He believed that the chief means are public or private prayer; "searching the Scriptures," which implies reading, hearing, and meditating on them (includes preaching); and receiving the Lord's Supper. Notice that he does not mention baptism. These are the "instituted" means of grace. But he also speaks of "provisional" means of grace, such as the bands, class meetings, and societies. See Sermon 16, "The Means of Grace," II.1, *Works of John Wesley* 5:185–201; see "Wesleyan Spirituality and Faith Development," 195; Maddox, *Responsible Grace*, 201–15; Runyon, *New Creation*, 107–28.

66. Sermon 16, "Means of Grace," II.3. *Works of John Wesley* 5.

67. See James Forbes, *The Holy Spirit and Preaching*, 21. He also writes, "To preach today in Jesus' name, and to do so with power, still requires the enabling presence of the Holy Spirit....There are many preachers who are waiting for and depending on the power from beyond themselves—and there are many who are aware that if that power is not present, the preaching will not be effective" (101).

68. Lee, *Sisters of the Spirit*, 48.

69. James Harris, *Preaching Liberation* (Minneapolis: Fortress Press, 1995), 34–35. Because the Word is the responsibility of God, Tom Troeger urges imaginative preachers, who engage in creative multimedia strategies for proclamation, to "pray for the Spirit," for the Spirit must be present if there is to be fruitful communication. Troeger also writes that "our strategies find their deepest origins not in human calculation but in prayer. The finest eloquence, the cleverest presentation, the liveliest and most up-to-date form of communication will only bear fruit if the Spirit is present." See Troeger, *Ten Strategies for Preaching in a Multi-Media Culture* (Nashville: Abingdon Press, 1996), 8, 120. In similar fashion, William Willimon writes, "Faithful sermons require the presence of the Holy Spirit to make them work." See his *Proclamation and Theology* (Nashville: Abingdon Press, 2005), 83.

70. Charles Spurgeon, *Second Series of Lectures to my Students: Addresses Delivered to the Students of the Pastors' College, Metropolitan Tabernacle* (London: Passmore and Alabaster, 1906), 179. Spurgeon was not alone in his thinking. According to H. Grady Davis, salvation is the functional form of proclamation. He writes, "It has pleased God, who somehow unaccountably loves mankind, to save men, to save the race from self-destruction if men will let themselves be saved, or, if they will not, still to save out of the destruction as many as will acknowledge and trust him." See Henry Grady Davis, *The Design for Preaching* (Philadelphia: Muhlenberg Press, 1958), 103. Even John Broadus and Phillips Brooks realize the ultimate purpose of preaching is salvation. Brooks claims the preacher's task is to bring the hearers to Christ so that they may find him and he save them. Broadus says the purpose of preaching is to spread the good tidings of salvation through Jesus Christ. See Phillips Brooks, *Lectures on Preaching* (New York: Dutton, 1877; reprint, New York: Seabury, 1964), 21, 32, 128. See John A. Broadus, *On the Preparation and Delivery of Sermons* (New York: Sheldon, 1870; reprint, New York: Harper and Bros., 1926), 3, 6.

71. Henry Mitchell, *Celebration and Experience in Preaching* (Nashville: Abingdon, 1990), 25. William Turner notes that the Spirit "imports faith" into people's hearts. See William Turner, "Preaching the Spirit: The Liberation of Preaching," paper presented at the annual meeting of the Academy of Homiletics, Williamsburg, VA, 2 December 2005, 182.

72. Herbert H. Farmer, *The Servant of the Word* (New York: Scribner, 1942), 29–31.

73. For one approach to the relationship between preaching and testimony, see Anna Carter Florence's *Preaching as Testimony* (Louisville: Westminster John Knox, 2007).

74. Lee, *Sisters of the Spirit*, 29.

75. King, "The Strength to Love," 502.

76. Ibid., 501.

77. James Earl Massey, *Designing the Sermon: Order and Movement in Preaching* (Nashville: Abingdon Press, 1980), 16.

78. Forbes, *Holy Spirit and Preaching*, 63, 78.

79. Jean-Jacque von Allmen, *Preaching and Congregation*, trans. B. L. Nicholas (London: Lutterworth Press, 1962), 31.

80. Mitchell, *Celebration and Experience in Preaching*, 147.

81. Paul Wilson believes that the theological structure of the four pages of a sermon "assists the Holy Spirit in bringing forth hope." See Wilson, The *Four Pages of a Sermon: A Guide to Biblical Preaching* (Nashville: Abingdon Press, 1999), 260.

82. Mitchell, *Celebration and Experience*, 148; cf. Mitchell, *Black Preaching*, 123, 126–27.

83. This homiletical collaboration may be described as "theonomic reciprocity," which describes human and divine agency in preaching as a reciprocal relationship, with priority given to the divine. Rudolf Bohren, who espouses this nomenclature, declares,

The Spirit becomes the speech teacher of the disciple, and the disciple the mouthpiece of the Spirit. It is not the disciple who speaks, but the Spirit. But the Spirit needs the mouth of the disciple, and the disciple himself must speak. If the disciple brings the Spirit into language, the Spirit also helps the disciple to speak. The Spirit gives not only the word but its articulation. The Spirit determines not only the word's advent and presence but also its future. For preaching this means first of all that the preacher receives the word from the Holy Spirit.

See "Rudolf Bohren: The Spirit as Giver and Gift of the Word," in *Theories of Preaching: Selected Readings in the Homiletical Tradition*, ed. Richard Lischer (Durham, NC: Labyrinth Press, 1987), 327–28. Fred Craddock states, "Any work of the Holy Spirit which relieves me of my work and responsibility is plainly false." See his *Preaching* (Nashville: Abingdon Press, 1985), 30.

4. The Spirit of Unity

1. For the story of Thurman's grandmother, see Howard Thurman, *Jesus and the Disinherited* (Nashville: Abingdon Press, 1949), 30, 31. For Weems's truthful essay about how African Americans negotiate biblical readings, see Renita J. Weems, "Reading *Her Way* through the Struggle: African American Women and the Bible," *Stony the Road We Trod: African American Biblical Interpretation*, ed. Cain Hope Felder (Minneapolis: Fortress, 1991), 57–77. Paul's mixed reception among African Americans is also detailed in Abraham Smith's "Paul and African American Biblical Interpretation," in *True to Our Native Land: An African American New Testament Commentary*, eds. Brain K. Blount, Cain Hope Felder, Clarice J. Martin, and Emerson B. Powery (Minneapolis: Fortress, 2007), 31–42.

2. See her essay "Paul and the African American Community," *Embracing the Spirit: Womanist Perspectives on Hope, Salvation, and Transformation*, ed. Emilie M. Townes (Maryknoll, NY: Orbis, 1997), 212–33.

3. Gordon D. Fee, *God's Empowering Presence: The Holy Spirit in the Letters of Paul* (Peabody, MA: Hendrickson, 1994), 84.

4. For more background information on the social divisions within the city of Corinth and the Corinthian church, see Gordon Fee, *The First Epistle to the Corinthians* (Grand Rapids, MI: Eerdmans, 1987); Wayne Meeks, *The First Urban Christians: The Social World of Apostle Paul* (New Haven: Yale University Press, 1983); and Gerd Theissen, *The Social Setting of Pauline Christianity* (Edinburgh: T & T Clark, 1982).

5. Richard B. Hays, *First Corinthians: Interpretation, A Bible Commentary for Teaching and Preaching* (Louisville: John Knox, 1997), 24.

6. Margaret Mitchell, *Paul and the Rhetoric of Reconciliation: An Exegetical Investigation of the Language and Composition of 1 Corinthians* (Louisville: Westminster John Knox, 1991), 1.

7. Ibid., 2, 66–67, 111. Mitchell notes that contrary to her opinion, historically, biblical scholars have argued that only chapters 1–4 are about factionalism.

8. Ibid., 112.

9. Hays, *First Corinthians*, 1.

10. Victor Furnish, *The Theology of the First Letter to the Corinthians* (Cambridge: Cambridge University Press, 1999), 14; cf. Fee, *First Epistle to the Corinthians*, 6–12. Fee boldly declares, "The letter is basically the apostle Paul vis-à-vis the whole Corinthian congregation."

11. Fee, *First Epistle*, 6.

12. Hays, *First Corinthians*, 24.

13. Theissen, *The Social Setting of Pauline Christianity* (Edinburgh: T & T Clark, 1982), 54.

14. Ibid., 13–14, 28, 31, 40, 42, 53, 104, 139.

15. Fee, *God's Empowering Presence*, 83. Meeks calls the Corinthians' view a "realized eschatology" that is contrary to Paul's "futurist eschatology." See Meeks, *The First Urban Christians*, 179.

16. Dale B. Martin, *The Corinthian Body* (New Haven: Yale University Press, 1995), 87.

17. Ibid., 96, 103.

18. Hays, *First Corinthians*, 18.

19. Fee, *God's Empowering Presence*, 84.

20. M. Mitchell, *Paul and the Rhetoric of Reconciliation*, 300.

21. Victor Furnish, "Theology in 1 Corinthians," *Pauline Theology*, vol. 2, *1 & 2 Corinthians*, ed. David M. Hay (Minneapolis: Fortress, 1993), 62.

22. M. Mitchell, *Paul and the Rhetoric of Reconciliation*, 211.

23. Fee, *First Epistle*, 230.

24. Theissen, *The Social Setting of Pauline Christianity*, 151–53.

25. Hays, *First Corinthians*, 194.

26. Ibid., 196–99.

27. Ibid., 199.

28. Furnish, *Theology of the First Letter*, 95.

29. Hays, *First Corinthians*, 8–11.

30. Howard Thurman, *The Search for Common Ground: An Inquiry into the Basis of Man's Experience of Community* (Richmond, IN: Friends United, 1986), 55.

31. Howard Thurman, *Disciplines of the Spirit* (Richmond, IN: Friends United, 1963), 104; cf. *The Search for Common Ground*, 28. Thurman believes there is even a unity between humanity and nature, which is why he says in *The Search for Common Ground,* "Man cannot long separate himself from nature without withering as a cut rose in a vase" (83–84).

32. Fee, *God's Empowering Presence*, 896.

33. Ibid., 849. Cf. N. T. Wright, *What Saint Paul Really Said: Was Paul of Tarsus the Real Founder of Christianity?* (Grand Rapids, MI: Eerdmans, 1997), 125.

34. Dale Martin writes that Paul uses rhetoric to decry rhetoric; thus he actually "stands in a great tradition of rhetorical disavowals of rhetorical activity." Martin also notes that it would have been impossible for an urban person like Paul to avoid exposure to a great deal of rhetoric. See Martin, *The Corinthian Body*, 45–55.

35. Fee, *First Epistle*, 90.

36. Anthony Thiselton, *The First Epistle to the Corinthians: A Commentary on the Greek Text* (Grand Rapids, MI: Eerdmans, 2000), 212.

37. Hays, *First Corinthians*, 45.

38. Fee, *First Epistle*, 100.

39. Ibid., 99.

40. Thiselton, *First Epistle to the Corinthians*, 224.

41. Fee, *First Epistle,* 101.

42. J. Paul Sampley, *Walking Between the Times: Paul's Moral Reasoning* (Minneapolis: Fortress, 1991), 88.

43. Furnish, "Theology in 1 Corinthians," 67.

44. Fee, *First Epistle*, 50.

45. Hays, *First Corinthians*, 32; Fee, "Theology of 1 Corinthians," 42.

46. Hays, *First Corinthians*, 245.

47. Wolfgang Schrage quoted by Hays, *First Corinthians*, 47, 49.

48. Thiselton, *First Epistle to the Corinthians*, 176.

49. Fee, *First Epistle*, 66.

50. James D. G. Dunn, *The Theology of Paul the Apostle* (Grand Rapids. MI: Eerdmans, 1998), 56, 61.

51. Fee, *First Epistle*, 264.

52. John A. T. Robinson, *The Body: A Study in Pauline Theology* (London: SCM, 1966), 29.

53. Howard Thurman, *Creative Encounter: An Interpretation of Religion and Social Witness* (New York: Harper and Bros., 1954), 123–24.

54. Martin Luther King, Jr., "The American Dream," *A Testament of Hope: Essential Writings and Speeches of Martin Luther King, Jr.*, ed. James Washington (San Francisco: Harper & Row, 1986), 210.

55. Martin, *The Corinthian Body*, 175.

56. Ibid.

57. Hays, *First Corinthians*, 102.

58. Charles H. Talbert, *Reading Corinthians: A Literary and Theological Commentary on 1 Corinthians* (New York: Crossroad, 1987), 32.

59. Fee, *First Epistle*, 250–51.

60. Ibid., 264.

61. Talbert, *Reading Corinthians*, 36.

62. Hays, *First Corinthians*, 108. Likewise, Pheme Perkins notes, "Belonging to the body of Christ has concrete implications for actions that Christians may engage in with their own bodies." See Perkins, "Paul and Ethics," *Interpretation* 38, no. 3 (1984): 271.

63. James H. Evans, *We Have Been Believers: An African-American Systematic Theology* (Minneapolis: Fortress Press, 1992), 135.

64. Zora Neale Hurston, *Sanctified Church* (Berkeley: Turtle Island, 1983), 91.

65. Thiselton, *First Epistle to the Corinthians*, 316.

66. M. Mitchell, *Paul and the Rhetoric of Reconciliation*, 104.

67. Thiselton, *First Epistle to the Corinthians*, 317.

68. Fee, *First Epistle*, 146–47.

69. Thiselton, *First Epistle to the Corinthians*, 317–18.

70. Thurman, *Disciplines of the Spirit*, 113.

71. This question, "Do you not know that . . . ?" is a rhetorical device used ten times in 1 Corinthians (see 5:6; 6:2, 3, 9, 15, 16, 19; 9:13, 24). Thiselton notes that this question "indicates both Paul's intensity of feeling (surely you know *this!*) and his belief that the principle at issue is axiomatic for the Christian and should not have escaped attention as a cardinal element in the community's thinking." See Thiselton, *First Epistle to the Corinthians*, 316.

72. Fee, *First Epistle*, 149.

73. Thiselton, *First Epistle to the Corinthians*, 466.

74. Ralph Martin, *The Spirit and the Congregation: Studies in 1 Corinthians 12–15* (Grand Rapids, MI: Eerdmans, 1984), 8.

75. Dunn, *Theology of Paul the Apostle*, 53.

76. Sampley, 37.

77. Hays, *First Corinthians*, 182. The spiritual problem is almost certainly the abuse of the gift of tongues (12:10, 28; 14:2, 4, , 6, 13, 18, 23, 27, 39; 13:8, 14:22, 26). For more about this high probability, see Fee, *First Epistle*, 571.

78. Meeks, 90.

79. "Give Me Jesus," *Songs of Zion* (Nashville: Abingdon Press, 1981), 165.

80. Hays, *First Corinthians*, 208.

81. Ibid., 218. James Dunn implicitly agrees with this when he says, "Spiritless Christian would have been a contradiction in terms for Paul" because by receiving the Spirit one becomes a Christian. See Dunn, *Theology of Paul*, 423.

82. Fee, *First Epistle*, 582.

83. M. Mitchell, *Paul and the Rhetoric of Reconciliation*, 267–68.

84. Talbert, *Reading Corinthians*, 82.

85. R. Martin, *The Spirit and the Congregation*, 15.

86. D. Martin, *Corinthian Body*, 87.

87. Sampley, 43.

88. Dunn, *Theology of Paul*, 553–59.

89. R. Martin, *The Spirit and the Congregation*, 15. Thiselton concurs when he writes, "Contextually and theologically the unity constitutes the major emphasis in vv. 4–11, since 'building' provides the cohesive goal and purpose of the gifts, whatever their variety." See Thiselton, *First Epistle to the Corinthians*, 928.

90. Talbert, *Reading Corinthians*, 84.

91. George Montague, *The Holy Spirit: Growth of a Biblical Tradition, A Commentary on the Principal Texts of the Old and New Testaments* (New York: Paulist Press, 1976), 144, 156.

92. See M. Mitchell, *Paul and the Rhetoric of Reconciliation*, 68–83, 119, 121, 157–64; D. Martin, *The Corinthian Body*, 38–68, 87–103.

93. M. Mitchell, *Paul and the Rhetoric of Reconciliation*, 161.

94. D. Martin, *The Corinthian Body*, 94.

95. Dunn, *Jesus and the Spirit*, 265.

96. R. Martin, *The Spirit and the Congregation*, 12; Dunn, *Jesus and Spirit*, 263.

97. Thurman, *The Search for Common Ground*, 3–4.

98. Ibid., 104. Elsewhere in this same book, Thurman states, "Mutual interdependence is characteristic of all of life. The need to care for and the need to be cared for is another expression of the same basic idea." See p. 3.

99. M. Mitchell, *Paul and the Rhetoric of Reconciliation*, 121; Cf. R. Martin, *The Spirit and the Congregation*, 25–30.

100. Martin Luther King, Jr., "A Christmas Sermon on Peace," *A Testament of Hope*, 254.

101. M. Mitchell, *Paul and the Rhetoric of Reconciliation*, 161; cf. n. 624, 168.

102. R. Martin, *The Spirit and the Congregation*, 50.

103. Fee, *First Epistle*, 572.

104. For more about the high status ascribed to the esoteric language of tongues, see D. Martin, *The Corinthian Body*, 87–103.

105. Hays, *First Corinthians*, 221.

106. Montague, *The Holy Spirit*, 162.

107. Hays, *First Corinthians*, 232.

108. Ibid., 227.

109. Fee, *First Epistle*, 248.

110. King, "A Christmas Sermon on Peace," *A Testament of Hope*, 256–57.

111. Hays, *First Corinthians*, 222.

112. Fee, *First Epistle*, 627.

113. Ibid., 627, n. 10.

114. Ibid., 628.

115. Furnish, "Theology in 1 Corinthians," 83.

116. It would appear from Paul's letter that the gift of tongues was a major problem in this community; thus Paul's focus on it in chapter 14 in his discussion about the practice of the gifts in the congregation. Ralph Martin asserts that the ultimate goal of Paul in chapters 12–14 is to "lower the assessment of glossolalia among the Corinthians." See R. Martin, *The Spirit and the Congregation*, 96.

117. Fee, *First Epistle*, 571.

118. Thiselton, *First Epistle to the Corinthians*, 1074. The entire theme of building up the church looms in Paul's mind as shown in *oikodomein* (to build up) and *oikodome* (upbuilding, edification), between them occurring seven times in chapter 14. Through her study of Pauline thought, Pheme Perkins argues that "'other-regarding' attitudes are fundamental to the Christian life. Christians are always willing to subject their concerns to the good of the neighbor." See Perkins, "Paul and Ethics," 279.

119. Hays, *First Corinthians*, 242.

120. Thurman, *Creative Encounter*, 139. The divided nature of the Church in the United States is also discussed in Amos Jones Jr., *Paul's Message of Freedom: What Does It Mean to the Black Church?* (Valley Forge, PA: Judson, 1984), 174–202.

121. Thomas G. Long, *The Witness of Preaching* (Louisville: Westminster John Knox, 1989), 10.

122. Paul Scott Wilson argues that every sermon should address one need in the congregation as a way of aiming for sermon unity. Cleo LaRue declares that preachers, in their sermons, should take into account the various "domains of concrete experience" rooted in the lives of people. Both scholars reveal a desire for contextually relevant sermons. See Wilson, *The Four Pages of a Sermon: A Guide to Biblical Preaching* (Nashville: Abingdon, 1999), 48; see LaRue, *The Heart of Black Preaching* (Louisville: Westminster John Knox, 2000), 20–27.

123. In this scriptural context, the Greek word for "foolishness" is *mōria*, from which we get the English word "moron," indicating the craziness of the gospel message and implying the foolish state of the messenger.

124. Teresa Fry Brown, *Weary Throats and New Songs: Black Women Proclaiming God's Word* (Nashville: Abingdon Press, 2003), 54.

125. Forbes, *Holy Spirit and Preaching*, 82.

126. See H. Mitchell, *Black Preaching*, 14, 18, 66, 104.

127. Other scholars who strive for attentive cultural and congregational analysis in order to connect with a listening community are Nora Tubbs Tisdale, James Nieman,

and Thomas Rogers. See Tisdale, *Preaching as Local Theology and Folk Art* (Minneapolis: Fortress, 1997) and Nieman and Rogers, *Preaching to Every Pew: Cross-Cultural Strategies* (Minneapolis: Fortress, 2001).

128. Fred Craddock, *Preaching* (Nashville: Abingdon Press, 1985), 25. For more about the role of listeners in preaching, see pp. 84–98. Also, see his *As One Without Authority* (Nashville: Abingdon Press, 1979) for an inductive sermon method that is geared towards the listener's participation.

129. Evans Crawford, *The Hum: Call and Response in African American Preaching* (Nashville: Abingdon, 1995), 39.

130. Ibid., 39, 42. Teresa Fry Brown lists many preaching clichés that are part of call and response in her book *Weary Throats and New Songs*, 168–69. It is important to note that call and response is not just "talk back" but "feel back" (body language, gestures). Cf. Brown, 166. Warren Stewart quotes Bishop Joseph Johnson from his book *Proclamation Theology*, who says:

> The Black preacher's style which included the pattern of call and response—a dialogue between preacher and congregation, who are, if you please, a trilogy in which the Holy Spirit moves the Black preacher, and the Black preacher speaks to the congregation and the congregation responds with, "Amen," "That's Right," "Tell it like it is," "Go ahead Son," "Let the Spirit have its way"—what takes place in the true Black worship is not superstition, but rather a real, natural dialogue.

See Stewart, *Interpreting God's Word in Black Preaching*, 63.

131. Ibid., 15, 16, 37.

132. H. Mitchell, *Black Preaching*, 108.

133. Ibid.

134. Paule Marshall, *Praisesong for the Widow* (New York: Putnam, 1983), 202.

135. Thurman, *Disciplines of the Spirit*, 123. In his *Luminous Darkness*, Thurman says that "The setting for hate often begins in situations where there are contacts without fellowship. That is, contacts that are devoid of the simple overtones of warmth, fellow-feeling, and genuineness." See *Luminous Darkness*, 38–39.

136. Boykin Sanders, "1 Corinthians," *True to Our Native Land: An African American New Testament Commentary*, eds. Brian K. Blount, Cain Hope Felder, Clarice J. Martin, and Emerson B. Powery (Minneapolis: Fortress, 2007), 297.

137. King, "An Experiment in Love," *A Testament of Hope*, 20.

5. The Spirit of Fellowship

1. Gerhard O. Forde, *Theology Is for Proclamation* (Minneapolis: Fortress, 1990), 2–3.

2. See *Songs of Zion* (Nashville: Abingdon Press, 1981), 83.

3. These words are from a poem by N. Lynne Westfield titled "Simile of In-Hospitality." This poem can be found in Westfield's book *Dear Sisters: A Womanist Practice of Hospitality* (Cleveland: Pilgrim, 2001), 55–56.

4. See the complete lyrics of the song "I am a Poor Wayfaring Stranger" on www.cyberhymnal.org.

5. See his autobiographical reflections entitled *Experiences of God*, trans. Margaret Kohl (Philadelphia: Fortress, 1980).

6. For these spirituals, see *Songs of Zion*, 170, 95.

7. Jürgen Moltmann, *Experiences in Theology* (Minneapolis: Fortress, 2000), 310.

8. Jürgen Moltmann, *The Trinity and the Kingdom of God: The Doctrine of God*, trans. Margaret Kohl (London: SCM, 1981), 126.

9. This relational nature of the triune God has led scholars, such as Moltmann, to "develop a social doctrine of the Trinity." For his approach, see his *The Trinity and the Kingdom of God*, 19.

10. Moltmann, *The Church in Power of the Spirit: A Contribution to Messianic Ecclesiology*, trans. Margaret Kohl (Minneapolis: Fortress, 1993), xv.

11. Moltmann, *Experiences in Theology*, 309–10.

12. James Weldon Johnson, *God's Trombones: Seven Negro Sermons in Verse* (New York: Penguin, 1927), 17.

13. Jürgen Moltmann, *The Church in the Power of the Spirit*, 55–56.

14. Ibid., 219. For more about the trinitarian open fellowship of the Holy Spirit, see pp. 217–221.

15. Howard Thurman, *Jesus and the Disinherited* (Nashville: Abingdon Press, 1949), 28–29.

16. Moltmann, *The Way of Jesus Christ: Christology in Messianic Dimensions*, trans. Margaret Kohl (Minneapolis: Fortress, 1993), 78, 94.

17. Ibid., 73.

18. Thurman, *Jesus and the Disinherited*, 89.

19. Thurman, "The Greatest of These," *The Growing Edge*, 27.

20. Arthur Sutherland, *I Was a Stranger: A Christian Theology of Hospitality* (Nashville: Abingdon Press, 2006), xviii.

21. Martin Luther King, Jr., "The Drum Major Instinct," *A Testament of Hope: The Essential Writing and Speeches of Martin Luther King, Jr.*, ed. James M. Washington (San Francisco: Harper & Row, 1986), 266.

22. Martin Luther King, Jr., "The Experiment of Love," *A Testament of Hope: The Essential Writing and Speeches of Martin Luther King, Jr.*, ed. James M. Washington (San Francisco: Harper & Row, 1986), 20.

23. Howard Thurman, *The Centering Moment* (New York: Harper & Row, 1969), 21.

24. Evans, *We Have Been Believers: An African-American Systematic Theology* (Minneapolis: Fortress, 1992), 136.

25. Moltmann, *Church in the Power of the Spirit*, 13, 36–37.

26. King, "Our God Is Marching On!" *A Testament of Hope*, 227.

27. Moltmann, *Church in the Power of the Spirit*, 295–96.

28. Ibid., 295, 303–7.

29. Thurman, *Jesus and Disinherited*, 12.

30. King, "A Time to Break Silence," *A Testament of Hope*, 234.

31. "De Gospel Train," *Songs of Zion*, 116.

32. Peter Paris, *The Spirituality of African Peoples: The Search for a Common*

Moral Discourse (Minneapolis: Fortress, 1995), 137. Paris claims that beneficence, or hospitality, is a moral virtue of Africans and African Americans.

33. Martin Luther King, Jr., "The Drum Major Instinct," 265–66.

34. Moltmann, *Church in the Power of the Spirit,* 278.

35. Thurman, "The Greatest of These," *The Growing Edge,* 28.

36. Moltmann, *Church in the Power of the Spirit,* 234–35.

37. Moltmann, *Theology of Hope: On the Ground and Implications of a Christian Eschatology,* trans. James Leitch (Minneapolis: Fortress, 1993), 22; cf. Richard Bauckham, *The Theology of Jürgen Moltmann* (Edinburgh: T & T Clark, 1995), 38.

38. King, "An Experiment in Love," *A Testament of Hope,* 20.

39. Moltmann, *Church in the Power of the Spirit,* 15.

40. Evans, *We Have Been Believers,* 137.

41. King, "A Time To Break Silence," 234.

42. Riggins R. Earl Jr., "Under Their Own Vine and Fig Tree: The Ethics of Social and Spiritual Hospitality in Black Church Worship," *Journal for the Interdenominational Theological Center* 14/2 (1987): 193. Similarly, Moltmann writes, "Pentecostal and charismatic experiences of the Spirit become spiritualistically insubstantial and illusory without the personal and political discipleship of Jesus." See his *Spirit of Life,* 121.

43. Moltmann, *The Church in the Power of the Spirit,* 284–87.

44. Ibid., 288.

45. Ibid., 65.

46. Howard Thurman, *Luminous Darkness: A Personal Interpretation of the Anatomy of Segregation and the Ground of Hope* (New York: Harper & Row, 1965), 112–13.

47. Moltmann, *Spirit of Life: A Universal Affirmation,* trans. Margaret Kohl (Minneapolis: Fortress, 1994), 24.

48. Thurman, *The Search for Common Ground: An Inquiry into the Basis of Man's Experience of Community* (Richmond, IN: Friends United, 1986), 29.

49. For an explicit case of this emphasis, see Moltmann's *The Source of Life: The Holy Spirit and the Theology of Life* (Minneapolis: Fortress, 1997). Cf. Moltmann, *The Spirit of Life,* 82.

50. Moltmann, *Spirit of Life,* xi.

51. Moltmann, *The Source of Life,* 11.

52. Moltmann, *Church in the Power of the Spirit,* 192.

53. Ibid., 97–98.

54. King, "A Time to Break Silence," 241.

55. Moltmann, *Source of Life,* 94.

56. Moltmann, *God in Creation,* 17. Thurman echoes this sentiment when he speaks of the "ground of community in the integrity of life itself" (A *Search for Common Ground,* 28).

57. Thomas G. Long, *The Witness of Preaching* (Louisville: Westminster John Knox, 1989), 172.

58. Arthur Van Seters, *Preaching and Ethics* (St. Louis: Chalice, 2004), 132.

59. David Buttrick states that "the Word of preaching (by the Spirit) sets us free to

respond to the Word (by the Spirit)." See *Homiletic: Moves and Structures* (Philadelphia: Fortress, 1987), 454.

60. Paul Wilson, *Imagination of the Heart: New Understandings in Preaching* (Nashville: Abingdon Press, 1988), 31.

61. Forbes, *The Holy Spirit and Preaching* (Nashville: Abingdon Press, 1989), 48.

62. James Harris, *Preaching Liberation* (Minneapolis: Fortress, 1995), 35.

63. Van Seters, *Preaching and Ethics*, 124. In his paradigm for preaching ethics, Van Seters maintains a cross-centeredness, with Jesus Christ as the "luminous center" of his ethical web of reflection (faith, moral character, norms, situation and context, authority), but by keeping ethics cross-centered, he keeps ethics Spirit-centered because the Spirit is of Jesus Christ. See Van Seters, *Preaching and Ethics*, 14, 53.

64. Sutherland, *I Was a Stranger*, 83. A wonderful example of the relationship between hospitality and preaching can be found in the work of Kathy Black, who focuses on the issue of disability. In *A Healing Homiletic: Preaching and Disability* (Nashville: Abingdon Press, 1996), she says, "God wills the well-being that is possible for each one of us." See p. 36.

65. Christine M. Smith, *Preaching as Weeping, Confession, and Resistance: Radical Response to Radical Evil* (Louisville: Westminster John Knox, 1994), 6.

66. Forbes, *Holy Spirit and Preaching*, 43.

67. "Rediscovering Lost Values," in *A Knock at Midnight: Inspiration from the Great Sermons of Rev. Martin Luther King, Jr.*, eds. Clayborne Carson and Peter Holloran (New York: Warner, 1998), 15.

68. For more insight into this idea of "death threat," please see the sermon by Luke A. Powery, "Death Threat," *The Princeton Seminary Bulletin* 28/3 (2007): 244–50.

69. Smith, *Preaching as Weeping, Confession, and Resistance*, 5.

70. William Willimon, *Proclamation and Theology* (Nashville: Abingdon Press, 2005), 94.

71. David Buttrick, *Preaching Jesus Christ: An Exercise in Homiletic Theology* (Philadelphia: Fortress, 1988), 51–53.

72. Forbes, *Holy Spirit and Preaching*, 88, 95.

73. Charles Campbell, *The Word Before the Powers: An Ethic of Preaching* (Louisville: Westminster John Knox, 2002), 43, 46, 69.

6. The Rhetoric of the Spirit through Lament and Celebration

1. Ron Allen says, "God, through the Holy Spirit, is active in all phases of the life of the sermon." See Allen, *Interpreting the Gospel: An Introduction to Preaching* (St. Louis: Chalice, 1998), 71. James Harris declares that the Holy Spirit gives the sermon "form and substance," but he does not elaborate on this idea, though he leads us in the direction for which I am calling. See Harris, *Preaching Liberation* (Minneapolis: Fortress, 1995), 35.

2. David Buttrick, *Homiletic: Moves and Structures* (Philadelphia: Fortress, 1987), 457. Though I disagree with Buttrick because he leaves no room for spiritual discernment in his statement, he does rightly state, "As Paul suggested, the test of the Spirit

in connection with preaching is the edification and upbuilding of Christian community."

3. I borrow this phrase from John Mason Stapleton, who argues that the ingredients of the Spirit's rhetoric are the following: gospel content, passionate expression, artistry of form, and caring for others. Stapleton helps us begin to think about what it means for a sermon to manifest the Spirit. See Stapleton, *Preaching in the Demonstration of the Spirit and Power* (Philadelphia: Fortress, 1988).

4. See Walter Brueggemann, *The Psalms and the Life of Faith*, ed. Patrick D. Miller (Minneapolis: Fortress, 1995), 105, 57.

5. See Campbell, *The Word Before the Powers: An Ethic of Preaching* (Louisville: Westminster John Knox, 2002), 107–10.

6. Emilie Townes, *Breaking the Fine Rain of Death: African American Health Issues and a Womanist Ethic of Care* (New York: Continuum, 1998), 23.

7. See Paul Wilson, *The Four Pages of a Sermon* (Nashville: Abingdon Press, 1999), pp. 73–154, and his overview of trouble in *Preaching and Homiletical Theory* (St. Louis: Chalice Press, 2004), 87–100.

8. Samuel D. Proctor, *The Certain Sound of the Trumpet: Crafting a Sermon of Authority* (Valley Forge, PA: Judson, 1994), 28.

9. LaRue, *The Heart of Black Preaching* (Louisville: Westminster John Knox, 2000), 112. Similarly, Warren Stewart says that God is the point of departure in the hermeneutical process for African American proclamation. See Stewart, *Interpreting God's Word in Black Preaching* (Valley Forge, PA: Judson, 1984), 14–15.

10. Charles Campbell says that truthfulness, anger, patience, and hope are key virtues of any preacher. See *The Word Before the Powers,* 169–88.

11. See James Cone, *The Spirituals and the Blues: An Interpretation* (Maryknoll, NY: Orbis, 1991); Howard Thurman, *Deep River and the Negro Spiritual Speaks of Life and Death* (Richmond, IN: Friends United, 1975); and Cheryl Kirk-Duggan, *Exorcizing Evil: A Womanist Perspective on the Spirituals* (Maryknoll, NY: Orbis, 1997).

12. Barbara A. Holmes, *Joy Unspeakable: Contemplative Practices of the Black Church* (Minneapolis: Fortress, 2004), 75.

13. Albert Raboteau, *A Sorrowful Joy* (New York: Paulist, 2002), 50.

14. William B. McClain, *Come Sunday: The Liturgy of Zion* (Nashville: Abingdon Press, 1990), 13. Cf. *Spirituals and the Blues*.

15. James Cone, *God of the Oppressed* (San Francisco: HarperSanFrancisco, 1975), 19.

16. As noted by Evans Crawford, *The Hum: Call and Response in African American Preaching* (Nashville: Abingdon Press, 1995), 68–69.

17. Harris, *Preaching Liberation*, 52.

18. Crawford, *The Hum*, 69–70.

19. Teresa Fry Brown, *Weary Throats and New Songs: Black Women Proclaiming God's Word* (Nashville: Abingdon Press, 2003), 16. For more about the preaching ministry of black women in the nineteenth and early twentieth century, see Chanta M. Haywood, *Prophesying Daughters: Black Women Preachers and the Word, 1823–1913* (Columbia: University of Missouri Press, 2003).

20. Harold Dean Trulear, "The Sacramentality of Preaching," in *Primary Sources of Liturgical Theology: A Reader*, ed. Dwight W. Vogel (Collegeville, MN: Liturgical, 2000), 266–72.

21. See Wilson, *Preaching and Homiletical Theory*, 98.

22. I thank Art Van Seters for this critical perspective in recognizing that balancing lament and celebration may be premature in certain circumstances. For instance, Rachel refuses to be consoled and only weeps for her children (Matt. 2:18; Jer. 31:15). Rushing to sermonic celebration in the case of Rachel could suppress anguish and lead to Spiritless preaching. On the story of Rachel, see Christopher Morse, *Not Every Spirit: Dogmatics of Christian Disbelief* (Valley Forge, PA: Trinity International, 1994), 9–11. Also, the poetic work of Ann Weems provides helpful insight into human situations of lament. See her *Psalms of Lament* (Louisville: Westminster/John Knox, 1995).

23. For more about the dialectical movement of hurt to joy, death to life in the Psalms, see Walter Brueggemann, *The Psalms and the Life of Faith*, 67–83, and Patrick Miller, "Heaven's Prisoners: The Lament as Christian Prayer," in *Lament*, 19.

24. See Wilson, *Preaching and Homiletical Theory*, 73–100. For antithesis and thesis as part of a sermon method, see Proctor, *The Certain Sound of a Trumpet*, 28, 53–92. For the ethical impulse of exposing and envisioning as sermon movements, see Campbell, *The Word Before the Powers*, 105–27.

25. James F. Kay, "The Word of the Cross at the Turn of the Ages," *Interpretation* 53, no. 1 (1999): 51. Kay also notes that this lens of "old age" and "new age" is "perceived not simply sequentially and not simply spatially, but both at once, as if looking through two lenses *simultaneously*."

26. Saliers, *Worship as Theology: A Foretaste of Glory Divine* (Nashville: Abingdon Press, 1994), 120–21.

27. See his *Holy Things: A Liturgical Theology* (Minneapolis: Fortress, 1998).

28. Amy Plantinga Pauw, "Dying Well," in *Practicing our Faith*, ed. Craig Dykstra and Dorothy Bass (San Francisco: Jossey-Bass, 1997), 170.

29. Long, *Witness*, 157. In a similar vein, Paul Wilson notes, "Grace does not cancel the reality of human sin and the need for change. Easter does not obliterate Good Friday, although it puts it in a different perspective. Both are true—they exist in a tension, the final outcome of which has been determined" (*Four Pages*, 22). Martin Luther King, Jr. preaches a similar ideal in "Guidelines for a Constructive Church" when he says "Good Friday's as much a fact of life as Easter." See this sermon in *A Knock at Midnight: Inspiration from the Great Sermons of Reverend Martin Luther King, Jr.*, eds. Clayborne Carson and Peter Holloran (New York: Warner, 1998), 108.

30. See Wilson, *Preaching and Homiletical Theory*, 92–93.

31. Elizabeth Achtemeier, "The Use of Hymnic Elements in Preaching," *Interpretation* 39, no. 1 (1985): 46, 59. In a similar manner, Richard Lischer says, "In the ecclesiastical Latin of the fourth century, four hundred years before it was exclusively associated with preaching, *praedicare* meant 'to praise,' 'to celebrate.'" See Lischer, *A Theology of Preaching: The Dynamics of the Gospel* (Nashville: Abingdon, 1981), 26. Henry Mitchell says that African American preaching, rooted in a history of pain,

"simply holds that no sermon *glorifies* God which avoids God's plan to uplift human-ity." See Mitchell, *Black Preaching: The Recovery of a Powerful Art* (Nashville: Abingdon Press, 1990), 130.

32. Paule Marshall, *Praisesong for the Widow* (New York: Putnam, 1983), 244–45.

33. Walter Brueggemann, *Israel's Praise: Doxology Against Idolatry and Ideology* (Philadelphia: Fortress, 1988), 133.

34. Ibid., 136.

35. Gordon Lathrop, *Holy Things* (Minneapolis: Fortress, 1993), 58.

36. See Wilson, *Four Pages*, 155–234.

37. This definition is taken from a chapter title in Samuel D. Proctor's *How Shall They Hear? Effective Preaching for Vital Faith* (Valley Forge, PA: Judson, 1992), 19.

38. See William Turner, "Musicality of Black Preaching: A Phenomenology," *Performance in Preaching: Bringing the Sermon to Life*, eds. Jana Childer and Clayton Schmit (Grand Rapids, MI: Baker Academic, 2008).

39. For more about tonal semantics, see Smitherman, *Talkin and Testifyin: The Language of Black America* (Boston: Houghton Mifflin, 1977), 134–47. For another in-depth study of the performance of African American sermons, see Gerald L. Davis, *I Got the Word in Me and I Can Sing It, You Know: A Study of the Performed African-American Sermon* (Philadelphia: University of Pennsylvania Press, 1985).

40. See Smith, *Preaching as Weeping, Confession, and Resistance: Radical Responses to Radical Evil* and Campbell, *The Word before the Powers*.

41. Mary Catherine Hilkert, *Naming Grace: Preaching and Sacramental Imagination* (New York: Continuum, 1997), 126.

42. Campbell names hope as another key virtue for Christian preachers. See *The Word before the Powers*, 183–88.

43. Some examples of texts that only focus on one particular arena of the holistic manifestation of the Spirit are the following: personal—André Resner, *Preacher and Cross: Person and Message in Theology and Rhetoric* (Grand Rapids, MI: Eerdmans, 1999) and Robert Dykstra, *Discovering a Sermon: Personal Pastoral Preaching* (St. Louis: Chalice, 2001); communal— Leonora Tubbs Tisdale, *Preaching as Local Theology and Folk Art* (Minneapolis: Fortress, 1997) and John McClure, *The Roundtable Pulpit: Where Leadership and Preaching Meet* (Nashville: Abingdon Press, 1995); social—Christine M. Smith, *Preaching as Weeping, Confession, and Resistance: Radical Responses to Radical Evil* (Louisville: Westminster John Knox, 1992) and Charles L. Campbell, *The Word before the Powers*. It should be no surprise, as has been mentioned, that this is an indication of the scarcity of homiletical works that focus on the Spirit; a homiletical consideration of the Spirit necessarily includes all realms of life.

44. LaRue, *The Heart of Black Preaching*, 16–25.

45. For a fair and critical presentation about these churches, see Milmon Harrison, *Righteous Riches: The Word of Faith Movement in Contemporary African-American Religion* (Oxford: Oxford University Press, 2005) and Marvin McMickle, *Where Have All the Prophets Gone? Reclaiming Prophetic Preaching in American* (Cleveland: Pilgrim, 2006).

46. See Mitchell, *Celebration and Experience in Preaching* (Nashville: Abingdon Press, 1990), 68.

47. Robert Hood, *Must God Remain Greek? Afro Cultures and God-Talk* (Minneapolis: Fortress, 1990), 205.

48. Hilkert, *Naming Grace*, 111.

49. Mitchell, *Black Preaching*, 123.

50. Mitchell, *Celebration and Experience*, 68.

51. Long, *Witness of Preaching*, 42–43.

52. This desired unity is expressed in the prayer of Christ, "that they may be one, as we are one." See John 17:11.

53. Smitherman, *Talkin' and Testifyin'*, 109.

54. Ibid., 108. She considers call and response to be a black mode of discourse. For more on her perspective, see *Talkin and Testifyin*, 104–18.

55. Long, *Witness of Preaching*, 86.

56. See Zora Neale Hurston, *Sanctified Church* (Berkeley: Turtle Island, 1981), 104.

57. See her article, "Context, Contours, Contents: Towards a Description of the Classical Reformed Teaching on Worship," *The Princeton Seminary Bulletin* 16, no. 2 (1995): 182.

58. Wilson, *Four Pages*, 57. He also notes that "listeners are led to mission by the Holy Spirit."

59. Smith's sermon can be found in *Power in the Pulpit: How America's Most Effective Black Preachers Prepare Their Sermons*, ed. Cleophus J. LaRue (Louisville: Westminster John Knox, 2002), 141–45. Blanks's sermon can be found in *This Is My Story: Testimonies and Sermons of Black Women in Ministry*, ed. Cleophus J. LaRue (Louisville: Westminster John Knox, 2005), 55–59.

60. J. Alfred Smith, "How Can They Hear without a Preacher?" in *Power in the Pulpit*, ed. Cleophus J. LaRue, 135.

61. Smith, "Foundations," 141.

62. Ibid., 142.

63. Ibid.

64. Ibid.

65. Ibid., 142–43.

66. Ibid., 142.

67. Ibid., 143.

68. Ibid.

69. Ibid., 143–44.

70. For a complete version of this hymn, see *The New National Baptist Hymnal* (Nashville: National Baptist Publishing Board, 1977), 106.

71. Smith, "Foundations," 144.

72. Ibid.

73. Blanks, "Telling God," 55.

74. Ibid., 56.

75. Ibid.

76. Ibid.

77. Ibid.

78. Ibid., 56–57.

79. Ibid., 57.

80. Ibid., 58.

81. Ibid., 58–59.

82. Ibid., 59.

83. See Paul Scott Wilson, *Four Pages of the Sermon.*

84. See "Preaching the Whole Counsel of God" in Gardner C. Taylor, *How Shall They Preach* (Elgin, IL: Progressive Baptist Publishing House, 1977), 77–94.

7. Practicing Lament and Celebration

1. Zan Holmes, "Are We for Real?" *Power in the Pulpit: How America's Most Effective Black Preachers Prepare Their Sermons*, ed. Cleophus J. LaRue (Louisville: Westminster John Knox, 2002), 87.

2. Carolyn Ann Knight, "When All Hell Breaks Loose," *Power in the Pulpit*, 101.

3. Prathia L. Hall, "Encounters with Jesus from Dying to Life," *Power in the Pulpit*, 68.

4. See Fry Brown's sermon "Just Preach" in *Weary Throats and New Songs: Black Women Proclaiming God's Word* (Nashville: Abingdon Press, 2003), 178.

5. Howard Thurman, *The Growing Edge* (Richmond, IN: Friends United, 1956), 19–20.

6. Gardner Taylor, "Look Up!" *Power in the Pulpit*, 157–58.

7. Knight, "When All Hell Breaks Loose," 104.

8. Holmes, "Are We for Real?" 87.

9. J. Alfred Smith, "Foundations of Our Faith," *Power in the Pulpit*, 143.

10. Ibid., 143–44.

11. James Earl Massey, "Looking Beyond Our Laments," *Sundays in the Tuskegee Chapel: Selected Sermons* (Nashville: Abingdon Press, 2000), 155.

12. Mitchell, *Celebration and Experience in Preaching* (Nashville: Abingdon Press, 1990), 69.

13. Ibid.

14. Mitchell, "African-American Preaching," *Concise Encyclopedia of Preaching*, eds. William H. Willimon and Richard Lischer (Louisville: Westminster John Knox, 1995), 3.

15. Brown, "Just Preach," *Weary Throats and New Songs*, 176–77.

16. Ibid., 179.

17. Vashti Murphy McKenzie, "Same No More," *Outstanding Black Sermons*, vol. 4, ed. Walter S. Thomas (Valley Forge, PA: Judson, 2001), 75–76.

18. Both Mitchell and Frank Thomas state that hyperbole is a key aspect of celebration. See Mitchell, *Celebration and Experience*, 67, and Thomas, *They Like to Never Quit*, 98.

19. Martin Luther King, Jr., "The American Dream," *A Knock at Midnight: Inspiration from the Great Sermons of Martin Luther King, Jr.*, eds. Clayborne Carson and Peter Holloran (New York: Warner, 1998), 98–99.

20. Frank A. Thomas, *They Like to Never Quit Praisin' God: The Role of Celebration in Preaching* (Cleveland: Pilgrim, 1997), 19–23.

21. Henry Mitchell, "Nevertheless," *Fire in the Well: Sermons by Ella and Henry Mitchell*, ed. Jacqueline B. Glass (Valley Forge, PA: Judson, 2003), 77–78.

22. Thomas, *They Like to Never Quit Praisin' God*, 31.

23. Blanks, "Telling God Where It Hurts," *This Is My Story: Testimonies and Sermons of Black Women in Ministry*, ed. Cleophus J. LaRue (Louisville: Westminster John Knox, 2005), 58–59.

24. Smith, "Foundations of Our Faith," 143–44.

25. Martin Luther King, Jr., "Drum Major Instinct," *Testament of Hope: The Essential Writings and Speeches of Martin Luther King, Jr.*, ed. James M. Washington (San Francisco: Harper & Row, 1986), 266.

26. Charles Booth, "Three Responses to a Miracle," *Power in the Pulpit*, 40.

27. Brown, "Resting but Remaining in Tune," *Weary Throats and New Songs*, 154.

28. Ella Mitchell, "To Heal the Brokenhearted," *Fire in the Well*, 9.

29. Smith, "Foundations of our Faith," 144.

30. Ibid.

31. Charles Adams, "Faith Critiques Faith," in Cleophus J. LaRue, ed., *Power in the Pulpit: How America's Most Effective Black Preachers Prepare Their Sermons* (Louisville: Westminster John Knox, 2002), 27.

32. Hall, "Encounters with Jesus from Dying to Life," *Power in the Pulpit*, 73.

33. Adams, "Faith Critiques Faith," 24ff.

34. Holmes, "Are We for Real?" 88.

35. Knight, "When All Hell Breaks Loose," 108.

36. Henry Mitchell, "Jesus as Investment Counselor," *Fire in the Well*, 89.

37. Smith, "Foundations of Our Faith," 144.

38. Mitchell, *Celebration and Experience in Preaching*, 69; cf. Thomas, *They Like to Never Quit*, 98.

39. Blanks, "Telling God Where It Hurts," 59.

40. Henry Mitchell, "Nevertheless," *Fire in the Well*, 78.

41. See Ella Mitchell, "To Heal the Brokenhearted," *Fire in the Well*, 159–60 and Gardner Taylor, "Look Up!" *Power in the Pulpit*.

42. Fry Brown, "Resting but Remaining in Tune," *Weary Throats and New Songs*, 155. For other instances of the use of poetic hymns in sermonic celebration, see Henry Mitchell, "Jesus as Investment Counselor," *Fire in the Well*, 90; cf. Charles Booth, "Three Responses to a Miracle," *Power in the Pulpit*, 41; cf. Zan Holmes, "Are We for Real?" *Power in the Pulpit*, 88.

43. Prathia L. Hall, "Encounters with Jesus from Dying to Life," *Power in the Pulpit*, 73.

Conclusion

1. See Harold Wells, *The Christic Center: Life-Giving and Liberating* (Maryknoll, NY: Orbis, 2004).

2. The idea that the Spirit is a life-creating, life-redeeming, and life-sustaining presence in every domain is crucial when it comes to discerning what is and what is not of the Spirit of God. Lament, celebration, grace, unity, and fellowship are life-giving signs of the Spirit in preaching that ultimately aim to build up individuals, communities,

and societies. Anything that seeks to destroy life and foster death and destruction toward oneself, others, God, or creation, is *not* of the Holy Spirit. For more about the issue of discernment, see pp. 100–103 in Arthur Van Seters, *Preaching and Ethics* (St. Louis: Chalice, 2004) and "Discernment" by Frank Rogers, Jr. in *Practicing Our Faith: A Way of Life for a Searching People*, ed. Dorothy C. Bass (San Francisco: Jossey-Bass Publishers, 1997), 105–18.

BIBLIOGRAPHY

Achetemeier, Elizabeth. "The Use of Hymnic Elements in Preaching." *Interpretation* 39, no. 1 (1985): 46–59.

Allen, Ronald J. *Interpreting the Gospel: An Introduction to Preaching.* St. Louis: Chalice, 1998.

Andrews, Dale P. *Practical Theology for Black Churches: Bridging Black Theology and African American Folk Religion.* Louisville: Westminster John Knox, 2002.

Andrews, William L., ed. *Sisters of the Spirit: Three Black Women's Autobiographies of the Nineteenth Century.* Bloomington: Indiana University Press, 1986.

Augustine. *On Christian Doctrine.* ca. 396–427. Reprint, translated by D. W. Robertson Jr., New York: Macmillan, 1987.

Austin-Broos, Diane J. *Jamaica Genesis.* Chicago: University of Chicago Press, 1997.

Baker-Fletcher, Karen. "Voice, Vision, and Spirit: Black Preaching Women in Nineteenth Century America." In *Sisters Struggling in the Spirit: A Women of Color Theological Anthropology*, ed. Nantawan Boonprasat Lewis, Lydia Hernandez, Helen Locklear, and Robina Marie Winbush, 31–42. Louisville: Women's Ministries Program Area and National Ministries Division, Presbyterian Church (U.S.A.), 1994.

Bartow, Charles L. *God's Human Speech: A Practical Theology of Proclamation.* Grand Rapids, MI: Eerdmans Company, 1997.

Basil. *On the Holy Spirit.* ca. 329–79. Reprint, New York: St. Vladimir's Seminary, 1980.

Bauckham, Richard. *The Theology of Jürgen Moltmann.* Edinburgh: T & T Clark, 1995.

Best, Wallace. "Lucy Smith and Pentecostal Worship in Chicago." In vol. 2, *Religions of the United States in Practice*, ed. Colleen McDannell, 11–22. Princeton, NJ: Princeton University Press, 2001.

Black, Kathy. *A Healing Homiletic: Preaching and Disability.* Nashville: Abingdon Press, 1996.

Bohren, Rudolf. *Preaching and Community.* Translated by David E. Green. Atlanta: John Knox, 1965.

Bond, L. Susan. *Contemporary African American Preaching: Diversity in Theory and Style.* St. Louis: Chalice, 2003.

Broadus, John A. *On the Preparation and Delivery of Sermons*, 1870. Reprint, New York: Harper and Bros., 1926.

Brooks, Phillips. *Lectures on Preaching.* New York: Dutton, 1877. Reprint, New York: Seabury, 1964.

Brown, Sally A. and Patrick D. Miller, eds. *Lament: Reclaiming Practices in Pulpit, Pew, and Public Square.* Louisville: Westminster John Knox, 2005.

Brown, Teresa L. Fry. *Weary Throats and New Songs: Black Women Proclaiming God's Word.* Nashville: Abingdon Press, 2003.

Brueggemann, Walter. *Finally Comes the Poet: Daring Speech for Proclamation.* Minneapolis: Fortress, 1989.

———. *Israel's Praise: Doxology against Idolatry and Ideology.* Philadelphia: Fortress, 1988.

———. *The Message of the Psalms: A Theological Commentary.* Minneapolis: Augsburg, 1984.

———. *The Psalms and the Life of Faith.* Edited by Patrick D. Miller. Minneapolis: Fortress, 1995.

Burton, Richard. *Afro-Creole: Power, Opposition, and Play in the Caribbean.* Ithaca, NY: Cornell University Press, 1997.

Buttrick, David G. *Homiletic: Moves and Structures.* Philadelphia: Fortress, 1987.

Campbell, Charles L. *The Word before the Powers: An Ethic of Preaching.* Louisville: Westminster John Knox, 2002.

Cannon, Katie Geneva. "Transformative Grace." In *Feminist and Womanist Essays in Reformed Dogmatics*, eds. Amy Plantinga Pauw and Serene Jones, 139–51. Louisville: Westminster John Knox, 2006.

Clayborne, Carson and Peter Holloran, eds. *A Knock at Midnight: Inspiration from the Great Sermons of Reverend Martin Luther King, Jr.* New York: Warner, 1998.

Cleage, Albert B. "Let's Not Waste the Holy Spirit." In *Black Theology: A Documentary History, 1966–1979*, ed. Gayraud Wilmore and James Cone, 332–39. Maryknoll, NY: Orbis, 1979.

Coleman, Will. *Tribal Talk: Black Theology, Hermeneutics, and African/American Ways of "Telling the Story."* University Park: Pennsylvania State University Press, 2000.

Cone, Cecil W. "The Black Religious Experience." In *Theology and Body*, ed. John Y. Fenton, 82–85. Philadelphia: Westminster, 1974.

Cone, James H. *God of the Oppressed.* San Francisco: HarperSanFrancisco, 1975.

———. *The Spirituals and the Blues: An Interpretation.* Maryknoll, NY: Orbis, 1991.

———. "Strange Fruit: The Cross and the Lynching Tree." *The African American Pulpit* 11, no. 2 (Spring 2008): 18–26.

Congar, Yves. *I Believe in the Holy Spirit*. Translated by David Smith. London: Geoffrey Chapman, 1986.

Cooper-Lewter, Nicholas C. and Henry H. Mitchell. *Soul Theology: The Heart of American Black Culture*. San Francisco: Harper & Row, 1986.

Costen, Melva and Mark Sturge. "Black Churches' Worship." In *The New Westminster Dictionary of Liturgy and Worship*, ed. Paul Bradshaw, 61–64. Louisville: Westminster John Knox, 2002.

Costen, Melva Wilson. *African American Christian Worship*. Nashville: Abingdon Press, 1993.

Craddock, Fred. *Preaching*. Nashville: Abingdon Press, 1985.

Crawford, Evans E., and Thomas H. Troeger. *The Hum: Call and Response in African American Preaching*. Nashville: Abingdon Press, 1995.

Cummings, George C. L. "The Slave Narratives as a Source of Black Theological Discourse: The Spirit and Eschatology." In *Cut Loose Your Stammering Tongue: Black Theology in the Slave Narratives*, ed. Dwight N. Hopkins and George C. L. Cummings, 33–46. Louisville: Westminster John Knox, 2003.

Davis, Gerald L. *I Got the Word in Me and I Can Sing It, You Know: A Study of the Performed African-American Sermon*. Philadelphia: University of Pennsylvania Press, 1985.

Davis, Henry Grady. *The Design for Preaching*. Philadelphia: Muhlenberg, 1958.

Dubois, W. E. B. *The Souls of Black Folk*. 1903. Reprint, New York: Penguin, 1969.

Dunn, James D. G. *The Theology of Paul the Apostle*. Grand Rapids, MI: Eerdmans, 1998.

Earl Jr., Riggins R. *Dark Salutations: Ritual, God, and Greetings in the African American Community*. Harrisburg, PA: Trinity, 2001.

———. *Dark Symbols, Obscure Signs: God, Self, and Community in the Slave Mind*. Maryknoll, NY: Orbis, 1993.

———. "Under Their Own Vine and Fig Tree: The Ethics of Social and Spiritual Hospitality in Black Church Worship." *Journal of the Interdenominational Theological Center* 14, no. 2 (1987): 181–93.

Evans, Jr., James H. *We Have Been Believers: An African-American Systematic Theology*. Minneapolis: Fortress, 1992.

Farmer, Herbert H. *The Servant of the Word*. New York: Scribner, 1942.

Fee, Gordon D. *The First Epistle to the Corinthians*. Grand Rapids, MI: Eerdmans, 1987.

———. *God's Empowering Presence: The Holy Spirit in the Letters of Paul*. Peabody, MA: Hendrickson, 1994.

———. "Toward a Theology of 1 Corinthians." In *Pauline Theology*. Vol. 2,

1 & 2 Corinthians, ed. David M. Hay, 37–58. Minneapolis: Fortress, 1993.

Forbes, James. *The Holy Spirit and Preaching*. Nashville: Abingdon Press, 1989.

Forde, Gerhard O. *Theology Is for Proclamation*. Minneapolis: Fortress, 1990.

Furnish, Victor. "Theology in 1 Corinthians." In *Pauline Theology*. Volume 2, *1 & 2 Corinthians*, ed. David M. Hay, 59–89. Minneapolis: Fortress, 1993.

———. *The Theology of the First Letter to the Corinthians*. Cambridge: Cambridge University Press, 1999.

Geertz, Clifford. "Deep Play: Notes on the Balinese Cockfight." In *Readings in Ritual Studies*, ed. Ronald L. Grimes, 217–29. Upper Saddle River, New Jersey: Prentice Hall, 1996.

Gilkes, Cheryl Townsend. "The 'Loves' and 'Troubles' of African-American Women's Bodies." In *A Troubling In My Soul: Womanist Perspectives on Evil and Suffering*, ed. Emilie M. Townes, 232–50. Maryknoll, NY: Orbis, 1993.

Glass, Jacqueline B., ed. *Fire in the Well: Sermons by Ella and Henry Mitchell*. Valley Forge, PA: Judson, 2003.

González, Justo L. and Gonzalez, Catherine G. *The Liberating Pulpit*. Nashville: Abingdon Press, 1994.

Hardy, Clarence E. *James Baldwin's God: Sex, Hope, and Crisis in Black Holiness Culture*. Knoxville: University of Tennessee Press, 2003.

Harris, James H. *Preaching Liberation*. Minneapolis: Fortress, 1995.

Hayes, Diana L. "Slain in the Spirit: Black Americans and the Holy Spirit." *Journal of the Interdenominational Theological Center* 20, no. 1–2 (Fall-Spring 1992–1993): 96–115.

Hays, Richard B. *First Corinthians*. Interpretation: A Bible Commentary for Teaching and Preaching. Louisville: Westminster John Knox, 1997.

Hilkert, Mary Catherine. *Naming Grace: Preaching and the Sacramental Imagination*. New York: Continuum, 1997.

Holmes, Barbara A. *Joy Unspeakable: Contemplative Practices of the Black Church*. Minneapolis: Fortress, 2004.

Hood, Robert E. *Must God Remain Greek? Afro Cultures and God-Talk*. Minneapolis: Fortress, 1990.

Hoyt, Thomas L., Jr. "Romans." In *True to Our Native Land: An African American New Testament Commentary*, eds. Brian K. Blount, Cain Hope Felder, Clarice J. Martin, and Emerson B. Powery, 249–75. Minneapolis: Fortress, 2007.

———. "Testimony." In *Practicing Our Faith*, ed. Dorothy Bass, 91–103. San Francisco: Jossey-Bass, 1997.

Hurston, Zora Neale. *Sanctified Church*. Berkeley: Turtle Island, 1983.

Johnson, Clifton H., ed. *God Struck Me Dead: Voices of Ex-Slaves*. Cleveland: Pilgrim, 1993.

Johnson, James Weldon. *God's Trombones: Seven Negro Sermons in Verse*. New York: Penguin Books, 1927.

Kay, James F. "The Word of the Cross at the Turn of the Ages." *Interpretation* 53, no. 1 (1999): 44–56.

LaRue, Cleophus J. *The Heart of Black Preaching*. Louisville: Westminster John Knox, 2000.

————, ed. *Power in the Pulpit: How American's Most Effective Black Preachers Prepare Their Sermons*. Louisville: Westminster John Knox, 2002.

————, ed. *This Is My Story: Testimonies and Sermons of Black Women in Ministry*. Louisville: Westminster John Knox, 2005.

Lincoln, C. Eric and Lawrence H. Mamiya. *The Black Church in the African American Experience*. Durham, NC: Duke University Press, 1990.

Lischer, Richard. *A Theology of Preaching: The Dynamics of the Gospel*. Nashville: Abingdon Press, 1981.

————, ed. "Rudolf Bohren: The Spirit as Giver and Gift of the Word." In *Theories of Preaching: Selected Readings in the Homiletical Tradition*. Durham, NC: Labyrinth, 1987.

Long, Thomas G. *The Witness of Preaching*. Louisville: Westminster John Knox, 1989.

Maddox, Randy. *Responsible Grace: John Wesley's Practical Theology*. Nashville: Abingdon Press, 1994.

Marshall, Paule. *Praisesong for the Widow*. New York: Putnam, 1983.

Martin, Dale B. *The Corinthian Body*. New Haven: Yale University Press, 1995.

Martin, Ralph P. *The Spirit and the Congregation: Studies in 1 Corinthians 12–15*. Grand Rapids, MI: Eerdmans, 1984.

Massey, James Earl. *Designing the Sermon: Order and Movement in Preaching*. Nashville: Abingdon Press, 1980.

————. *Sundays in the Tuskegee Chapel: Selected Sermons*. Nashville: Abingdon Press, 2000.

Mays, James L. *Psalms*. Interpretation: A Bible Commentary for Teaching and Preaching. Louisville: Westminster John Knox, 1994.

Mbiti, John S. *African Religions and Philosophy*. New York: Doubleday, 1970.

McClain, William B. *Come Sunday: The Liturgy of Zion*. Nashville: Abingdon Press, 1990.

Meeks, M. Douglas, ed. *The Future of the Methodist Theological Traditions*. Nashville: Abingdon Press, 1985.

Meeks, Wayne A. *The First Urban Christians: The Social World of the Apostle Paul*. New Haven: Yale University Press, 1983.

Miller, Patrick D. *Interpreting the Psalms*. Philadelphia: Fortress, 1986.

Mitchell, Henry H. "African-American Preaching." In *Concise Encyclopedia of Preaching*, ed. William H. Willimon and Richard Lischer, 2–9. Louisville: Westminster John Knox, 1995.

———. *Black Belief: Folk Beliefs of Blacks in America and West Africa*. New York: Harper & Row, 1975.

———. *Black Preaching: The Recovery of a Powerful Art*. Nashville: Abingdon Press, 1990.

———. *Celebration and Experience in Preaching*. Nashville: Abingdon Press, 1990.

———. "The Holy Spirit: A Folk Perspective." *The Living Pulpit* 5, no. 1 (January–March 1996): 40–41.

Mitchell, Margaret M. *Paul and the Rhetoric of Reconciliation: An Exegetical Investigation of the Language and Composition of 1 Corinthians*. Louisville: Westminster John Knox, 1991.

Moltmann, Jürgen. *The Church in the Power of the Spirit: A Contribution to Messianic Ecclesiology*. Translated by Margaret Kohl. Minneapolis: Fortress, 1993.

———. *The Crucified God: The Cross of Christ as the Foundation and Criticism of Christian Theology*. Translated by R. A. Wilson and John Bowden. Minneapolis: Fortress, 1993.

———. *Experiences in Theology: Ways and Forms of Christian Theology*. Translated by Margaret Kohl. Minneapolis: Fortress, 2000.

———. *Experiences of God*. Translated by Margaret Kohl. Philadelphia: Fortress, 1980.

———. *God in Creation: A New Theology of Creation and the Spirit of God*. Translated by Margaret Kohl. Minneapolis: Fortress, 1993.

———. *The Source of Life: The Holy Spirit and the Theology of Life*. Translated by Margaret Kohl. Minneapolis: Fortress, 1997.

———. *The Spirit of Life: A Universal Affirmation*. Translated by Margaret Kohl. Minneapolis: Fortress, 1994.

———. *Theology of Hope: On the Ground and the Implications of a Christian Eschatology*. Translated by James W. Leitch. Minneapolis: Fortress, 1993.

———. *The Trinity and the Kingdom of God: The Doctrine of God*. Translated by Margaret Kohl. London: SCM, 1981.

———. *The Way of Jesus Christ: Christology in Messianic Dimensions*. Translated by Margaret Kohl. Minneapolis: Fortress, 1993.

Montague, George T. *The Holy Spirit: Growth of a Biblical Tradition: A*

Commentary on the Principal Texts of the Old and New Testaments. New York: Paulist, 1976.

Moyd, Olin P. *The Sacred Art: Preaching and Theology in the African American Tradition.* Valley Forge, PA: Judson, 1995.

Murphy, Joseph M. *Working the Spirit: Ceremonies of the African Diaspora.* Boston: Beacon, 1995.

Old, Hughes Oliphant. *Themes and Variations for a Christian Doxology: Some Thoughts on the Theology of Worship.* Grand Rapids, MI: Eerdmans, 1992.

———. *Worship That Is Reformed According to Scripture.* Atlanta: John Knox, 1984.

Outler, Albert C., ed. *John Wesley.* New York: Oxford University Press, 1964.

———, ed. *The Works of John Wesley*, 3rd edition. Grand Rapids, MI: Baker, 1996.

Paris, Peter J. *The Spirituality of African Peoples: The Search for a Common Moral Discourse.* Minneapolis: Fortress, 1995.

Pasquarello III, Michael. *Christian Preaching: A Trinitarian Theology of Proclamation.* Grand Rapids, MI: Baker Academic, 2006.

Pauw, Amy Plantinga. "Dying Well." In *Practicing our Faith*, ed. Dorothy Bass, 163–78. San Francisco: Jossey-Bass, 1997.

Pinn, Anthony B. "Black Theology, Black Bodies, and Pedagogy," *Cross Currents* 50, no.1–2 (2000): 196–202.

———. *Terror and Triumph: The Nature of Black Religion.* Minneapolis: Fortress, 2003.

Pitts, Walter F., Jr. *Old Ship of Zion: The Afro-Baptist Ritual in the African Diaspora.* Oxford: Oxford University Press, 1993.

Powery, Emerson B. "The Groans of 'Brother Saul': An Exploratory Reading of Romans 8 for 'Survival,'" *Word and World* 24, no. 3 (Summer 2004): 315–22.

Proctor, Samuel D. *The Certain Sound of the Trumpet: Crafting a Sermon of Authority.* Valley Forge, PA: Judson, 1994.

———. *How Shall They Hear? Effective Preaching for Vital Faith.* Valley Forge, PA: Judson, 1992.

Raboteau, Albert J. *Slave Religion: The "Invisible Institution" in the Antebellum South.* Oxford: Oxford University Press, 1978.

———. *A Sorrowful Joy.* New York: Paulist, 2002.

Reid, Stephen Breck. *Listening In: A Multicultural Reading of the Psalms.* Nashville: Abingdon Press, 1991.

Roberts, J. Deotis. "The Holy Spirit and Liberation: A Black Perspective." *Mid-Stream* 24, no. 4 (October 1985): 398–410.

Robinson, John A. T. *The Body: A Study in Pauline Theology.* London: SCM, 1966.

Runyon, Theodore. *The New Creation: John Wesley's Theology Today.* Nashville: Abingdon Press, 1998.

————, ed. *Sanctification and Liberation: Liberation Theologies in Light of the Wesleyan Tradition.* Nashville: Abingdon Press, 1981.

Saliers, Don E. *Worship as Theology: Foretaste of Glory Divine.* Nashville: Abingdon Press, 1994.

————. *Worship Come to Its Senses.* Nashville: Abingdon Press, 1996.

Sampley, J. Paul. *Walking Between the Times: Paul's Moral Reasoning.* Minneapolis: Fortress, 1991.

Sanders, Boykin. "1 Corinthians." In *True to Our Native Land: An African American New Testament Commentary,* eds. Brian K. Blount, Cain Hope Felder, Clarice J. Martin, Emerson B. Powery, 276–306. Minneapolis: Fortress, 2007.

Sanders, Cheryl J. "African-American Worship in the Pentecostal and Holiness Movements." *Wesleyan Theological Journal* 32, no. 2 (Fall 1997): 105–120.

————. *Saints in Exile: The Holiness-Pentecostal Experience in African American Religion and Culture.* Oxford: Oxford University Press, 1996.

Schweizer, Eduard. *The Holy Spirit.* Translated by Reginald H. and Ilse Fuller. Philadelphia: Fortress, 1980.

Smith, Christine M. *Preaching as Weeping, Confession, and Resistance: Radical Responses to Radical Evil.* Louisville: Westminster John Knox, 1992.

Smitherman, Geneva. *Black Talk: Words and Phrases from the Hood to the Amen Corner.* Boston: Houghton Mifflin, 2000.

————. *Talkin and Testifyin: The Language of Black America.* Boston: Houghton Mifflin, 1977.

Songs of Zion. Nashville: Abingdon Press, 1981.

Spencer, Jon Michael. "The Heavenly Anthem: Holy Ghost Singing in the Primal Pentecostal Church (1906–1909)." *Journal of Black Sacred Music* 1, no. 1 (Spring 1987): 1–33.

Spurgeon, Charles H. *Lectures to my Students: A Selection from Addresses Delivered to the Students of the Pastors' College, Metropolitan Tabernacle.* London: Passmore and Alabaster, 1875.

————. *Second Series of Lectures to my Students: Addresses Delivered to the Students of the Pastors' College, Metropolitan Tabernacle.* London: Passmore and Alabaster, 1906.

Stapleton, John Mason. *Preaching in the Demonstration of the Spirit and Power.* Philadelphia: Fortress, 1988.

Stewart, Sr., Warren H. *Interpreting God's Word in Black Preaching*. Valley Forge, PA: Judson, 1984.

Suchocki, Marjorie Hewitt. *The Whispered Word: A Theology of Preaching*. St. Louis: Chalice, 1999.

Sutherland, Arthur. *I Was a Stranger: A Christian Theology of Hospitality*. Nashville: Abingdon Press, 2006.

Talbert, Charles H. *Reading Corinthians: A Literary and Theological Commentary on 1 and 2 Corinthians*. New York: Crossroad, 1987.

Taylor, Gardner C. *How Shall They Preach*. Elgin, IL: Progressive Baptist Publishing House, 1977.

Terrell, JoAnne Marie. *Power in the Blood? The Cross in the African American Experience*. Maryknoll, NY: Orbis, 1998.

Theissen, Gerd. *The Social Setting of Pauline Christianity*. Edited and Translated by John H. Schütz. Edinburgh: T & T Clark, 1982.

Thiselton, Anthony. *The First Epistle to the Corinthians: A Commentary on the Greek Text*. Grand Rapids, MI: Eerdmans, 2000.

Thomas, Frank A. *They Like to Never Quit Praisin' God: The Role of Celebration in Preaching*. Cleveland: Pilgrim, 1997.

Thomas, Walter S., ed. *Outstanding Black Sermons*. Volume 4. Valley Forge, PA: Judson, 2001.

Thurman, Howard. *The Centering Moment*. New York: Harper & Row, 1969.

———. *Creative Encounter: An Interpretation of Religion and Social Witness*. New York: Harper and Bros., 1954.

———. *Deep Is the Hunger*. New York: Harper and Bros., 1951.

———. *Disciplines of the Spirit*. Richmond, IN: Friends United, 1963.

———. *The Growing Edge*. Richmond, IN: Friends United, 1956.

———. *The Inward Journey*. New York: Harper and Bros., 1961.

———. *Jesus and the Disinherited*. Nashville: Abingdon Press, 1949.

———. *Luminous Darkness: A Personal Interpretation of the Anatomy of Segregation and the Ground of Hope*. New York: Harper & Row, 1965.

———. *Meditations of the Heart*. New York: Harper and Bros., 1953.

———. *Mysticism and the Experience of Love*. Wallingford, PA: Pendle Hill, 1961.

———. *The Search for Common Ground: An Inquiry into the Basis of Man's Experience of Community*. Richmond, IN: Friends United, 1986.

Townes, Emilie M. *Breaking the Fine Rain of Death: African American Health Issues and a Womanist Ethic of Care*. New York: Continuum, 1998.

Troeger, Thomas H. *Imagining the Sermon*. Nashville: Abingdon Press, 1990.

————. *Preaching While the Church is Under Reconstruction: The Visionary Role of Preachers in a Fragmented World*. Nashville: Abingdon Press, 1999.

————. *Ten Strategies for Preaching in a Multi-Media Culture*. Nashville: Abingdon Press, 1996.

Trulear, Harold Dean. "The Sacramentality of Preaching." In *Primary Sources of Liturgical Theology: A Reader*, ed. Dwight W. Vogel, 266–72. Collegeville, MN: Liturgical, 2000.

Turner, William C. "Holy Spirit and Preaching." In *Concise Encyclopedia of Preaching*, eds. William H. Willimon and Richard Lischer, 227–29. Louisville: Westminster John Knox, 1995.

————. "The Musicality of Black Preaching: A Phenomenology." In *Performance in Preaching: Bringing the Sermon to Life*, eds. Jana Childers and Clayton Schmit, Grand Rapids, MI: Baker Academic, 2008.

————. "Preaching the Spirit: The Liberation of Preaching." Paper presented at the annual meeting of the Academy of Homiletics, Williamsburg, VA, 2 December 2005.

Uzukwu, Elochukwu E. *Worship as Body Language: Introduction to Christian Worship, An African Orientation*. Collegeville, MN: Liturgical, 1997.

Van Seters, Arthur. *Preaching and Ethics*. St. Louis: Chalice, 2004.

Venable-Ridley, C. Michelle. "Paul and the African American Community." In *Embracing the Spirit: Womanist Perspectives on Hope, Salvation, and Transformation*, ed. Emilie M. Townes, 212–33. Maryknoll, NY: Orbis, 1997.

von Allmen, Jean-Jacques. *Preaching and Congregation*. Translated by B. L. Nicholas. London: Lutterworth, 1962.

Wainwright, Geoffrey. *Doxology: The Praise of God in Worship, Doctrine, and Life*. Oxford: Oxford University Press, 1980.

Walker, David. *Appeal to the Coloured Citizens of the World, but in Particular, and Very Expressly, to Those of the United States of America*. Boston, 1829. Reprint, New York: Hill and Wang, 1965.

Walker, Wyatt Tee. *The Soul of Black Worship*. New York: Martin Luther King Fellows, 1984.

Washington, James M., ed. *A Testament of Hope: The Essential Writings and Speeches of Martin Luther King, Jr.* San Francisco: HarperCollins, 1986.

Weems, Renita J. "Reading *Her Way* through the Struggle: African American Women and the Bible." In *Stony the Road We Trod: African American Biblical Interpretation*, ed. Cain Hope Felder, 57–77. Minneapolis: Fortress, 1991.

Welker, Michael. *God the Spirit*. Translated by John F. Hoffmeyer. Minneapolis: Fortress, 1994.

Wells, Harold. *The Christic Center: Life-Giving and Liberating.* Maryknoll, NY: Orbis, 2004.

Westermann, Claus. *The Praise of God in the Psalms.* Translated by Keith R. Crim. Atlanta: John Knox, 1965.

———. *Praise and Lament in the Psalms.* Atlanta: John Knox, 1981.

Westfield, N. Lynne. *Dear Sisters: Womanist Practice of Hospitality.* Cleveland: Pilgrim, 2001.

Willimon, William H. *Proclamation and Theology.* Nashville: Abingdon Press, 2005.

Wilson, Paul Scott. *The Four Pages of a Sermon: A Guide to Biblical Preaching.* Nashville: Abingdon Press, 1999.

———. *Imagination of the Heart: New Understandings in Preaching.* Nashville: Abingdon Press, 1988.

———. *Preaching and Homiletical Theory.* St. Louis: Chalice, 2004.

Wimberly, Edward P. "The Black Christian Experience and the Holy Spirit." *Quarterly Review* 8, no. 2 (Summer 1988): 19–35.

Witvliet, Theo. "In Search of a Black Christology." *Cross Currents* 37, no. 1 (1987): 17–32.

Wolterstorff, Nicholas. *Lament for a Son.* Grand Rapids, MI: Eerdmans, 1987.

INDEX OF SCRIPTURE